American English File

Third Edition

MULTI-PACK B
Student Book | Workbook

Christina Latham-Koenig
Clive Oxenden
Jerry Lambert

Paul Seligson

Paul Seligson and Clive Oxenden
are the original co-authors of
English File 1 and *English File* 2

OXFORD
UNIVERSITY PRESS

Contents

Course overview

American English File
Third Edition

Welcome to **American English File Third Edition**. This is how to use the Student Book, Online Practice, and the Workbook in and out of class.

Student Book

All the language and skills you need to improve your English, with Grammar, Vocabulary, Pronunciation, and skills work in every File.

Use your Student Book in class with your teacher.

Workbook

Grammar, Vocabulary, and Pronunciation practice for every lesson.

Use your Workbook for homework or for self-study to practice language and to check your progress.

ACTIVITIES AUDIO VIDEO RESOURCES

ONLINE

Go to
americanenglishfileonline.com
and use the code on
your Access Card to
log into the Online
Practice.

LOOK AGAIN

- Review the language from every lesson.
- Watch the video and listen to all the class audio as many times as you like.

PRACTICE

- Improve your skills with extra Reading, Writing, Listening, and Speaking practice.
- Use the interactive video to practice Practical English.

CHECK YOUR PROGRESS

- Test yourself on the language from the File and get instant feedback.
- Try a Challenge activity.

SOUND BANK

- Use the Sound Bank video to practice and improve your pronunciation of English sounds.

Online Practice

Look again at Student Book language you want to review or that you missed in class, do extra *Practice* activities, and *Check your progress* on what you learned so far.

Use the Online Practice to learn outside the classroom and get instant feedback on your progress.

americanenglishfileonline.com

Course overview   5

7A First day nerves

G uses of the infinitive **V** verbs + infinitive: *try to*, *forget to*, etc. **P** weak form of *to*, linking

> What do I need to do?
>
> It's important not to be late.

How to survive your first day in a new office

Everybody gets nervous on their first day at any job, but these tips can help you to get it right...

Hey Karen! Kylie? Chris?

6:30
Wake up early, have breakfast, shower, and get dressed. Wear formal work clothes, but not too formal. Check the weather forecast to make sure your clothes are right, and if you're driving, check traffic reports to see if there are any problems.

TOP TIP: ¹_____

8:50
Plan to arrive at least ten minutes early, but not more than 20 – you don't want to look too enthusiastic. Say hello to people, smile, and use this time to ask questions.

TOP TIP: ²_____ **If you can't, admit it and say "Sorry, I forgot your name."**

11:00
Offer to make coffee or to bring water for your colleagues.

TOP TIP: ³_____ **If it's very bad, people will always remember it. If it's very good, they'll always ask you to make it.**

12:00
Don't be the first person to ask about lunch. Wait to see what everybody else does.

TOP TIP: ⁴_____

1:00
Be prepared to have problems. Many bosses give new employees some difficult work on their first day to see how they manage.

TOP TIP: ⁵_____ **If you can't, don't be afraid to ask for help.**

3:00
If you go to a meeting, listen, keep quiet, and take notes.

TOP TIP: ⁶_____ **You don't want to annoy other people on day one.**

5:00
Don't think that staying late will impress your boss. It won't, at least not on your first day. Go home.

TOP TIP: ⁷_____ **If you made any mistakes, make sure you don't make them again tomorrow.**

1 READING

a Imagine that somebody you know is starting a new office job tomorrow. Think of two important tips you could give him or her to make the first day go well.

+ Do _____
  _____

− Don't _____
  _____

b Now read the article. Are your tips there?

c Read *Top tips* A–G. Then read the article again, and put them in the correct place (1–7).

   A **Don't make it either very well or very badly.**
   B **Try to remember everybody's name.**
   C **If they invite you to go with them, go!**
   D **Decide what to wear the night before.**
   E **Think about everything that you've learned today.**
   F **Keep your good ideas for the next meeting.**
   G **Try to solve the problem yourself first.**

d Which tip do you think is the most important? Do you think any of the tips could also be useful for the first day in a new class or on a course?

2 LISTENING

a 🔊 7.1 Listen to Simon and Claire describing their first day at work. What problems did they have? What advice from the article in **1** would you give them?

54

b Listen again. Answer with **S** (Simon), **C** (Claire), or **B** (both of them).

Who...?

1 _____ wasn't expecting to work on his / her first day
2 _____ didn't have the training to do the job
3 _____ made a wrong decision because of his / her interview
4 _____ couldn't answer the questions that people asked him / her
5 _____ felt bad when he / she spoke to the boss
6 _____ never had the same problem again

c Have you ever had a problem on your first day in a new job, or in a new class or school? What was it?

3 VOCABULARY & GRAMMAR
verbs + infinitive; uses of the infinitive

a Complete the missing verbs from the article.

1 Pl_____ to arrive at least ten minutes early.
2 O_____ to make coffee.
3 You don't w_____ to annoy other people on day one.
4 Tr_____ to solve the problem yourself first.

b Ⓥ p.158 **Vocabulary Bank** Verb forms Do Part 1.

c Match sentences a–c to rules 1–3.

a _____ Check the weather forecast **to make sure** your clothes are right.
b _____ Decide what **to wear** the night before.
c _____ ...don't be afraid **to ask** for help.

> Use the infinitive...
> 1 after adjectives
> 2 to give a reason for doing something
> 3 after a question word, e.g., *who, what, how*

d Ⓖ p.138 **Grammar Bank 7A**

e Ⓒ **Communication** How to survive... **A** p.104 **B** p.110 Read and re-tell two more *How to survive...* articles.

f Do you think the tips you have read in this lesson are appropriate in your country? If not, why not?

4 PRONUNCIATION & SPEAKING weak form of *to*, linking

a ◑7.4 Listen to three sentences. Is *to* stressed? How is it pronounced?

I want to come.   It's difficult to say.   Try not to be late.

> 🔍 Linking words with the same consonant sound
> When a word ends in a consonant sound and the next word begins with the same sound, we often link the words together and only make the consonant sound once. This happens when a word ends in /t/ before *to*, so, e.g., *want to* is pronounced /ˈwɒntə/.

b ◑7.5 Listen and complete questions 1–10 with three or four words.

1 Have you ever _____ something new and failed?
2 How important is it to know_____?
3 How long do you usually spend deciding _____ in the morning?
4 Have you ever _____ your phone during a class or concert?
5 Where are you _____ for your next vacation?
6 Are you _____ next weekend?
7 Would you like _____ in another country?
8 Have you ever _____ when you weren't?
9 Do you think it's important _____ at school?
10 Do you think it's possible _____ with an ex-boyfriend or girlfriend?

c Work in pairs. **A** ask **B** the first five questions. **B** give as much information as you can. Change roles for the last five questions.

5 WRITING

With a partner, write a *How to survive...* article. Choose one of the titles below, and try to think of at least four tips. Organize your tips in a logical order. Start each one with an imperative, e.g., *Don't be late, Wear the right clothes...* Then explain why.

How to survive... • a job interview
  • a party where you don't know anyone
  • a family vacation

🕐 **Go online** to review the lesson

G uses of the gerund (verb + *-ing*) **V** verbs + gerund **P** *-ing*, the letter *o*

1 VOCABULARY & GRAMMAR
verbs + gerund; uses of the gerund

a Talk to a partner. Is there a book, a movie, or a song that makes you feel happy? What is it?

b Read about *Happiness is…*, and look at the Instagram posts. Check (✓) the ones you most agree with. Then compare with a partner.

c Look at the first cartoon. Which verb form do we use after the verb "finish"?

d **V** p.158 Vocabulary Bank Verb forms Do Part 2.

e Look at the cartoons again. Find an example of a gerund (verb + *-ing*):
1 after a preposition _____
2 used as a noun _____
3 in the negative form _____

f **G** p.138 Grammar Bank 7B

g Write your own continuation for *Happiness is…*

h Work in small groups. Read your idea to the group. Do you agree with the other students' ideas of happiness?

Illustrators **Ralph Lazar** and **Lisa Swerling** got the idea for *Happiness is…* while sitting together one day in a hot tub at their home in California. Lisa had just finished answering all her emails, and she said, "Happiness is having an empty inbox." Ralph replied, "Happiness is getting into a hot tub." They began to list things that made them happy, and illustrated them. Later they asked people on Facebook "What makes you happy?" and Ralph drew and posted on Instagram the ones they liked best.

HAPPINESS IS

…when a song ends the exact moment you finish parking.

HAPPINESS IS

…a free coffee refill without asking.

HAPPINESS IS

…fitting in to jeans that you haven't worn for a very long time, and THEN, finding money in one of the pockets.

HAPPINESS IS

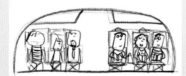

…sitting next to someone nice on a plane.

HAPPINESS IS

…finding a delicious food with no calories or fat or cholesterol.

HAPPINESS IS

…landing in a new country.

HAPPINESS IS

…reading a really good book and then finding it's a series.

HAPPINESS IS

…finding the other ear ring.

HAPPINESS IS

…not having to set the alarm for the next day.

2 LISTENING & SPEAKING

a You're going to listen to part of a radio money program about the Bank of Happiness in Tallinn, the capital of Estonia. What do you think the bank does?

Airi Kivi from the Bank of Happiness

b 🔊 7.8 Listen once. How does the bank work? Choose the correct description.

1 You pay money into the bank, and receive help in return.
2 You help somebody, and the bank pays you.
3 You help somebody, and then somebody else helps you.

c Listen again and choose a, b, or c.

1 Tallinn is one of the world's smart cities because __.
  a the people who live and work there use a lot of technology
  b the people are very intelligent
  c the government wants the people to be more intelligent

2 The Bank of Happiness makes it possible for people to __.
  a borrow money cheaply
  b get services without paying for them
  c buy property in other countries

3 Which of the following could you post on the Bank of Happiness?
  a I'm looking for a partner.
  b I need somebody to lend me money.
  c I need somebody to give me English lessons.

4 Airi Kivi started the Bank of Happiness because she wanted __.
  a people to help each other
  b to make people richer
  c to help people who didn't have jobs

5 In the Bank of Happiness, if somebody takes your dog for a walk __.
  a you then need to take their dog for a walk
  b you don't need to do anything for them
  c you need to do something for them

6 The principle of the Bank is that __ makes people happy.
  a having a lot of money and possessions
  b having a lot of friends
  c helping other people

d Answer the questions with a partner.

1 Do you think the Bank of Happiness is a good idea? Do you think it could work in your country?
2 Have you heard of any similar projects? Do they work well?
3 Imagine you're a member of the bank. What can you offer to do? What would you like other people to do for you?

3 PRONUNCIATION
-ing, the letter o

a 🔊 7.9 Listen and repeat some words ending in -ing.

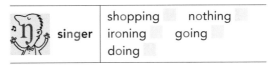

singer	shopping nothing
	ironing going
	doing

b Listen again. How is the letter o pronounced in the five words in **a**? Match them to the sound pictures. Then practice saying the words.

1 phone	2 computer	3 clock
4 boot	5 up	

c 🔊 7.10 Listen to the pairs of words. Can you hear the difference?

1 a bang b bank   3 a sing b sink
2 a thing b think   4 a ping b pink

d 🔊 7.11 Now listen to four sentences. Which word in **c** did you hear?

4 SPEAKING

a Choose five things to talk about from the list below.

SOMETHING...
- you don't mind doing in the house
- you like doing with your family
- you don't feel like doing on the weekend
- you spend too much time doing
- you are very good (or very bad) at doing

SOMEWHERE...
- you love going to in the summer
- you don't like going to alone
- you are thinking of going to this weekend
- you dream of going to in the future
- you hate going to

b Work in pairs. **A** tell **B** about the five things. Say why. **B** ask for more information. Then change roles.

I don't mind cooking. I really like it, and I often cook on the weekend.

Go online to review the lesson

What do I have to do?

You have to take four tests.

G have to, don't have to, must, must not, can't   **V** adjectives + prepositions: *afraid of*, etc.   **P** stress on prepositio

1 SPEAKING

Talk in small groups.

Have you ever...

- spoken to a tourist in English? When? Why?
- needed to speak in English on the phone? Who to? What about?
- sent an email in English? Who to? What was it about?
- seen a movie or video clip in English? Which? How much did you understand?
- read a book or magazine in English? Which one(s)?
- asked for directions in English in a foreign city? Where?
- used an app or website to improve your English? Which one?

2 READING

a Are people from your country good at learning languages? Why (not)? Do you think Americans are good at learning your language?

> 🔍 **Topic sentences**
> Paragraphs usually begin with a topic sentence.
> This tells you what the paragraph is about.

b Read an article about a language learning experiment. Complete each paragraph with a topic sentence, A–F.

A So what happened after four weeks?
B But what happens when an American tries to learn a new language after leaving school?
C Max decided to learn Spanish.
D Motivation is obviously a problem.
E Americans are famous for being bad at learning languages.
F The situation in American schools doesn't help either.

c Read the article again. Answer the questions with a partner.

1 What two examples does the writer give to show that Americans are bad at learning languages?
2 Why does he / she think that Americans aren't motivated to learn languages?
3 What reason do many schoolchildren give for not wanting to study a foreign language?
4 How did a newspaper try to find out if Americans really are bad at learning languages?
5 Why did Max decide to learn Spanish? How did he learn?
6 What did he do when he finished the course?

Por favor...

Are AMERICANS really so bad at learning languages?

1 *E* That's been true for a long time. In any city around the world you can hear American tourists asking for the restaurant menu in English. Sometimes they try to say a couple of phrases in the local language, but they stop making an effort as soon as they discover that the waiter knows a little English. Some Americans who live abroad often spend all their time with other Americans, and never learn the language at all.

2 ___ Many Americans think "I don't have to learn a foreign language because everyone speaks English nowadays." This is partly true. In many multinational companies, for example, employees have to speak English because it is the company's official language of communication.

3 ___ Most American children only have to learn a language until they are 14 or 15. After that, they don't have to continue if they don't want to. Many young people say that they don't want to continue studying a foreign language because "it's too difficult."

4 ___ A newspaper decided to find out by sending Max, one of its journalists, on an intensive language course. He then had to go to the country and do some "tests" to see if he could "survive" in different situations.

5 ___ "I'd like to visit Puerto Rico and Latin America in the future. If I go, I don't want to be the typical American who expects everyone else to speak English." He did a one-month intensive course at a language school in Washington, D.C.

6 ___ When his course ended, he went to San Juan, Puerto Rico for the weekend to take his tests. A teacher called Nilda met him there and gave him a score out of ten for each test and then a final score for everything.

3 GRAMMAR have to, don't have to, must, must not, can't

a ◉7.12 Listen to Max talking about the tests and fill in the blanks.

> ### THE TESTS
> **You have to**
> – order a drink and a ¹_____ in a café, ask how much it is, and understand the price.
> – ask for directions on the street (and ²_____ them).
> – get a ³_____ to a historical building.
> – leave a message on somebody's voicemail.
>
> ### THE RULES
> – You must not use a ⁴_____ or phrase book app.
> – You must only ⁵_____ _____.
> – You can't use your ⁶_____ or mime, or write anything down.

b Look at the highlighted phrases. Which phrases mean…?

   1 Do this. It's important. _____ _____

   2 Don't do this. It's a bad idea. _____ _____

c Now look at an extract from the article in **2**. Does the highlighted phrase mean…?

> Many Americans think "I don't have to learn a foreign language because everyone speaks English nowadays."

   1 I don't need to do this

   2 I can't do this

d ⓖ p.138 Grammar Bank 7C

e ⓒ Communication What are the rules? **A** p.105 **B** p.110 Complete the rules.

4 LISTENING

a ◉7.15 Look at Max's tests again. Which test do you think was the easiest for him? Which do you think was the most difficult? Listen and check your answers.

b Listen again. Mark the sentences **T** (true) or **F** (false). Correct the **F** sentences.

   1 The waiter didn't understand Max.

   2 The bill was $6.90.

   3 The drugstore was the first street on the left.

   4 The driver understood the name of the fort.

   5 Max made a grammar mistake when he left the voicemail message.

   6 Max's final score was eight.

   7 Max says you can learn the language in a month.

c How well do you think you could do Max's four tests in English? What do you have to say…?

   1 to order a drink and a sandwich and ask the price

   2 to ask somebody on the street for directions, e.g., to the nearest drugstore

   3 to tell a taxi driver where you want to go

   4 to leave a voicemail message that you have called and would like the person to call you back

5 VOCABULARY & PRONUNCIATION adjectives + prepositions; stress on prepositions

> 🔎 **Adjectives + prepositions**
> Some adjectives are usually followed by certain prepositions, e.g., *Americans are famous **for** being bad **at** learning languages.* It's useful to learn the prepositions with the adjectives.

a Complete the sentences with a preposition from the list.

at (x2) for (x2) from in of (x2) to with

Languages

   1 Do you think you're good ____ learning languages?

   2 Is there anything about learning English that you're bad ____? What?

   3 Do you think listening to pop music is good ____ your English? Why (not)?

   4 Are you afraid ____ going to places where you don't speak the language? Why (not)?

   5 What English-speaking countries are you most interested ____? Why?

Tourism

   6 Which towns or cities in your country are full ____ tourists in the summer?

   7 What tourist attractions is your country famous ____?

   8 Are people in your country usually nice ____ tourists?

   9 Do you get angry ____ tourists who don't try to speak your language? Why (not)?

   10 Are people in the big cities very different ____ people in the rest of the country?

b ◉7.16 Listen and check.

c ◉7.17 Listen to questions 1 and 2, and 3 and 7 again. In which questions are *at* and *for* a) stressed and b) unstressed?

d Ask and answer all the questions in **a** with a partner.

6 WRITING

Ⓦ p.117 Writing A formal email Write an email asking for information.

Go online to review the lesson

Practical English At the pharmacy

going to a pharmacy V feeling sick

1 ▶ RUNNING IN CENTRAL PARK

a ◀)**7.18** Watch or listen to Rob and Jenny. Are they enjoying their run?

b Watch or listen again and answer the questions.

1 How does Rob say he feels?
2 What does Jenny say about Central Park?
3 Is Rob happy he came to New York?
4 What is Rob tired of doing?
5 What does Jenny invite him to do?
6 How many more times are they going to run round the park?

2 VOCABULARY feeling sick

a Match the phrases and photos.

What's the matter?

☐ I have a <u>hea</u>dache. /ˈhɛdeɪk/
☐ I have a cough. /kɒf/
☐ I have the flu. /fluː/
☐ I have a <u>tem</u>perature. /ˈtɛmprətʃər/
☐ I have a <u>sto</u>machache. /ˈstʌməkeɪk/
☐ I have a cold.

b ◀)**7.19** Listen and check. Then cover the phrases and practice with a partner.

What's the matter? 🔵 🔵 *I have a headache.*

3 ▶ GOING TO A PHARMACY

a ◀)**7.20** Cover the conversation below and watch or listen. Circle the correct answer.

1 Rob thinks he has *a cold / the flu*.
2 The pharmacist gives Rob *ibuprofen / penicillin*.
3 He has to take the medicine every *four hours / eight hours*.
4 It costs *$16.99 / $6.99*.

b Watch or listen again. Complete the **You hear** phrases.

You hear	You say
Good morning. Can I help you?	I'm not feeling very well. I think I have flu.
What are your symptoms?	I have a headache and a cough.
Do you have a ¹_____?	No, I don't think so.
Are you allergic to any drugs?	I'm allergic to penicillin.
No ²_____. This is ibuprofen. It'll make you feel ³_____.	How many do I have to take?
⁴_____ every four hours.	Sorry? How often?
⁵_____ every four hours. If you don't feel better in ⁶_____ hours, you should see a doctor.	OK, thanks. How much is that?
That's $6.99, please.	Thank you.
You're ⁷_____.	

> **American and British English**
> *pharmacy* = American English (and sometimes British English)
> *chemist's* = British English
> *drugs* = *medicine* in American English
> *drugs* = *illegal substances* in American and British English
> *the flu* = American English
> *flu* = British English

c ◉ 7.21 Watch or listen and repeat the **You say** phrases. Copy the <u>rhy</u>thm.

d Practice the conversation with a partner.

e 👥 In pairs, role-play the conversation.
   A (book closed) You don't feel very well. Decide what symptoms you have. Are you allergic to anything?
   B (book open) You are the pharmacist. You begin *Can I help you?*

f Change roles.

4 ▶ DINNER AT JENNY'S APARTMENT

a ◉ 7.22 Watch or listen to Rob and Jenny. Mark the sentences **T** (true) or **F** (false).
  1 Rob broke up with his girlfriend a year before he met Jenny.
  2 Jenny hasn't had much time for relationships.
  3 Jenny knew that Rob wasn't feeling well in the morning.
  4 Rob wants to go back to his hotel because he's tired.
  5 Jenny is going to call a taxi.

b Watch or listen again. Say why the **F** sentences are false.

c ◉ 7.23 Read the information box about *have got*. Listen and repeat the phrases.

> 🔍 **have got**
> In British English, *have got* is sometimes used instead of *have* to talk about possession.
> **I've got** a busy day tomorrow.
> **Have you got** any children? **Yes, I have. I've got** a girl and a boy.
>   **No, I haven't. I haven't got** any children.
>
> See **appendix** p.165.

d Ask and answer with a partner. Use *Have you got...? Yes, I have. / No, I haven't.* Give more information if you can.
  A any pets a bike or motorcycle a garden
  B any brothers and sisters a car a laptop

Have you got any pets?)
  (*Yes I have. I've got two dogs.*

e Look at the **Social English** phrases. Can you remember any of the missing words?

> 💬 **Social English**
> 1 **Rob**   That was a lovely _____.
> 2 **Rob**   That isn't very _____ for you.
> 3 **Jenny** I'm _____ you're feeling better.
> 4 **Rob**   I think I _____ get back to the hotel now.
> 5 **Rob**   I'm _____ I'll be fine.
> 6 **Rob**   Thanks again for a _____ evening.

f ◉ 7.25 Watch or listen and complete the phrases. How do you say them in your language? Then watch or listen and repeat the phrases.

g Complete conversations A–F with **Social English** phrases 1–6. Then practice them with a partner.

A	My cold has completely disappeared.	▮
B	▮ Thanks so much for inviting me.	It was a pleasure.
C	It's getting late. ▮	I'll call a taxi for you.
D	Do you think you'll be OK for tonight?	▮ Don't worry.
E	This is my third coffee this morning.	▮ You won't sleep tonight.
F	I hope you enjoyed the party.	We certainly did. ▮

CAN YOU...?

▮ describe symptoms when you feel sick
▮ get medicine at a pharmacy
▮ talk about possessions with *have got*

8A Should I stay or should I go?

Should I leave him?

No, I think you should stay.

1 READING & LISTENING

a If you have a problem that you need to talk about, do you talk to a friend or to a member of your family? Why?

b TV talk show host Graham Norton has an advice column in a newspaper. Read a problem that was sent to him and three possible options. Then talk to a partner. Which of the three pieces of advice do you agree with? Why?

c ◉ 8.1 Now listen to Tracey reading Graham's advice. Which of the three options does Graham think is right? Why?

Dear Graham,

I'm 24 and my partner is 46. We've been together for two years, and we have a wonderful relationship. I also have a great relationship with his children from his previous marriage. But I feel worried when I think about our future together. He has already lived life. He's been married, he's had children, and he's owned a business. I'm just starting my life. I want to have children, but he's not sure. I love him and I want to be with him, but I also want to share the adventures of life with someone. Should I leave him? Am I making my life more difficult by choosing to be with someone who's more than 20 years older than me?

Tracey

What should Tracey do?

a She should leave him and find somebody who is closer to her age and shares her interests.

b She should think hard about what kind of man she really wants to be with before making a decision.

c She should stay with him if she loves him. Being with an older man has advantages as well as disadvantages.

2 GRAMMAR *should*

a Look at the sentences. Answer questions 1–3.

Should I leave him?
She should stay with him.
You shouldn't make a decision in a hurry.

1 What do we use *should* for?
   a rules b advice c permission
2 Does *should* change in sentences with the third person?
3 How do we make negatives and questions with *should*?

b **G** p.140 Grammar Bank 8A

c Read the messages. What should the people do? Write a short answer to each message.

> My neighbors have noisy parties every weekend. I can't sleep and it's driving me crazy!

> It was my girlfriend's birthday yesterday, and I forgot to get her a present. She isn't happy.

> I share an apartment with a friend, but she never does any housework.

> My ten-year-old son wants a smartphone – he says all his friends have one.

3 PRONUNCIATION /ʊ/ and /u/

a ◉ 8.3 Listen and repeat the words and sounds. What's the difference between the two sounds? Which consonant isn't pronounced in *should* and *would*?

🐂	bull	should would good put
👢	boot	choose do truth you

b ◉ 8.4 Put the words in the correct row. Then listen and check.

book cool could flew food look lose pull push shoes school

c Practice saying the sentences.
1 What should I do?
2 You shouldn't lose your cool.
3 You should tell the truth.
4 What school should they choose?

4 SPEAKING & LISTENING

a Look at some advice for another problem. With a partner, say what you think the problem is.

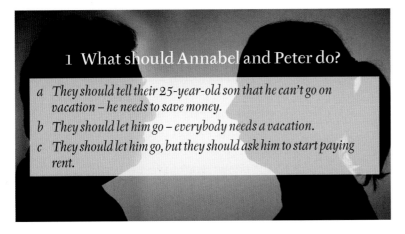

1 What should Annabel and Peter do?

a *They should tell their 25-year-old son that he can't go on vacation – he needs to save money.*

b *They should let him go – everybody needs a vacation.*

c *They should let him go, but they should ask him to start paying rent.*

b 🔊 8.5 Listen to Annabel and Peter calling a radio show called *What's the problem?* and make notes about the problem with their son. Were you right?

c Talk to your partner and choose the best advice for Annabel and Peter. Check (✓) a, b, or c and say why.

d 🔊 8.6 Listen to an expert giving them advice. Is it the advice you chose? Is it good advice? Why (not)?

e 🔊 8.7 / 8.8 Repeat **a–d** for Nick.

2 What should Nick do?

a *He should stay where he has a job, and see his girlfriend on weekends.*

b *He should go with her and start a new life.*

c *He should tell her to stay where they are if she wants to stay together.*

f 🔊 8.9 / 8.10 Now repeat **a–d** for Jane.

3 What should Jane do?

a *She should go on vacation with both friends.*

b *She should get to know her friend's friend Angie better, and then decide.*

c *She should refuse to go if Angie goes too.*

5 VOCABULARY & SPEAKING
get

a Look at three sentences from this lesson. Match *get* in sentences 1–3 to meanings a–c.

a buy / obtain   b receive   c become

1 He will never **get** as excited as you about, for example, a wedding.

2 He should save his money so that he can **get** his own place to live.

3 I **get** a good salary.

b 🅥 p.159 **Vocabulary Bank** *get*

c In pairs, ask and answer the questions with *get*.

1 When was the last time you **got a present**? What was it? Who was it from?

2 Do you usually **get nervous** before exams or presentations? What do you do to feel more relaxed?

3 What website do you use if you want to **get tickets** a) to travel or b) for the movies / theater / concerts?

4 Who do you **get along with** best in your family? Is there anybody you don't get along with?

5 How do you **get to work / school / college**? How long does it usually take you?

6 What's the first thing you do when you **get home** from work / school / college?

7 How many **messages** do you **get** a day on your phone? How many **emails** do you **get**? Who are they usually from? Do you answer them?

8 Do you have a good sense of direction, or do you often **get lost**?

G *if* + present, *will* + base form (first conditional) **V** confusing verbs **P** homophones

> If we don't take umbrellas, it'll rain.

> Yes, that always happens!

1 READING

a If you're waiting in a long line at the supermarket and you change to a different line, what will usually happen?

b Read the first two paragraphs of the article and check. Who was Murphy? What is his "law"?

If something can go wrong...

If you're in a long line at the supermarket and you change to another line that is moving more quickly, what will happen? The line you were in before will suddenly start moving faster. What will happen if you take your umbrella because you think it's going to rain later? It won't rain, of course. It will only rain if you forget to take your umbrella. These are examples of Murphy's Law, which says, "If there is something that can go wrong, it will go wrong."

Murphy's Law took its name from Captain Edward Murphy, an American aerospace engineer from the 1940s. He was trying to improve safety for pilots flying military planes. Not surprisingly, he got a reputation for always thinking of the worst thing that could happen in every situation. Here are some more examples of Murphy's Law.

Shopping
1 If you lose a glove and buy a new pair,...
2 If you order something online,...

Transportation
3 If you stop waiting for a bus and start walking,...
4 If you're in a taxi and you're late for something important,...

Technology
5 If a technician comes to fix your computer,...
6 If you need to urgently print a document,...

Air travel
7 If you get to the airport early,...
8 If you're late for your flight,...

c Now look at the eight examples of Murphy's Law in the article and match them to sentences A–H.

- A it will immediately start working.
- B three will come at the same time.
- C all the traffic lights will be red.
- D you'll find the lost one.
- E your flight will be delayed.
- F the printer won't have any paper.
- G there'll be a long line at security.
- H you'll be out when they deliver it.

d Do any of these things (or things like this) often happen to you?

2 GRAMMAR *if* + present, *will* + base form

a In pairs, cover A–H and look at 1–8 in the article. How many of the laws can you remember?

b Look at the laws again. What tense is the verb after *if*? What form is the other verb?

c **G** p.140 **Grammar Bank 8B**

d In pairs, complete these examples of Murphy's Law.
1 If you find a pair of shoes that you really like in a store,...
2 If you're on the street and you need a taxi,...
3 If you wear a new white shirt,...
4 If you leave your phone at home,...
5 If there's a soccer game on TV and you leave the room for 30 seconds,...

e Compare your answers with other students. Do you have the same (or similar)?

3 LISTENING

a **◉ 8.13** You're going to listen to two stories. First listen to six extracts, and ⟨circle⟩ the words and phrases that you hear. What do you think they mean?

Peter wanted to get a job

1 It was the *recession / depression* and it was very difficult to get a job.
2 I *tried for / applied for* lots of different jobs.
3 We *got cut off / got off* because the bus went into a tunnel.

Sue wanted to see a tiger

4 I was interested in *either / neither* a trip to see birds *nor / or* a trip to see a tiger.
5 I thought it would be really cool to see a tiger *in the wild / in Thailand.*
6 We spent *the whole morning / all morning* looking for the tiger.

b **◉ 8.14** Listen to the stories once. Why are they examples of Murphy's Law?

c Listen again. Mark the sentences **T** (true) or **F** (false). Correct the **F** sentences.

1 Peter didn't have a college degree.
2 He wasn't expecting to get a phone call about a job.
3 He couldn't call them back because his phone had no battery.
4 Sue didn't have much free time at the conference.
5 The guide was optimistic about seeing the tiger.
6 Sue didn't really enjoy her trip.

d Whose experience was more annoying? Have you ever had a Murphy's Law experience?

4 VOCABULARY & SPEAKING
confusing verbs

a Look at the sentences about Peter and Sue. The underlined verbs are mistakes. What verbs should they be?

1 Peter was unemployed, and was <u>finding</u> a job.
2 The guide <u>said</u> Sue that there was only one tiger in the whole park.

b **Ⓥ p.160 Vocabulary Bank** Confusing verbs

c ⟨Circle⟩ the correct verb. Then ask and answer the questions with a partner.

1 Who do you *look / look like* in your family?
2 How many English classes have you *missed / lost* this year?
3 What music do you like *hearing / listening to* in the car?
4 Do you think soccer players *win / earn* too much money?
5 What is the best way to *know / meet* new friends?
6 Is it sometimes OK to *say / tell* a lie?
7 Have you ever *lent / borrowed* money to a family member?
8 Do you know anyone who's *looking for / finding* an apartment?
9 What clothes do you usually *carry / wear* during the week?
10 Do you ever *look at / watch* movies on your phone?

5 PRONUNCIATION homophones

> 🔍 **Homophones**
> Homophones are words with different spellings, but the same pronunciation. Some of the confusing verbs in **4** are homophones, e.g., *I can't **hear** you. Please come **here**.*

a **◉ 8.16** Listen to the pairs of sentences, and complete sentence b with a homophone of the **bold** word.

1 a What are you going to **wear** tonight?
  b A _____ are you from? B I'm from Toronto.
2 a I don't **know** what to do.
  b There's _____ milk in the refrigerator!
3 a Hi. Nice to **meet** you.
  b Do you want _____ or fish?
4 a The maximum **weight** for carry-on bags is 25 pounds.
  b I'm coming! _____ for me!
5 a Please **write** soon.
  b Is it on the left or on the _____?
6 a There's only **one** ticket left.
  b Brazil _____ the game 5–1.
7 a I can't **see** the board!
  b I love swimming in the _____.
8 a Have you ever read ***War and Peace***?
  b It was cold, so she _____ a coat.

b **◉ 8.17** Listen and write four sentences. Then practice saying them.

You must be mine.

Yes. I'll be yours.

G possessive pronouns **V** adverbs of manner **P** reading aloud

1 READING

a You are going to read and listen to a short story. First, look at the photos on this page. In what century do you think the story takes place? Why?

b ◀》8.18 Read and listen to Part 1. Then answer the questions with a partner.

1 What did the detective give Hartley?
   What did he offer to do?
2 What did Hartley do when he got the address?
3 What did Vivienne look like?
4 Why was Hartley angry with her?

Think about the story so far: Why do you think Vivienne didn't answer Hartley's letter?

c ◀》8.19 Read and listen to Part 2. Then answer the questions with a partner.

1 Why wasn't Vivienne sure about accepting Hartley's offer?
2 How did Hartley try to persuade her?
3 Where did Hartley and Vivienne first meet?
4 What did Hartley think was the reason why Vivienne didn't say yes to his offer?
5 What do you think Hartley wanted Vivienne to do?

Think about the story so far: Who do you think Héloise is?

Girl – O. Henry

ᘒᘓ ᘒᘓ ᘒᘓ

Part 1

"I've found where she lives," said the detective quietly. "Here is the address."

Hartley took the piece of paper. On it were the words "Vivienne Arlington, No. 341 East 49th Street."

05 "She moved there a week ago," said the detective. "I can follow her if you want. It will only cost you $7 a day and expenses…"

"No, thank you," interrupted Hartley. "I only wanted the address. How much is it?"

10 "One day's work," said the detective. "Ten dollars."

Hartley paid the man. Then he left his office and took a tram to Broadway. After walking a short distance he arrived at the building that he was looking for. He went up the stairs, into her apartment, and saw her

15 standing by the window.

Vivienne was about twenty-one. Her hair was red gold, and her eyes were sea-blue. She was wearing a white top and a dark skirt.

"Vivienne," said Hartley angrily, "you didn't answer

20 my last letter. It took me a week to find your new address! Why didn't you answer me? You knew I was waiting to see you and hear from you."

2 PRONUNCIATION reading aloud

a ◀》8.20 Listen to the last four lines of Part 2. What tells the speakers…?

a where to pause
b in what way to say the dialogue

> 🔍 **Reading aloud**
> Reading stories or poems aloud gives you the opportunity to focus on pronunciation, especially sentence rhythm.

b ◀》8.21 Listen and repeat the names from the story.

Hartley /ˈhɑrtli/   the Montgomerys /mɑntˈgɑməriz/
Vivienne /ˈvɪviən/   Héloise /ɛloʊˈiz/

c Practice reading aloud with a partner. **A** read Part 2 until "…*when I was at the Montgomerys*'." Use the adverbs to help you, and remember to pause at the commas. Then **B** read the rest of Part 2.

Part 2

The girl looked out the window dreamily.

"Mr. Hartley," she said slowly, "I don't know what to
say to you. I understand all the advantages of your offer,
and sometimes I feel sure that I could be happy with you.
But, then sometimes I am less sure. I was born a city girl,
and I am not sure that I would enjoy living a quiet life in the
suburbs."

"My dear girl," said Hartley, "You will have everything
that you want. You can come to the city for the theater, for
shopping, and to visit your friends as often as you want. You
can trust me, can't you?"

"I can trust you completely," she said, smiling at him. "I
know you are the kindest of men, and that the girl who you
get will be very lucky. I heard all about you when I was at
the Montgomerys'."

"Ah!" exclaimed Hartley, "I remember so well the evening
I first saw you at the Montgomerys'. I will never forget that
dinner. Come on, Vivienne, promise me. I want you. Nobody
else will ever give you such a happy home."

Vivienne didn't answer. Suddenly Hartley was
suspicious. "Tell me, Vivienne, is there," he asked, "is there
someone else?"

"You shouldn't ask that, Mr. Hartley," she said. "But
I will tell you. There is one other person – but I haven't
promised him anything."

"Vivienne," said Hartley masterfully, "You must be mine."
Vivienne looked him in the eye.

"Do you think for one moment," she said calmly, "that
I could come to your home while Héloise is there?"

Glossary
advantage *n* a positive thing
suburb *n* an area where people live outside a city
trust *v* believe that somebody is good, honest, etc.
suspicious *adj* feeling that somebody has done something wrong
masterfully *adv* in a dominant way

3 GRAMMAR possessive pronouns

a Look at some sentences from the story. Complete
them with *my* or *mine*.

1 "Vivienne, you didn't answer _____ last letter."
2 "Vivienne…you must be _____."

b 🄖 p.140 Grammar Bank 8C

c ◆)8.23 Listen. Say the sentences with a possessive
pronoun.

》 *It's my book.* (*It's mine.*

4 ▶ VIDEO LISTENING

a ◆)8.18, 8.19 Close your books and watch
or listen to Parts 1 and 2 of the story.

b ◆)8.24 Watch or listen to Part 3 of
the story. Answer the questions.

1 What did Hartley say about Héloise?
2 What did Vivienne promise to do?

Think about the story so far: Who do you think the
lady on the stairs is?

c ◆)8.25 Watch or listen to Part 4 of the story.

1 Who was the lady on the stairs?
2 Who was Vivienne?
3 Who was Héloise?

d Did the ending surprise you? Why (not)?

5 VOCABULARY & WRITING
adverbs of manner

a Look at Part 2 of the story and <u>underline</u>
six adverbs that describe how Vivienne and
Hartley are behaving, speaking, or feeling.

b Make adverbs from the following adjectives.

angry lazy quiet sad serious slow

c ◆)8.26 Listen to some lines from stories. Add
an adverb from **b** after "said" to show how the
person is speaking.

1 "I'm sorry, but I don't love you," he said _____.
2 "Give me back all my letters," she said _____.
3 "I think…I have an idea," he said _____.
4 "Don't make a noise. Everyone is asleep," she
said _____.
5 "I don't feel like doing anything," he said _____.
6 "This is a very important matter," she said _____.

d In pairs, write a short final scene between
Hartley and Héloise. Include at least two
adverbs of manner after *said*.

🄖 **Go online** to watch the video and review the lesson

7&8 Review and Check

GRAMMAR

Circle a, b, or c.

1 I need ____ some emails.
   a to answer b answer c answering
2 The situation is difficult ____.
   a for explain b explain c to explain
3 I don't know what ____.
   a do b to do c that I do
4 I don't really mind ____ housework.
   a do b to do c doing
5 ____ is one of the best forms of exercise.
   a Swiming b Swimming c Swim
6 ____ bring our books tomorrow?
   a Do we have to
   b Have we to
   c Do we must
7 It's free. You ____ pay.
   a don't have to b must not c haven't to
8 You must ____ your grandmother.
   a to call b calling c call
9 You ____ drink so much coffee.
   a not should
   b don't should
   c shouldn't
10 I think you should ____ to her about it.
   a to talk b talk c talking
11 If she ____, she won't come back.
   a goes b went c 'll go
12 If they don't come soon, we ____ them.
   a don't see b won't see c aren't see
13 Call me if you ____ a taxi.
   a won't find b don't find c didn't find
14 A Whose book is that? B It's ____.
   a my b the mine c mine
15 She forgot his birthday, but he didn't forget ____.
   a her b hers c she

VOCABULARY

a Circle the correct verb.
1 When did you *know / meet* your husband?
2 Did you *tell / say* Mark about the party?
3 If we don't run, we'll *miss / lose* the train!
4 I really *wait / hope* she passed the exam.
5 My mother always *carries / wears* a lot of jewelry.

b Complete with a verb from the list.

enjoy feel like finish forget hate learn mind promise

1 Don't _____ to turn off the light before you go.
2 I want to _____ to speak Chinese before my trip to Beijing.
3 Do you _____ going out for dinner later?
4 I _____ to pay you back next week.
5 My parents are very punctual – they _____ being late.
6 Do you _____ waiting here until I'm ready?
7 I really _____ making cakes. It's so relaxing.
8 When are you going to _____ using the printer? I need it!

c Complete the sentences with a preposition.
1 She was really angry _____ me because I was late.
2 Are you interested _____ this TV show?
3 When I was a child, I was afraid _____ dogs.
4 I'd really like to be good _____ dancing.
5 Eating too many cookies and cakes is bad _____ you.

d Complete the *get* phrases.
1 We didn't have the GPS, and we got l_____ on the way home from Boston.
2 I'm always really hungry when I get h_____ from school.
3 She was very sick, but luckily she's getting b_____.
4 We got two t_____ for the theater to see a show.
5 I get a_____ very well with my brothers and sisters.
6 They were married for ten years, but six months ago they got d_____.
7 When I was young, I got a lot of pr_____ on my birthday.

PRONUNCIATION

a Practice the words and sounds.

Vowel sounds   **Consonant sounds**

bull boot singer vase bag monkey nose

b p.166–7 **Sound Bank** Say more words for each sound.

c What sound in **a** do the pink letters have in these words?
1 choose 2 look 3 love 4 doing 5 know

d Underline the stressed syllable.
1 sur|vive 2 ha|ppi|ness 3 a|fraid 4 pre|tend 5 borr|ow

CAN YOU understand this text?

a Read the article. Does it give you...?
1 explanations and tips about waiting in line
2 the history of waiting in line
3 stories about waiting in line

HOW TO BE A LINE WINNER

Do you know why the lines at the other checkouts in the supermarket always seem to move faster than yours? A new book by David Andrews, *Why Does the Other Line Always Move Faster?*, has the answer: because you only notice how fast the other lines are moving when yours is moving slowly. If your line moves fast, then you won't notice the slower lines at all, because you're busy unloading your shopping cart, putting things into bags, and paying.

Of course, another part of the answer is simple probability. If there are three lines in the supermarket and you join the middle one, there is a two in three chance that one of the other lines will be the fastest, whereas yours only has a one in three chance.

SO HOW CAN YOU BE A LINE WINNER?
According to Andrews, this is what you should do:

1 CHOOSE A LINE THAT HAS MORE MEN IN IT. Men are less patient than women, and sometimes give up and leave the line if it's moving very slowly.

2 CHOOSE A LINE ON THE LEFT. Most people are right-handed, and choose lines on the right, so lines on the left are often shorter.

3 DON'T USE THE EXPRESS LANE. Lots of people with a few items can be slower than a few people with lots of items.

4 IF YOU CAN, CHOOSE A CHECKOUT THAT IS "CASH ONLY." Using cash is usually quicker than paying by card.

5 DON'T THINK TOO MUCH! Sometimes it's best just to join the line with the fewest people.

b Read the article again. Match the sentence halves.
1 If your line moves fast, ▨
2 If there are three lines, ▨
3 If there are a lot of women in the line, ▨
4 If you choose a line on the left, ▨
5 If there are a lot of people in the express lane, ▨
6 If people pay cash, ▨

a yours will probably not be the fastest.
b it will move more slowly than a normal lane.
c you'll be too busy to notice the other lines.
d they'll pay more quickly than with cards.
e you will probably spend less time waiting.
f it will move more slowly than a line with lots of men.

▶ CAN YOU understand these people?

🔊 8.27 Watch or listen and answer the questions.

1 Susie   2 Frank   3 Katelyn   4 Joseph   5 Alison

1 For Susie happiness is _____ and having good food and music.
   a going out with friends   b being at home with friends
   c going to a friend's house
2 Frank speaks German _____.
   a fluently   b fairly well   c only a little bit
3 Katelyn doesn't usually ask her parents for advice _____.
   a because she doesn't get along with them
   b because they are much older than she is
   c because she lives far away from them
4 Joseph suggests that people who can't sleep _____.
   a should have the window open at night
   b should buy a really comfortable bed
   c shouldn't have their phone in their bedroom
5 Alison thinks Americans and the British are bad at learning languages _____.
   a because they don't think they need to
   b because they don't have good teachers
   c because English is easier than most other languages

CAN YOU say this in English?

Check (✓) the box if you can do these things.
   Can you...?
1 ▨ talk about something you would like to learn to do, and someone you think would be interesting to meet
2 ▨ talk about three things you like, love, and hate doing
3 ▨ talk about the rules in your (language) school using *must* and *have to*
4 ▨ give someone advice about learning English using *should* and *shouldn't*
5 ▨ remember three examples of Murphy's Law in English
6 ▨ say two true sentences using *mine* and *yours*

Go online to watch the video, review Files 7 & 8, and check your progress

What would you do if you saw a bear?

I'd run away.

G *if* + past, *would* + base form (second conditional) **V** animals and insects **P** word stress

1 VOCABULARY & PRONUNCIATION
animals and insects; word stress

a ◀))9.1 Listen. Which animals can you hear?

b **V** p.161 **Vocabulary Bank** Animals

> 🔍 **Stress in words that are similar in other languages**
> Some words in English, e.g., for animals, are similar to the same words in other languages, but the stress is often in a different place.

c Look at the animal words below. Can you remember which syllable is stressed? <u>Underline</u> it.

ca|mel	cro|co|dile	dol|phin	e|le|phant
gi|raffe	kan|ga|roo	li|on	mo|squi|to

d ◀))9.3 Listen and check. Are any of these words similar in your language? Is the stress in the same place?

e In pairs, ask and answer the questions.
1 Do you have (or have you ever had) a pet? What was it?
2 What's your favorite movie about an animal?
3 What's your favorite cartoon animal?
4 What animal would you most like to see on a safari?
5 Are there any animals or insects you are really afraid of?
6 Are you allergic to any animals or insects?
7 What are the most dangerous animals or insects in your country?

2 LISTENING

a Look at the pictures of the five most dangerous land or sea animals in North America. Which do you think is the most and least dangerous?

b ◀))9.4 Listen and check. Complete 5th to 1st in the chart with the names of the land or sea animals.

c Listen again and complete the facts about the land or sea animals with one or two words in each blank.

5th _____
- They can be over ^{1}_____ long.
- They only attack when people walk, play, or ^{2}_____ in areas where they live.

4th _____
- More than ^{3}_____ of the attacks happen in the ^{4}_____ near California and Florida.
- The place where people are most likely to be attacked is Smyrna Beach, especially if you ^{5}_____.

3rd _____
- They can be about ^{6}_____ long with bands of black, red, and ^{7}_____.
- They only attack when people ^{8}_____ on them by accident.

2nd _____
- The ^{9}_____ is the most dangerous kind.
- They can weigh as much as ^{10}_____ pounds. They have powerful jaws, ^{11}_____, and sharp claws.

1st _____
- They cause about ^{12}_____ deaths a year.
- You need to be especially careful in ^{13}_____.
- They cause about ^{14}_____ car accidents a year.

d Are any of these animals dangerous where you live? Have you ever had a bad experience with any of them?

3 READING & SPEAKING

a Read the quiz questions and answers. Complete each question with an animal or insect from the list.

bee   cows   dog   jellyfish   shark   snake   wasp

WOULD YOU KNOW WHAT TO DO?

We all love seeing animals on TV and in zoos, but some animals can be dangerous. If you met one in real life, would you know the right thing to do? Read about some common and some less common situations and decide what you would do.

IN THE CITY

1 **What would you do...**if a large, aggressive _____ ran towards you?
  a I would shout "down" at it several times.
  b I would put my hands in my pockets and walk slowly backwards.
  c I would keep completely still and look in its eyes.

2 **What would you do...**if you were driving and a _____ or _____ flew into the car?
  a I would open all the windows and wait for it to fly out.
  b I would try to kill it with a map or a newspaper.
  c I would wave my hand to make it go out.

IN THE COUNTRY

3 **What would you do...**if a poisonous _____ bit you on the leg, and you were more than 30 minutes from the nearest town?
  a I would put something very cold on it, like a water bottle.
  b I would suck the bite to get the poison out.
  c I would tie something, e.g., a scarf, on my leg above the bite.

4 **What would you do...**if you were walking a dog on a leash and some _____ started moving towards you?
  a I would let the dog run free.
  b I would pick the dog up in my arms.
  c I would shout and wave my arms.

IN THE WATER

5 **What would you do...**if you were in the ocean and a _____ stung you?
  a I would rub the sting with a towel to clean it.
  b I would wash the sting with fresh water.
  c I would wash the sting with vinegar or ocean water.

6 **What would you do...**if you were in the ocean near the shore and you saw a _____?
  a I would swim to the shore as quickly and quietly as possible.
  b I would float and pretend to be dead.
  c I would shout for help.

b Look at the highlighted verbs and verb phrases. With a partner, try to guess their meaning from the context.

c Read the quiz again and circle your answers, a, b, or c.

d **© Communication** Would you know what to do? **A** p.105 **B** p.110 **C** p.107   Read the answers to one section and tell the others. Did you all choose the right answers?

e Have you ever been in any of these situations? What did you do?

4 GRAMMAR *if* + past, *would* + base form

a Look at quiz questions 1–6 again. Are they about a past situation or an imagined future situation? What tense is the verb after *if*? What form is the other verb?

b **G p.142 Grammar Bank 9A**

5 SPEAKING

Work in groups of three. Take turns choosing a question and asking the others in the group. Then answer it yourself.

WHAT WOULD (OR WOULDN'T) YOU DO...?

...if you saw a mouse in your kitchen
...if you saw a dog attacking someone
...if a bird or a bat flew into your bedroom
...if you saw a large spider in the bathtub
...if it was a very hot day and you were on a beach that was famous for shark attacks
...if someone offered to buy you a fur coat
...if your neighbor's dog barked all night
...if a friend asked you to take care of their cat or dog for the weekend
...if you went to somebody's house for dinner and they gave you...?
  a horse meat   b goat   c kangaroo

> 🔎 Talking about imaginary situations with *would* / *wouldn't*
> I'd (definitely)...
> I think I'd (probably)...
> I (probably) wouldn't...
> I (definitely) wouldn't...
> I don't think I'd...

Go online to review the lesson

Do you have any phobias?

Yes, I've been afraid of heights since I was a child.

G present perfect + *for* and *since* **V** words related to fear, phrases with *for* and *since* **P** sentence stress

1 READING

a Look at all the photos in this lesson. Are you afraid of any of these things?

b Read some information from *fearof.net*, a website about phobias. Complete each phobia with the correct heading from the list.

Fear of butterflies   Fear of crowds
Fear of doctors   Fear of driving   Fear of heights

FEAROF.net
THE ULTIMATE LIST OF PHOBIAS AND FEARS

1

Some people with this phobia find it difficult to pass the test. Others are anxious on freeways or certain roads. In extreme cases, people are afraid of being a passenger in a vehicle. *Comment*

2

People say that actress Nicole Kidman suffers from this phobia. It is closely linked to a general fear of insects. People with this phobia are afraid of most insects with wings, and they feel nauseous or they panic if they see them. *Comment*

3

This phobia is very common in young children, but adults suffer from it, too. Many are especially afraid of having vaccinations or blood tests. *Comment*

4

This fear affects nearly one in every 20 adults. People with this phobia usually avoid tall buildings, skiing, or standing on balconies. *Comment*

5

This phobia affects many people, but women more than men. These people feel very anxious or scared if they are in a noisy place where there are a lot of people, for example a shopping mall or a sports stadium. They often avoid these kinds of places. *Comment*

c Now read some comments posted on the website. Match comments A–E to fears 1–5.

A I am so scared that I haven't been to see one for more than 15 years. I hate thinking about them! I feel the same way about dentists, too. *Carl*

B I have a fear of going over bridges, and on freeways at over 60 mph. I'm OK at 45 mph. I once went over a bridge and I had to stop in the middle – I was really frightened. I haven't driven that way since then, and that was seven years ago. *Becky*

C I thought I was the only person that had this fear! I'm OK with the small ones, but I'm terrified of the big ones. I'm OK if they aren't close to me, but as soon as they start flying near me I run away. I like looking at pictures of them because they can be beautiful, but if they fly towards me, especially towards my face, I panic. *Mina*

D I suffer from this phobia, and what works best for me, if I know that I'm going to be in a situation where there'll be a lot of people, is to arrive early. Then other people arrive little by little, and that helps me. The worst thing is walking into a place that is already full of people. *Simon*

E I've had this phobia for about 20 years. It started when I was a child, about six I think. I had a bad dream where I was in an apartment building high up on a hill and I almost fell out of the window. I woke up and started crying. I haven't been to any really high places since then. Even if I imagine I'm in a high place, I feel dizzy. *Keith*

d Look at the highlighted words in the phobias and comments and match them to the definitions.

1 the noun made from the adjective *afraid* _____
2 one adjective that means *very afraid* _____
3 two synonyms for *afraid* _____, _____
4 an adjective for the feeling that everything is going around in circles _____
5 to suddenly feel afraid and not be able to think _____
6 to be badly affected by something _____

e Do you have or does anyone you know have a phobia? When and how did it start? How does it affect your or their life?

My brother is really scared of flying. He gets very nervous before he flies somewhere. It started about ten years ago when…

2 LISTENING & SPEAKING

a 🔊 9.6 Listen to interviews with two women, Julia and Chloe, about their phobias. Answer the questions.

	Julia	Chloe
1 What is she afraid of?		
2 How long has she had the phobia?		
3 What does she think started it?		
4 How does/did it affect her life?		
5 Has she had any therapy?	Yes / No	Yes / No

b Listen again. What do you find out about their therapy or why they didn't have therapy? Are their phobias better now?

c Which of the phobias in this lesson do you think is the most rational / the most irrational?

3 GRAMMAR & VOCABULARY present perfect; phrases with *for* and *since*

a Look at this extract from the first interview in **2**. Answer the questions.

"How long have you had this phobia?"
"I've had it since I was about 12, so for more than 30 years."

1 When did she begin to be afraid of spiders?
2 Is she afraid of spiders now?
3 What tense do we use to talk about something that started in the past and is still true now?

b 🄖 p.142 Grammar Bank 9B

c Fill in the blanks with *for* or *since*.

_____ 1990	_____ a long time
_____ about 20 years	_____ ages
_____ I was a child	_____ six months
_____ May 4th	_____ a few weeks
_____ then	_____ I got up this morning
_____ 8:15	_____ five minutes

d 🔊 9.8 Listen and check. Practice saying the phrases.

4 PRONUNCIATION sentence stress

a 🔊 9.9 Listen and repeat. Copy the rhythm.

1	I've worked	I've worked here	I've worked here for ten years.
2	We've lived	We've lived in Vancouver	We've lived in Vancouver since 2012.
3	How long	How long have you known	How long have you known your best friend?

b 🔊 9.10 Listen and write five sentences. Practice saying them.

5 SPEAKING

a Look at the questions below. Which two tenses do you need to use? What are the missing words in each question?

		Name
have	/ a pet? What is it? How long / it?	
	/ a tablet? What kind? How long / it?	
live	/ in a modern apartment? How old is it? How long / there?	
	/ near this school? Where exactly? How long / there?	
know	/ anybody from another country? Where's he (or she) from? How long / him (or her)?	
be	/ a fan of a soccer team? Which team? How long / a fan?	
	/ a member of a club or organization? Which one? How long / a member?	
	/ married? What's your partner's name? How long / married?	

b 🔊 9.11 Listen and check.

c Move around the class and ask other students the questions. If they answer *Yes, I do* or *Yes, I am* to the first question, ask the second question. Try to find a different person for each question.

Do you have a pet? (*Yes, I do.*

What is it? (*A dog.*

How long have you had it?

9C Scream queens

> She's written several books.

> Really? Her mother also wrote books.

1 VOCABULARY & PRONUNCIATION
biographies; word stress, /ɔːr/

a Number the events in what you think is a logical order. Compare with a partner. Do you agree?

- *1* be born
- ___ marry somebody / get married
- ___ go to elementary school
- ___ have children
- ___ go to high school
- ___ go to college
- ___ graduate from high school
- ___ separate
- ___ get a job
- ___ divorce somebody / get divorced
- ___ retire
- ___ fall in love
- *13* die

b 🔊 9.12 Look at the highlighted words in the list above. Which syllable is stressed? Listen and check.

c 🔊 9.13 Listen and repeat the words and sound.

horse	born	divorced	four

d Practice saying these words. (Circle) the ones with the /ɔːr/ sound.

more	work	world	boring	door	worse	sports
wear	form	near	score	word		

e 🔊 9.14 Listen and check. What rule can you hear for words with *wor* + consonant?

2 READING

a Look at the photos of Janet Leigh and her daughter and read the introduction. Have you seen any of their movies?

b Read ten paragraphs about the lives of the two women. In pairs, decide which five are about Janet Leigh (**JL**) and which five are about Jamie Lee Curtis (**JLC**).

c Work in pairs. **A** Re-read the facts about Janet Leigh and **B** about Jamie Lee Curtis. Close your books and tell your partner what you can remember.

Like mother, like daughter

Janet Leigh (1927–2004) was one of movie director Alfred Hitchcock's favorite actresses, and was in more than 50 movies and many TV shows. Her daughter Jamie Lee Curtis (1958–) is also a successful actress.

1 ___ She had two children from her third marriage to actor Tony Curtis. The marriage lasted 11 years. She then married again, and this marriage lasted for the rest of her life.

2 ___ She has been in many different kinds of movies, including the comedies *Trading Places*, *A Fish Called Wanda*, and *True Lies*, for which she won a Golden Globe Award for Best Actress in a Musical or Comedy. She has also starred in the comedy-horror TV series *Scream Queens*. In one episode she recreated the famous scream from *Psycho*.

3 ___ She has been married for more than 20 years to actor, screenwriter, and director Christopher Guest. She became Lady Haden-Guest when her husband became Baron Haden-Guest after the death of his father.

4 ___ She was married four times. At the age of 15 (pretending to be 18) she married 18-year-old John Kenneth. They got divorced four months later.

5 ___ She has written several bestselling children's books. She says she finds the inspiration for her writing all around her – in the experiences of her children, her godchildren (one is actor Jake Gyllenhaal), her friends, and of course in her own life.

3 GRAMMAR present perfect or simple past? (2)

a Cover the text. Which sentences are about Janet Leigh? Which are about Jamie Lee Curtis? Why are the tenses different?

1 **She was** in more than 50 movies.
2 **She's been** in many different kinds of movies.
3 **She was** married four times.
4 **She's been** married for more than 20 years.
5 **She's written** several best-selling children's books.
6 **She wrote** four books.

b Ⓖ **p.142 Grammar Bank 9C**

6 [   ] She is a fan of *World of Warcraft*, and has been to events such as ComicCon and BlizzCon.

7 [   ] Her most famous role was the victim in *Psycho*, for which she won the Golden Globe Award for Best Supporting Actress and received an Oscar nomination. However, she was traumatized by the iconic shower scene, and for the rest of her life she never took showers, only baths.

8 [   ] She is close friends with actress Sigourney Weaver. In an interview, she admitted that she has never watched Weaver's film *Alien* the whole way through because she was too scared.

9 [   ] She was in five movies, including *Houdini*, with Tony Curtis, and also starred opposite Frank Sinatra and Paul Newman.

10 [   ] She wrote four books. The first, the memoir *There Really Was a Hollywood*, became a *New York Times* best seller.

4 LISTENING

a Look at the photo of a famous father and his son. Do you know who they are? Do you know anything about them?

b 🔊 9.16 Listen to a radio show about the son and check your answers. What's the son's real name? How well did he and his father get along?

c Listen again. What is the connection between the son and 1–9? Make notes.

1 Zowie Bowie
   His name when he was very young.
2 UK, 1971
3 Angie
4 the drums, the saxophone, and the piano
5 an 8mm video camera
6 the London Film School
7 commercials for French Connection and Heinz ketchup
8 *Moon*
9 *Source Code* and *Warcraft*
10 paparazzi

d Do you think Jamie Lee Curtis and Duncan Jones have been successful because their parents were famous, or because they are genuinely talented? Do you think it's more common for children to want to do the same job as their parents, or to do something completely different?

5 SPEAKING & WRITING

a Think about an older person (a friend or a member of your family) who is alive and who you know well. Prepare to answer the questions below about their life and to tell your partner any other interesting information about them.

The past		The present	
When was	born?	Where does	live now?
Where was	born?	How long has	lived there?
What did	do after graduated from high school? (e.g., get a job, go to college, get married, have children, etc.)	What does	do? (job)
		What does	do in free time?
		Do you think	has had a good life? Why (not)?

b Interview your partner about his / her person. Ask for more information. Do your two people have anything in common?

I'm going to tell you about my grandmother.

When was she born?

c Ⓦ **p.118 Writing** A biography Write a biography of a person you know, or a famous person.

 Go online to review the lesson

1 ▶ HOLLY AND ROB IN BROOKLYN

a ◀ 9.17 **Watch or listen to Rob and Holly. Mark the sentences T (true) or F (false).**

1 Rob has just done an interview.
2 He is in a hurry.
3 He has another interview in Manhattan.
4 He has another coffee.
5 Barbara calls Rob.
6 The restaurant is booked for seven o'clock.

> 🔍 **American and British English**
> *restroom* = American English
> *toilet* = British English
>
> *the subway* = American English
> *the underground* = British English

b **Watch or listen again. Say why the F sentences are false.**

2 VOCABULARY directions

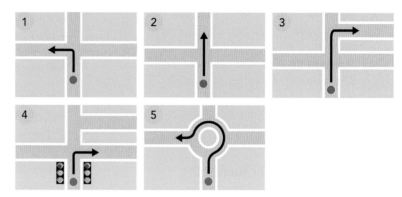

a **Look at the pictures and complete the phrases.**

1 Turn _____.
2 Go _____ ahead.
3 Take the _____ turn on the right.
4 Turn right at the _____ lights.
5 Go around the _____ and take the third exit.

b ◀ 9.18 **Listen and check.**

c **Cover the phrases and look at the pictures. Say the phrases.**

> 🔍 **American and British English**
> *go straight ahead* = American English
> *go straight on* = British English

3 ▶ ASKING HOW TO GET THERE

a ◀ 9.19 **Cover the conversation on p.77 and watch or listen. Mark Rob's route on the map.**

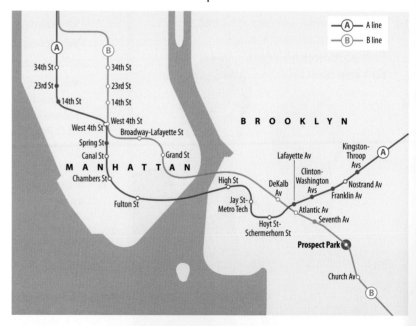

b Watch or listen again. Complete the **You hear** phrases.

You say	You hear
How do I get to Greenwich Village on the subway?	Go to the subway station at Prospect Park. ¹_____ the B train to West 4th Street.
How many stops is that?	Six or seven.
OK. And then?	From West 4th Street take the A train, and get ²_____ at 14th Street.
Could you say that again?	OK. From Prospect Park take the B train to West 4th Street, and then take the A train to 14th Street. That's only one ³_____.
Where's the restaurant?	Come out of the subway on Eighth Avenue, go ⁴_____ on for about 50 yards and take the ⁵_____ left. That's Greenwich Avenue. The restaurant's on the ⁶_____. It's called The Tea Set.
OK, thanks. See you later.	And don't get ⁷_____!

c ▶9.20 Watch or listen and repeat the **You say** phrases. Copy the rhythm.

d Practice the conversation with a partner.

e 👥 In pairs, role-play the conversation.

   A **B** is at Prospect Park. Choose a destination on the subway map. Give **B** directions. You start with *Go to the subway station at…*

   B Follow **A**'s directions, and tell **A** which subway stop you have arrived at. Were you right?

f Change roles.

(*Take the B train to… Then…*

---

4 ▶ **ROB IS LATE…AGAIN**

a ◀9.21 Watch or listen to Rob and Jenny. Is the date a success?

b Watch or listen again and answer the questions.

   1 What excuse does Rob give for being late?
   2 How long has Jenny waited for him?
   3 What does Rob suggest they do?
   4 What does Jenny say that Rob could do?
   5 Who is Rob interested in: Holly or Jenny?

c Look at the **Social English** phrases. Can you remember any of the missing words?

> 🎈 **Social English**
> 1 **Rob**   I'm so _____.
> 2 **Rob**   I _____ I'm sorry.
> 3 **Jenny**   I don't _____ like a walk.
> 4 **Jenny**   It's been a _____ day.
> 5 **Jenny**   I didn't _____ to say that.

d ◀9.22 Watch or listen and complete the phrases. How do you say them in your language? Then watch or listen and repeat the phrases.

e Complete conversations A–D with **Social English** phrases 1–5. Then practice them with a partner.

A	Let's go to the park.	And anyway, it's raining.
B	You're half an hour late!	▨
	The dinner's cold.	The traffic was terrible.
C	Your mother is so annoying!	My mother? Annoying?
	Sorry, ▨	
D	Let's watch a movie on TV.	No, I'm tired. ▨

CAN YOU…?

▨ give and understand directions on the street
▨ give and understand directions for using public transportation
▨ apologize

🔵 **Go online** to watch the video, review the lesson, and check your progress

G expressing movement   **V** sports, expressing movement   **P** word stress

> Where did you run?
>
> I ran around the park.

1 VOCABULARY & PRONUNCIATION sports; word stress

a What sports can you see in the photos?

b ◄)10.1 <u>Underline</u> the stressed syllable in these sports. Listen and check.

> base|ball   bas|ket|ball   cy|cling   gym|na|stics   hand|ball   ka|ra|te
> rug|by   ski|ing   so|ccer   te|nnis   track and field   vo|lley|ball
> wind|sur|fing   yo|ga

c Put the sports in the correct column. Add two more sports to each column.

play (sports with a ball)	go (+ verb + *-ing*)	do
baseball	*cycling*	*gymnastics*

2 SPEAKING

Ask and answer with a partner. Give and ask for as much information as you can.

SPORTS – YOU LOVE THEM OR YOU HATE THEM

- Do you play any sports or do any exercise?
  - Yes. What? Do you enjoy it?
  - No. Why not? Did you play more sports or do more exercise in the past? Why do you do less now?
- Which sports do you think are the most exciting to watch?
- Which sports do you think are the most boring?
- Are you (or is anyone in your family) a fan of a sports team? Which one? Do you (or they) go to their games?
- Have you ever been to any live sporting events?
- What is the most exciting sporting event you have ever been to or watched on TV?

3 VOCABULARY & GRAMMAR expressing movement

a ◄)10.2 Listen to the soccer commentary. Complete the sentences.

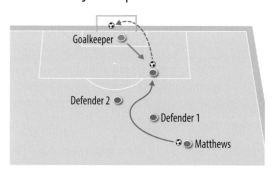

He goes ¹_____ one defender, and another! The goalkeeper's coming ²_____ him. Matthews shoots. And the ball goes ³_____ the goalkeeper and ⁴_____ the goal!

b **V** p.162 Vocabulary Bank Expressing movement

c Complete the sentences with a verb from the list.

> hit   kick   run   throw

1 In basketball you have to _____ the ball **through a hoop**.
2 In soccer you have to _____ the ball **into a goal**.
3 In tennis you have to _____ the ball **over a net**.
4 In the 800-meter race you have to _____ twice **around the track**.

d **G** p.144 Grammar Bank 10A

e Look at the photos in **1** again and complete the sentences with a verb and a preposition.

1 She's *jumping* *over* the bar.
2 He's _____ the ball _____ the hoop.
3 She's _____ the ball _____ the net.
4 She's _____ _____ the mountain.
5 He's _____ _____ the track.
6 He's _____ the ball _____ the goal.
7 He's _____ _____ the line.

4 READING & SPEAKING

a Do you ever watch women's sports? Are they team sports or individual sports? In your country, are there any women's sports that are as popular as men's?

b Read some comments people posted on a forum. Find one person who obviously prefers women's sports and one who obviously prefers men's sports.

c Read comments A–F again and match them to the main point that each person is making.

1 ☐ Women soccer players don't complain as much as men.
2 ☐ Men's tennis matches are more boring than women's.
3 ☐ People will never enjoy watching women playing team sports as much as watching men.
4 ☐ Men are always better athletes than women.
5 ☐ We should let men and women play together on the same teams.
6 ☐ Watching women doing individual sports is as interesting as watching men.

d Look at the highlighted sport words in the comments. What do they mean? How do you pronounce them?

e Check (✓) the comments you agree with on the website. Then compare with a partner. Say why you agree, and what you think about the other comments.

5 WRITING

a Do you see people playing sports or exercising in your town or city? What do you see them doing?

b Ⓦ p.119 Writing An article
Read about parkrun, and then write an article.

Why aren't women's sports as popular as men's?

Send us your thoughts

A I actually prefer watching women's tennis. Men usually hit the ball so hard, especially when they serve, that their opponent can't return it, so it's less exciting to watch.
RichSmith *12:22 pm*

B I think we should open up men's soccer to women. Then we could compare, person to person, how well each player performs, and teams could be made up of the best players, both men and women. That's true of most team sports, actually.
WayneKeys *12:27 pm*

C Women's sports that are identical to men's sports – soccer and basketball, for example – will never be as popular as men's, because men are faster, stronger, and more athletic. On the other hand, sports that highlight the strengths of female athletes – tennis, gymnastics, ice skating – are popular. But it's interesting that none of those are team sports.
Brandi *3:02 pm*

D Brandi, I think you're right about the difference between team and individual sports. When I watch the Olympics (winter and summer), I enjoy the women's and men's individual events equally. The women probably run / swim / ski a little slower than the men, but I can't really tell, and it's just as exciting.
Lynn228 *3:12 pm*

E Most people want to watch the best sports people perform at the highest level. If you compare top male and female athletes, physical differences mean that women are always inferior athletes to men.
SimonB *12:58 pm*

F In men's soccer, the players fall all the time and act like babies. The women don't do that. I've read research that says that women hardly ever pretend to be hurt. And when they *are* hurt, they get up again 30 seconds faster than men.
ZoeCruz *8:25 pm*

The alarm goes off at 2:35 a.m.

Do you get up then?

G word order of phrasal verbs **V** phrasal verbs **P** linking

1 READING & SPEAKING

a Answer the questions with a partner.

1 What time do you wake up during the week?
2 Do you use an alarm to wake up? If not, what makes you wake up?
3 Do you get up immediately after you wake up?
4 When you first get up do you feel…?
 a awful
 b sleepy
 c awake and energetic

b Look at the photos and read the information about Ella and Peter. What time do you think they have to get up?

c **C** Communication Early birds **A** p.105 **B** p.111 Read about Ella or Peter and tell your partner about her / him.

(*Ella gets up very early, at…*

d In general are you a morning or an evening person? Would you like to work the hours that Ella or Peter work? Why (not)? Do you know people who get up very early for work?

2 VOCABULARY & GRAMMAR phrasal verbs

> **Phrasal verbs**
> *Wake up, get up, go out, give up*, etc., are common phrasal verbs (verbs with a preposition or adverb).
>
> Sometimes the meaning of the two separate words can help you guess the meaning of the phrasal verb, e.g., *go out*. Sometimes the meaning of the two words does not help you, e.g., *give up*.

a Look at some things that Ella and Peter say. With a partner, explain what the highlighted verbs mean.

1 "The alarm goes off at 2:35."
2 "I wake up on time because I have an alarm that repeats."
3 "I get up at about 4:45."
4 "During the week we don't go out at all."
5 "I really love my breakfast show, and I never want to give it up."

b Can you think of a phrasal verb that means…?

1 to try to find something   l_____ f_____
2 to put on clothes in a store to see if they are the right size   tr_____ o_____
3 to have a friendly relationship (with somebody)   g_____ a_____ w_____

c **V** p.163 **Vocabulary Bank** Phrasal verbs

Ella White is a baker and has her own small shop.

Peter Gordon is the host of the *Breakfast Show* on Eagle Radio.

1 Turn off the alarm clock.
2 Turn the alarm clock off.
3 Turn it off.

d Look at the photo and <u>underline</u> the object of the phrasal verb in each sentence.

e Complete the rules about separable phrasal verbs with *noun* or *pronoun*.

> 1 If the object of a phrasal verb is a _____, you can put it **after** the verb + *up*, *on*, etc., **OR between** the verb + *up*, *on*, etc.
> 2 If the object of a phrasal verb is a _____, you **must** put it **between** the verb + *up*, *on*, etc.

f **G** p.144 Grammar Bank 10B

3 LISTENING

a 🔊 10.7 You're going to listen to a radio show about getting up early. Listen to the first part. What does Tim Powell do at these times/for these periods of time?

1 5:45 *He wakes up at 5:45.*
2 30 minutes
3 Just before 9:00 a.m.
4 9:00 a.m.
5 5:20 a.m. on Thursdays
6 70 hours

b Listen again. Complete the sentence about Tim.

Tim gets up early because _____
_____ .

c 🔊 10.8 Now listen to the second part of the show. Complete three reasons why it's good to get up early.

1 The first reason why it's good to get up early is that the early morning is _____.
2 The second reason is that if you get up early, you _____ _____ _____ early.
3 The third reason is that it's better to _____ _____ in the morning, when you have _____.

d Listen again. What examples does the host give to explain each reason? What advice does he give to people who have problems getting up early?

e Do you think getting up very early is a good idea? If you got up an hour earlier, what would you do with your extra hour?

4 PRONUNCIATION linking

a 🔊 10.9 Listen and write the missing words.

1 I can't concentrate with the radio on. Please *turn* ___ *it* ___ *off*. ___
2 There's a wet towel on the floor. _____ _____ _____ .
3 If you don't know what the word means, _____ _____ _____ .
4 Why have you taken your coat off? _____ _____ _____ !
5 This book was very expensive. Please _____ _____ _____ .
6 Why are you wearing your coat in here? _____ _____ _____ !

b Listen again. Practice saying the sentences. Try to link the phrasal verbs and pronouns, e.g., *turn‿it‿off*, and say them as one word.

5 SPEAKING

a Read the questions in the questionnaire and think about your answers.

b Work in pairs. Interview your partner with the questions.

Phrasal verb
questionnaire

▶ Do you ever **get up** very late or very early? Why? When?

▶ What's the first thing you **turn on** after you **wake up** in the morning?

▶ Have you ever forgotten to **turn** your phone **off** at a concert or the movies?

▶ Do you **throw away** old clothes or do you give them to other people?

▶ Do you enjoy **trying on** clothes when you go shopping?

▶ When you go shopping, do you usually **write down** what you have to buy? Do you only buy what's on the list?

▶ What kind of stores do you enjoy **looking around**? What kind don't you enjoy?

▶ Do you often **go away** on the weekend? Where to?

▶ Do you enjoy **looking after** small children? Why (not)?

▶ Have you ever asked your neighbors to **turn** the TV or the music **down**? What happened?

▶ How do you usually **get around** your town or city during the day? What about late at night?

Go online to review the lesson

G the passive **V** people from different countries **P** /ʃ/, /tʃ/, and /dʒ/

The saxophone was invented by a Belgian.

When was it invented?

1 VOCABULARY & PRONUNCIATION
people from different countries; /ʃ/, /tʃ/, and /dʒ/

a What are the nationality adjectives for these countries? What do the first group have in common?

1 the United States Belgium Italy	**2** China Switzerland France the Netherlands England Spain

> 🔍 **Talking about people from different countries**
>
> We usually use *the* + nationality adjective + *-s* to talk about the people from a country, e.g., *the Americans, the Belgians*, etc.
>
> If the nationality adjective ends with /s/, /z/, /ʃ/, or /tʃ/, we don't add *-s*, e.g., *the English, the Chinese, the Dutch*, etc.
>
> For some countries there is a special word for the people, e.g., *Thailand > the Thais, Turkey > the Turks*.

b Read the information box and complete the chart.

	nationality adjective	people from that country
1 England		the
2 Brazil		the
3 Russia		the
4 Turkey		the
5 Argentina		the
6 Morocco		the
7 Japan		the
8 Spain		the

c 🔊 10.10 Listen and check.

d 🔊 10.11 Listen and repeat the words and sounds.

a shower	b chess	c jazz

e 🔊 10.12 What sound do the pink letters make, a, b, or c? Listen and check. Practice saying the sentences.

1 It's a Chinese invention. ____
2 I love French cheese and Spanish olives. ____
3 He has a Japanese watch. ____
4 It's a German technology company. ____
5 He's a Belgian musician. ____

2 GRAMMAR the passive

a In small groups, try to complete the sentences with the things in the photos.

CDs   dynamite   fireworks   glasses
the hot-air balloon   Lego   the cell phone
the saxophone   stamps   the watch

9th century

1 _____ were invented by the Chinese.

13th century

2 _____ were invented by the Italians.

18th century

3 _____ was invented by two French brothers.

19th century

4 _____ were invented by an English teacher.

5 _____ was invented by a Belgian musician.

6 _____ was invented by a Swedish scientist.

7 _____ was invented by the Swiss.

20th century

8 _____ was invented by the Americans.

9 _____ was invented by a Danish businessman.

10 _____ were invented by a Dutch company.

b 🔊 10.13 Listen and check.

c Listen again. Write down one other piece of information about each invention.

d Make five true sentences using the words in the chart.

Glasses	are produced	after the inventor of dynamite.
The first stamp	~~were invented~~	by Adolphe Sax.
Twenty billion pieces of Lego	was invented	the Penny Black.
The saxophone	is named	every year.
The Nobel Prize	was called	~~in about 1286.~~

Glasses were invented in about 1286.

e Look at the two sentences below and answer the questions.

    a The Swiss invented the watch.
    b The watch was invented by the Swiss.

    1 Do the sentences mean the same thing?
    2 In which sentence is the focus more on the watch?
    3 In which sentence is the focus more on the Swiss?

f **G** **p.144 Grammar Bank 10C**

3 SPEAKING

C **Communication** Passives quiz **A** p.106 **B** p.111
Make sentences for your partner.

4 ▶ VIDEO LISTENING

a Look at the photos. Which six things do you think were invented by women?

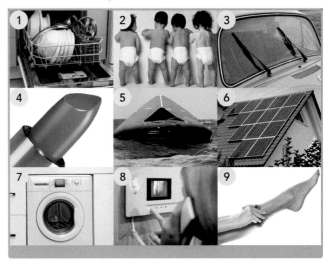

b Watch the video *Invented by women* and check.

c Watch again and answer the questions.

    1 **Marion Donovan (1917–1998)**
    What did her father and uncle do? What were diapers made of before? What happened to her invention in 1951?

    2 **Josephine Cochrane (1839–1913)**
    What often happened after her dinner parties? Who were the first customers for her invention?

    3 **Mary Anderson (1866–1953)**
    When and where did she get the idea for her invention? What did drivers have to do at that time when it was raining?

    4 **Marie Van Brittan Brown (1922–1999)**
    What was her job? What kind of neighborhood did she live in? Who helped her with her invention? What could you do if you saw an unwelcome stranger at the door?

    5 **Maria Beasley (1847–1904?)**
    Which famous ship were her inventions used on? How many survivors had used her invention?

    6 **Mária Telkes (1900–1995)**
    What nationality was she? What was her nickname? What did she design in 1948?

d Which three of the inventions in this lesson do you think are the most important? Which ones could you live without?

C **Go online** to watch the video and review the lesson

GRAMMAR

Circle a, b, or c.

1 If I ____ a snake, I'd be terrified.
   a see   b saw   c seen
2 What ____ if a large dog attacked you?
   a you would do
   b will you do
   c would you do
3 I ____ that bike if I were you.
   a wouldn't buy   b didn't buy   c won't buy
4 I ____ in this house since I was 12.
   a live   b lived   c have lived
5 We haven't seen my uncle ____ a long time.
   a since   b during   c for
6 ____ have you had this car?
   a How long
   b How much time
   c How long time
7 I ____ married for 15 years. I got divorced in 2017.
   a 've been   b am   c was
8 When ____ John F. Kennedy die?
   a did   b has   c was
9 The golf ball ____ the hole.
   a went on   b went   c went into
10 The door opened and two men ____.
   a came out   b came out of   c out
11 Your phone's on the floor. ____!
   a Pick up it   b Pick up   c Pick it up
12 I've lost my keys. Can you help me ____?
   a look them for
   b look for them
   c look after them
13 The first book in the series was ____ ten years ago.
   a write   b written   c wrote
14 The watch ____ in the nineteenth century.
   a were invented
   b is invented
   c was invented
15 *The Milkmaid* was painted ____ Vermeer.
   a for   b by   c to

VOCABULARY

a **Circle** the word that is different.

1 butterfly   goat   fly   mosquito
2 pig   sheep   cow   lion
3 spider   shark   jellyfish   whale
4 marry   separate   divorce   retire
5 basketball   cycling   rugby   volleyball

b Complete with *for* or *since*.

1 _____ three weeks
2 _____ a very long time
3 _____ 2015
4 _____ I was ten years old
5 _____ five years

c Complete with a word from the list.

along   down   forward   into   off   out   past   through   toward   up

1 We drove _____ a lot of tunnels in the Rocky Mountains.
2 When it started to rain, we went _____ a café to wait until it stopped.
3 She walked _____ the street, looking in the store windows.
4 When the cow started running _____ me, I was terrified.
5 Go _____ the gas station, and it's the next turn on the right.
6 You have to take _____ your shoes before going into the temple.
7 If you don't know the meaning of a word, look it _____.
8 Can you turn the heat _____? It's very hot in here.
9 She's looking _____ to her vacation.
10 Can you find _____ what time the movie ends?

d Complete with nationality words.

1 The _____ are very good at judo. (Japan)
2 There are three _____ students in my class. (Thailand)
3 I'd love to have a _____ watch. (Switzerland)
4 Some _____ speak French, and some speak Arabic. (Morocco)
5 We met a really friendly _____ couple. (Turkey)

PRONUNCIATION

a Practice the words and sounds.

Vowel sounds		Consonant sounds			
horse	bird	shower	chess	jazz	television

b **(P)** p.166–7 **Sound Bank** Say more words for each sound.

c What sound in **a** do the pink letters have in these words?

1 giraffe   2 work   3 divorce   4 invention   5 Dutch

d Underline the stressed syllable.

1 bu|tter|fly   3 pho|bi|a   5 ka|ra|te
2 re|tire   4 e|le|phant

CAN YOU understand this text?

a Read the article once. Who do you think behaved the worst? Why?

b Read the article again and answer with a name. Which of the bad losers…?

1 insulted the people in the crowd
2 became very emotional when he couldn't take part
3 attacked two officials
4 tried to hit an opponent
5 said he was sorry after the event

▶ CAN YOU understand these people?

🔊 **10.15** Watch or listen and answer the questions.

1 Bettina   2 Mairi   3 Dave   4 Sarah   5 Kathy

1 Bettina would like to see ____ in the wild.
  a a black bear   b a brown bear   c a polar bear
2 Mairi has been frightened of spiders ____.
  a since she was five or six   b for five or six years
  c since 2005 or 2006
3 Dave's great aunt ____.
  a is travelling to California
  b is more than a hundred years old
  c has had a difficult life
4 Sarah ____.
  a prefers running to hiking   b does yoga and pilates
  c prefers outdoor activities to indoor activities
5 Kathy gets up early ____.
  a every day   b during the week   c at weekends

CAN YOU say this in English?

Check (✓) the box if you can do these things.

Can you…?

1 ☐ say what you would do if…
  a a dog attacked you   b you won the lottery
  c you had more free time
2 ☐ talk about how long you have…
  a lived where you are now
  b had your laptop or phone   c been at this school
3 ☐ describe your life story
4 ☐ describe three things that you have to do in certain sports, using a verb and a preposition of movement
5 ☐ make true sentences with *take off*, *turn down*, and *look after*
6 ☐ talk about when three things were invented or built

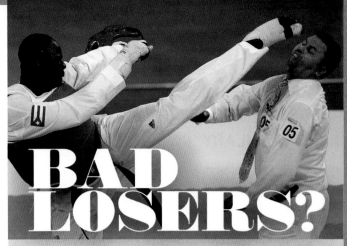

BAD LOSERS?

The hardest lesson to learn in sports is how to lose like a true sportsperson, without blaming your defeat on others. Here are some famous moments when losing was just too hard…

In the 1982 German Grand Prix, Nelson Piquet was winning the race. He was trying to pass Eliseo Salazar (who was last in the race), but Salazar didn't let him go past him, so Piquet crashed into Salazar. Piquet jumped out of his car and started trying to hit and kick Salazar (without much success!).

South Korean soccer player Ahn Jung-Hwan scored the goal that sent Italy out of the 2002 World Cup when they beat them 2-1. But Jung-Hwan also played for the Italian soccer team Perugia. After the game, the president of the club, Luciano Gaucci, announced that the player's contract would not be renewed. "That gentleman will never set foot in Perugia again," Gaucci said. "I have no intention of paying a salary to somebody who has ruined Italian soccer." Gaucci later apologized, but Ahn Jung-Hwan left the club and never went back to an Italian club.

In the 2003 Track and Field World Championship, the 100-meter runner Jon Drummond was disqualified for a false start. Drummond lay down on the track and began to cry. Two hours later his coach told reporters, "He's still crying. We're making him drink water because he's becoming dehydrated."

In the 2008 Beijing Olympics, Angel Matos of Cuba was trying to win a bronze medal in tae kwon do when the referee disqualified him for a technical error. Matos was furious, and after several minutes of arguing he kicked the referee in the head, and then attacked a Swedish judge. He was immediately banned from all competitions for life.

In 2016, at the Olympics in Rio de Janeiro, the German men's soccer team lost to the host nation in the final. Brazil won their first ever Olympic gold medal in the event and the local fans were delighted. As they celebrated, one very disappointed German player, Robert Bauer, decided to show seven fingers to the fans, to remind them of the time Germany beat Brazil 7-1 in the 2014 World Cup semi-final.

🔄 **Go online** to watch the video, review Files 9 & 10, and check your progress

Did you like school?

Yes, I did. I used to have a great time.

1 VOCABULARY school subjects

a ◑ **11.1** Listen. Match the lessons you hear to the subjects.

- art
- foreign languages (English, etc.)
- geography
- history
- IT (= information technology)
- literature
- math
- PE (= physical education)
- science: physics, chemistry, and biology

b ◑ **11.2** Listen and check. Which words helped you to identify the subjects?

c ◑ **11.3** Listen and repeat the subjects.

d Did you have any other subjects in elementary school, middle school, or high school? Which subjects were you…?

a good at   b OK at   c bad at

(*I was very bad at math.*

2 READING

a Look at the three photos. What do you know about the people? When they were at school, who do you think was probably…?

- the most popular student
- the most talented student
- the quietest student

b Read the article and check your answers.

c Read the article again. Answer with the name of the famous person (e.g., *J.K. Rowling*) or their teacher (e.g., *J.K. Rowling's teacher*).

Who…?

1 told older students his / her old student was too young to date
2 had family problems while he / she was at school
3 sometimes sees his / her old student perform
4 thinks he / she is similar to a character in his / her student's books
5 took part in a musical production
6 was not very interested in what he / she became famous for

d When you were at school, what do you think your teachers thought of you?

Fame Academy

They grew up to become famous. But what were they like when they were in school? Did they already have that "spark" that made them different? We asked their teachers.

Alex Turner lead singer and songwriter of Arctic Monkeys

Mark Coleman, *his PE teacher*

Everyone liked Alex at school. He was very good at English. Mr. Baker, his English teacher, really liked poetry, and I'm sure Alex was inspired by him because his song lyrics are incredible. But he didn't use to be very interested in music; he was much more interested in sports. He was possibly the best in the school at basketball. When he was 14, he broke his arm in my PE class. He was in the hospital for a week, and we collected money and bought him a CD, so he was probably beginning to get interested in music. Everyone at the school is very proud of the band, and I'm sometimes invited to their concerts.

J.K. Rowling author

John Nettleship, *her science teacher*

Joanne was about 12 when I taught her. Her school days weren't very happy. The school was a little like a prison, and then her mom, Anne, got very sick. Anne worked as my technician, and Joanne used to come and wait outside the science building for her mom, so that they could walk home together. She was obviously very worried about her mom. She was a very quiet child. I don't remember her ever answering a question. I think she was keeping all her experiences in her head to use later in her stories.

Joanne has said that no characters in Harry Potter are based more than 10% on a real person. So maybe it's just a coincidence that I used to have long, black hair. But to be honest, I think Professor Snape, especially in the later books, is very much like me.

3 GRAMMAR used to

a Look at sentences 1–3. Does *used to / didn't use to* refer to…?

1 a the present   b the past
2 a things that happened repeatedly, or that were true for a long time
   b things that happened once

1 Kristen Bell used to get asked out on dates by older boys.
2 Alex Turner didn't use to be very interested in music.
3 J.K. Rowling used to come and wait outside the science building for her mom.

b **G** p.146 Grammar Bank 11A

4 PRONUNCIATION used to / didn't use to

> 🔍 **Pronouncing used to**
> When we say *used to* or *(didn't) use to* we link the two words together. They are both pronounced /ˈyustə/.

a 🔊 11.5 Listen and repeat. <u>C</u>opy the <u>rhy</u>thm.

1	I used to	I used to be good	I used to be good at French.
2	She didn't	She didn't use to	She didn't use to wear glasses.
3	Did you	Did you use to	Did you use to walk to school?

b 🔊 11.6 Now listen and make affirmative or negative sentences or questions with *used to*.

1))) *have a lot of friends* (*I used to have a lot of friends.*

Kristen Bell actor

Marylee Petty, her English teacher

Kristen was in my ninth-grade English class. She was nice, friendly, and very pretty. I remember older boys used to ask her out on dates, and I told them all to stay away from her. She was too young for them! In her junior year, she auditioned for the role of Dorothy in our school's production of *The Wizard of Oz* and got it. She was – and still is – so talented. That particular show was one of my favorite student productions in all the years I've worked here. When Kristen was in *Frozen* – one of my favorite movies, I recognized her voice right away – it's so beautiful!

> **Glossary**
> **Professor Snape** the potions teacher in the Harry Potter books

5 LISTENING & SPEAKING

a Look at some answers to the question *Did you like school?* Mark them **P** (= positive), **N** (= negative), or **B** (= both negative and positive).

	P	I didn't like it. I absolutely loved it!
		No, not really. I didn't like it at all.
		I didn't hate school, but I don't think I liked it very much.
		Sometimes. Yeah, most of the time.
		Well, yes and no.
		Yes, definitely. I really enjoyed school.

b 🔊 11.7 Now listen to three men and three women answering the question *Did you like school?* Match the speakers 1–6 to their answers in **a**. Did the men or the women enjoy school more, or were they about the same?

c Listen again. For each speaker, write down the subjects they liked and didn't like.

d Think about when you were at school (if you are in high school, think about when you were in elementary school). Prepare your answers to the questions below. Think of examples you could give.

1 **Did you like school? Why (not)?**
2 **Did you love or hate certain subjects?**
3 **Did you use to…?**
  • be disorganized or very organized
  • be late for school or on time
  • get a lot of homework or a little
  • have a teacher you really liked
  • have a teacher you hated
  • wear a uniform

e Work in groups of three and have a conversation. Take turns answering a question, and then ask the others *What about you?*

Help! I can't decide!

G *might* **V** word building: noun formation **P** diphthongs

> Why are you taking a raincoat?

> Because it might rain.

1 GRAMMAR *might*

a Interview your partner with the questionnaire. Ask for more information. Which of you is more indecisive?

Are you indecisive?

> Well, I might need it...

> Why are you packing that?

Do you have problems deciding...?

* what to pack when you're going away
* what to buy when you go shopping
* what to wear in the morning
* what to order in a restaurant
* where to go on vacation

Do you often change your mind about things? What kind of things?

Do you think you are indecisive?

Yes   No   I'm not sure

b 🔊 11.8 Nancy and Brian are going on vacation. Nancy is packing. Listen to their conversation. What four things does Brian think Nancy <u>doesn't</u> need to take?

1 _____   2 _____   3 _____   4 _____

c Listen again. Complete Nancy's reasons for taking the things.

1 I might _____.
2 It might _____.
3 The hotel might not _____.
4 They're _____.

d 🔊 11.9 Listen to them at the airport. What happens?

e Look at sentences 1–3 in **c**. Do we use *might* for...?

1 an obligation OR 2 a possibility

f 🄶 p.146 Grammar Bank 11B

g In pairs, take turns asking and answering the questions below. Use *I'm not sure. I might… or I might…* and give two possibilities each time.

1 What are you going to do after class?
2 What are you going to have for dinner tonight?
3 What are you going to do on Saturday night?
4 Where are you going to have lunch on Sunday?
5 Where are you going to go for your next vacation?

What are you going to do after class?

(*I'm not sure. I might go home or I might…*

2 PRONUNCIATION diphthongs

a 🔊 11.11 Listen and repeat the words and sounds.

1		bike	might buy decide since
2		train	may fail key break
3		phone	know although blouse won't
4		chair	fear there wear scared
5		ear	here engineer souvenir where
6		tourist	sure bus Europe curious
7		owl	round towel south throw
8		boy	town noisy enjoy annoy

b Look at the words next to the sounds. Which one has a different sound?

c 🔊 11.12 Listen and check.

d 🔊 11.13 Listen and repeat the sentences.

3 LISTENING & SPEAKING

a Look at the photos. What style of jeans do you usually buy? What color? Do you sometimes have problems finding the right ones?

JEANS: STYLE & FIT

ripped   bootcut   straight   skinny   boyfriend

b ◀)) 11.14 Listen to a talk called *Is too much choice making us unhappy?* Does the speaker think the answer is yes or no?

c Listen again. What are the five main points in the talk? Choose a, b, or c.

1 Nowadays, it is __ to buy jeans than in the past because there is so much choice.
   a easier   b more difficult   c more fun

2 One of the examples the speaker gives of where we have a lot of choice today is __.
   a buying coffee in supermarkets
   b choosing which airline to travel with
   c finding a boyfriend or girlfriend

3 Research has shown that when we have a lot of choice we often __.
   a worry that we've chosen the wrong thing
   b can't decide what to buy
   c buy more than we really need

4 In another study, about jams, Professor Lepper found that people were happier when they had __ jams to choose from than when they had 24.
   a sixteen   b six   c sixty

5 Professor Lepper suggests that when we go shopping we should __.
   a do research in advance
   b look at all the options carefully
   c relax and choose quickly

d In your country, is there a lot of choice in the following? Do you think it's a good or bad thing?

1 in supermarkets   4 in coffee shops
2 on TV   5 in restaurants
3 in clothes stores

4 VOCABULARY & SPEAKING
word building: noun formation

a Look at some extracts from the listening. Are the highlighted words verbs or nouns?

Being able to **choose** from a lot of **options** is a good thing.

We feel happier when we have less **choice**.

We should try to relax when we have to **decide** what to buy.

We get stressed every time we have to make a **decision**.

b Read the information about making nouns from verbs. Write the verbs next to the nouns in the chart.

> 🔍 **Making nouns from verbs**
> With some verbs you can make a noun by adding *-ion*, *-sion*, or *-ation*, *-ition*, e.g., *decide* → *decision*.
> With some other verbs, the noun is a new word, e.g., *choose* (verb) → *choice* (noun).

Verb	Noun + -ion, -sion, or -ation / -ition	Verb	Noun new words
1 *decide*	de**ci**sion	9	choice
2	election	10	advice
3	confusion	11	flight
4	invention	12	life
5	competition	13	death
6	education	14	success
7	invitation		
8	pronunciation		

c ◀)) 11.15 Listen and check. Underline the stressed syllable in the multisyllable verbs and nouns.

d Complete the questions with a noun from **b**.

When was the last time you…?
1 had to make a big _____
2 got an _____ to a wedding or party
3 went on an international _____
4 got excited about a new _____

Have you ever…?
5 won a _____
6 given someone _____ about something, e.g., a relationship
7 been in a _____ or _____ situation
8 not understood somebody because of their _____

e Ask and answer the questions with a partner.

Go online to review the lesson

11C Twinstrangers.net

> I have a son named James.
>
> So do I.

G *so, neither* + auxiliaries   **V** similarities and differences   **P** /ð/ and /θ/

1 READING & LISTENING

Thomas and Toby

Cordelia and Ciara

Niamh and Luisa

a Look at the photos. One of them is of identical twins, but two of them are of complete strangers. Which one do you think is of twins?

b Read about the project *Twin Strangers* and check your answers.

Two women recently met by chance at Bremen University, in Germany. One was English, and one was Irish, and they were both on Erasmus scholarships. Nothing unusual there, except for one thing. The two girls look identical. Their hair is the same color and length, they're the same age and size, and when you see them together, in the photo they put on social media, you would think that they were identical twins. In fact, Cordelia Roberts and Ciara Murphy are unrelated.

It seems that it is not uncommon for people who are unrelated to look almost identical. Niamh Geaney, from Dublin, and two friends were so interested in trying to find their "twins" that they set up an online project called Twin Strangers. Very quickly, Niamh found a remarkably similar-looking stranger who lived just a few miles away. It's perhaps not so surprising since both young women look typically Irish, with dark hair and very pale skin, but then Niamh found another lookalike – Luisa Guizzardi, who is from Genoa in Italy!

Glossary
Erasmus scholarships
a program that allows students from the European Union to study in another country

c Read the text again. Who set up the website? What was surprising about one of the "twins" that Niamh found?

d ◀))11.16 Journalist Maggie Alderson decided to try the website for herself. Listen to her talking. Did she find a "twin"? How did she feel about the experience?

e Listen again and answer the questions.

1 How does Maggie describe her appearance?
2 What was her first reaction when she saw her "twins"?
3 Who in Maggie's family did one woman look like?
4 What did her husband think of one of her "twins"? Did Maggie agree?
5 How did she change her profile?
6 What did Maggie's brother think of the woman who she put on her Facebook page?
7 In what ways does Maggie look like this woman?
8 Have they been in contact with each other?

f Talk to a partner.

1 Would you like to try the website? Why (not)?
2 Do you know any identical twins? Can you tell the difference between them?
3 Do you know anyone who looks very much like you?

2 VOCABULARY similarities and differences

a Look at some sentences about the people in **1**. Complete them with a word from the list.

as	both	from	identical	like	similar

1 Cordelia and Ciara were _____ on Erasmus scholarships.
2 The two girls looked _____.
3 The first photos Maggie looked at were totally different _____ her.
4 Maggie found one woman who looked just _____ her brother.
5 Her husband said "She has the same mouth _____ you."
6 Maggie's "twin" looks very _____ to her.

b ◀))11.17 Listen and check.

c Complete the sentences about you and your family. Tell your partner.

1 I have the same colour eyes as my _____.
2 I look like my _____.
3 My personality is quite similar to my _____'s.
4 My _____ and I both like _____.

3 GRAMMAR *so, neither* + auxiliaries

a Read about two more twins and answer the questions.

1 Who are Jim Springer and Jim Lewis?
2 Why didn't they know each other?
3 What did Jim Lewis decide to do when he was 39?
4 How long did it take him?

In the US, identical twin brothers were adopted soon after they were born. One brother was adopted by a couple named Lewis in Lima, Ohio, and his brother was adopted by a couple named Springer in Dayton, Ohio. By coincidence, both boys were named "Jim" by their new parents. Jim Springer's parents told him that he had an identical twin brother, but that he was dead. But Jim Lewis knew the truth. For many years he did nothing about it, but when he was 39, he decided to try to find his brother. Six weeks later, the two Jims met for the first time in a café in Dayton, and they probably had a conversation something like this...

"I'm **Jim.**"

"So am **I.**"

b �))11.18 Cover the conversation below. Listen once. Try to remember three things they have in common.

c Listen again and fill in the blanks. Which coincidence do you find the most surprising?

> **A** Hi! I'm Jim.
> **B** So ¹_____ I. Great to meet you. Sit down. Are you married, Jim?
> **A** Yes...well, I've been married twice.
> **B** Yeah? So ²_____ I. Do you have any children?
> **A** I have one son.
> **B** So ³_____ I. What's his name?
> **A** James Allen.
> **B** That's amazing! My son's name is James Allen, too!
> **A** Did you go to college, Jim?
> **B** No, I didn't.
> **A** Neither ⁴_____ I. I was a terrible student.
> **B** So ⁵_____ I. Hey, this is my dog Toy.

> **A** I don't believe it! My dog's named Toy, too!
> **B** He wants to go outside. My wife usually takes him. I don't do any exercise at all.
> **A** Don't worry. Neither ⁶_____ I. I drive everywhere.
> **B** What car do you have?
> **A** A Chevrolet.
> **B** So ⁷_____ I!
> **A** Hey, let's go have a hamburger, OK?
> **B** Sure. You know, I once worked in a hamburger restaurant.
> **A** Unbelievable! So ⁸_____ I!

d Look at the conversation again. Answer the questions with a partner.

1 Find two phrases that the twins use…
   when they have something ⊞ in common.
   when they have something ⊟ in common.
2 What part of the phrases changes?

e Ⓖ p.146 Grammar Bank 11C

f �))11.20 Listen and respond. Say you're the same.

1 ◉) *I take the bus to work.* (*So do I.*)

4 PRONUNCIATION /ð/ and /θ/

a ◉)11.21 Listen and repeat the words and sounds.

 🧘 mother	neither they brother
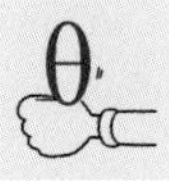 👍 thumb	both thirty throw

b ◉)11.22 Listen and write four more words in each group. Practice saying the words you added.

5 SPEAKING

a Complete the sentences so they are true for you.

Me	Someone who's the same as me
I love _____. (a kind of music)	
I don't like _____. (a drink)	
I'm very _____. (adjective of personality)	
I'm not very good at _____. (sport or activity)	
I'm going to _____ after class. (an activity)	
I have to _____ every day. (an obligation)	
I don't eat _____. (a kind of food)	

b Move around the class saying your sentences. For each sentence try to find someone like you, and write down their name. Respond to other people's sentences:

If you have something in common say *So do / am I*, or *Neither do / am I.*

A *I love heavy metal.* (**B** *So do I.*)

A *I don't like soda.* (**B** *Neither do I.*)

If you are different, say *Really?* and then say how you are different.

A *I love classical music.* (**B** *Really? I don't like it.*)

A *I don't like milk.* (**B** *Really? I like it in coffee.*)

🔄 **Go online** to review the lesson

91

Practical English Time to go home

on the phone

1 ▶ ROB AND JENNY TALK ABOUT THE FUTURE

a ◀))11.23 **Watch or listen to Rob and Jenny. Mark the sentences T (true) or F (false).**

1 Rob is going home today.
2 He says it will be difficult to stay in touch.
3 Jenny suggests that she could go to London.
4 Rob thinks it's a good idea.
5 They're going to a restaurant tonight.
6 Barbara wants to talk to Jenny.

> 🔍 **American and British English**
> *You just missed him* = American English
> *You've just missed* him = British English
> *(cell) phone* = American English
> *(mobile) phone* = British English

b Watch or listen again. Say why the F sentences are false.

2 ▶ ON THE PHONE

a ◀))11.24 **Cover the conversations below and watch or listen. Answer the questions.**

1 Who does Rob want to speak to?
2 How many times does he have to call?

b Watch or listen again. Complete the You hear phrases.

You hear	You say
Hello. Broadway Grill.	Oh, sorry. I have the wrong number.
NewYork 24seven. ¹_____ can I help you?	Hello. Can I speak to Barbara Keaton, please?
Just a second. I'll ²_____ you through…Hello.	Hi, is that Barbara?
No, I'm sorry. She's not at her ³_____ right now.	Can I leave a message, please?
Sure.	Can you tell her Rob Walker called? I'll call back later.
I'll give her the ⁴_____. You could try her cell phone.	Yes, I'll do that. Thank you.
I'm sorry, I can't take your ⁵_____ at the moment. Please ⁶_____ a message after the beep.	Hello, Barbara. This is Rob returning your call.
NewYork 24seven. How can I help you?	Hello. It's Rob again. Can I speak to Barbara, please?
Just a second. I'm sorry, the line's ⁷_____. Do you want to hold?	OK, I'll hold.
Hello.	Hi, Barbara. It's me, Rob.
Rob, hi! I tried to call you earlier.	What did you want to talk about?

c 🔊 11.25 Watch or listen and repeat the **You say** phrases. Copy the rhythm.

d Practice the conversations with a partner.

e 🗣️ In pairs, role-play the conversations.
   A (book open) You are the Broadway Grill, the receptionist, etc. You start *Hello. Broadway Grill.*
   B (book closed) You want to speak to Barbara.

f Change roles.

3 ▶ IN CENTRAL PARK AGAIN

a 🔊 11.26 Watch or listen to Rob and Jenny. Is it a happy ending or a sad ending?

b Watch or listen again and answer the questions.
   1 Who has some news?
   2 What did Barbara offer Rob?
   3 What did Jenny do this morning?
   4 What does Jenny ask Barbara to do?

c Look at the **Social English** phrases. Can you remember any of the missing words?

> 💬 **Social English**
> 1 **Rob**   You _____ first.
> 2 **Jenny**   That's great _____.
> 3 **Jenny**   I'll _____ her.
> 4 **Jenny**   I'll explain _____.
> 5 **Barbara** Is everything _____?
> 6 **Jenny**   _____ better.

d 🔊 11.27 Watch or listen and complete the phrases. How do you say them in your language? Then watch or listen and repeat the phrases.

e Complete conversations A–F with **Social English** phrases 1–6. Then practice them with a partner.

A	Carol needs to speak to you. It's urgent.	OK, ▨
B	So what's the problem with your parents?	It's very complicated. ▨
C	You look worried. ▨	No. I just heard that my sister's sick.
D	Did you hear that Mark and Allie are getting married?	Wow! ▨
E	Are you OK, Roz?	Yes, I'm fine. ▨
F	I have some news for you.	So do I. ▨

CAN YOU...?

☐ call somebody and say who you are / who you want to talk to
☐ leave a message for somebody
☐ respond to news

🖱️ **Go online** to watch the video, review the lesson, and check your progress

G past perfect **V** time expressions **P** the letter *i*

Why was she so angry?

Because her husband had left her behind.

1 READING & VOCABULARY time expressions

a Look at the pictures and the headlines for three news stories. What do you think the stories are about?

b Read the stories and check. Match them to the headlines.

IN THE MAIL

LEFT BEHIND

FALSE ALARM

1

Last Sunday at about 2:00 a.m., police in Sydney, Australia, received several phone calls about shouting and loud noises that were coming from an apartment in a suburb of the city. The callers had heard a woman screaming, a man shouting "I'm going to kill you! You're dead!," and somebody throwing furniture.

A police car went to the apartment immediately. A man opened the door.

"Where's your wife?" the officer asked.

"I don't have one," the man replied.

"Where's your girlfriend?"

"I don't have one," the man replied again.

The officer told the man that his neighbors had heard shouting and screaming.

"Come on, what have you done to her?" the officer asked.

"It was a spider," the man replied. "A really big one."

"What about the woman who was screaming?"

"Yes, sorry, that was me," the man said. "I really, really hate spiders. I was trying to kill it."

The police looked around the apartment and confirmed that nobody was hurt. Except the spider.

2

A woman in West Sussex, England, got a big surprise yesterday when she opened a large box of DVDs that she had bought on eBay and a cat suddenly jumped out. The cat, named Cupcake, had gotten into the box eight days earlier, when her owner Julie Baggott was packing the box to send to her customer. Julie didn't notice that Cupcake had climbed into the box and fallen asleep.

Julie's customer called the RSPCA, who took the cat and brought it to a vet. Dr. Ben Colwell, who treated Cupcake, said that she was very frightened and very thirsty – the cat had survived the 260-mile trip with no food or water. Luckily, Cupcake had a microchip in her neck, so the vet found Julie's information and called her.

Julie had been very sad about losing her cat. She had put up posters and looked for Cupcake for days. "I feel terrible," said Julie. "I put the DVDs in the box and I closed it right away, so I don't know how she got in there. It was a miracle she was alive."

3

An Argentinian family was driving home after a vacation in Brazil when the husband, Walter, made an unfortunate mistake. He stopped at a gas station, filled up the car with gas, and used the restroom. But when he drove off, he didn't notice that his wife Claudia wasn't in the car.

Claudia had been asleep in the back seat. While her husband was in the restroom, she woke up and went into the store to buy some cookies, but when she came back outside she found that her husband had left without her. The couple's 14-year-old son didn't notice that his mother wasn't there because he was playing on his phone in the front seat.

Walter only realized his wife wasn't in the car after he'd driven 60 miles. Meanwhile, Claudia tried to call him, but she couldn't get a signal, so she asked the gas station manager for help. He contacted the local police, who took her to the police station.

Her husband eventually returned to pick her up two hours later. When he arrived, Claudia was so angry that all she could do was scream and kick the car.

Glossary
RSPCA Royal Society for the Prevention of Cruelty to Animals

c Read the stories again. For each story, put the events in the order that they happened.

Story 1

☐ The police arrived at the apartment.
`1` The neighbors heard someone screaming.
☐ The man explained what had happened.
☐ The man killed the spider.

Story 2

☐ Julie put up posters.
☐ Julie lost her cat.
☐ The vet contacted Julie.
☐ The cat jumped out of the box.

Story 3

☐ Walter got back into the car and drove off.
☐ Walter realized what had happened.
☐ Claudia went into the store.
☐ Walter used the restroom.

d Look back at the stories and complete the sentences with time expressions.

1 A police car went to the apartment _____.
2 A cat _____ jumped out.
3 I put the DVDs in the box and I closed it _____.
4 _____, Claudia tried to call him.
5 Her husband _____ returned two hours later.

e Match the time expressions in **d** to their meaning.

1 quickly and unexpectedly _____
2 after a long time _____
3 while something else was happening _____
4 without delay _____ _____

2 GRAMMAR past perfect

a Look at a sentence from one of the stories. Which action happened first? Number the sentences 1 and 2.

Walter only realized his wife wasn't in the car after he'd driven 60 miles.

☐ Walter realized his wife wasn't in the car.
☐ Walter drove 60 miles.

b What do you think '*d* is a contraction of? What form of the verb is *driven*?

c Underline two more examples of the past perfect in each story.

d **Ⓖ p.148 Grammar Bank 12A**

e Complete the sentences in your own words. Use the past perfect.

1 When I got to the airport, I suddenly realized that…
2 When we arrived home from our vacation, we found that…
3 When the movie started, I immediately realized that…
4 I couldn't answer any of the exam questions because I…
5 We spent 20 minutes in the parking lot looking for the car because we couldn't remember…

f Compare with a partner. Are your sentences the same or different?

g **Ⓒ Communication** What had happened? **A p.106 B p.112** Try to guess your partner's sentences.

3 PRONUNCIATION the letter *i*

> 🔍 **The letter *i***
> The letter *i* is usually pronounced /aɪ/ before a consonant + *e*, e.g., *drive* and is pronounced /ɪ/ between two consonants if there is no *e*, e.g., *mistake*.

a Put the words from the stories in the correct row.

| alive arrive driven kill miracle notice outside signal |
| spider surprise survive while wife |

fish		bike	

b 🔊 **12.2** Listen and check. Practice saying the words. Which two words in the /ɪ/ column don't follow the rules?

4 SPEAKING

a Look at the pictures from two more newspaper stories. What do you think the stories are about?

b **Ⓒ Communication** Two more stories **A p.107 B p.112** Read your story and tell it to your partner.

c Which of the stories in this lesson do you find the most unbelievable? Have there been any funny or unusual stories in the news recently? What happened?

Ⓖ **Go online** to review the lesson

12B Think before you speak

She told me that she didn't want to marry him.

Really? Did she say why?

G reported speech **V** *say* or *tell*? **P** double consonants

1 LISTENING

a Look at the photo of two women, Rosemary and Iris. What do you think they're talking about?

You'll never guess what's happened.

No! That can't be true!

b ◀))12.3 Listen to the conversation between the two women. Who are Jack and Emma? What has happened to them?

c Listen again and answer the questions.

1 Rosemary thinks she heard them…
   a arguing.
   b having a party.
   c having a conversation.
2 According to Rosemary, Emma said she was…
   a seeing another man.
   b looking for a new job.
   c going to stay with her mother.
3 Emma said she had…
   a left the dog with a neighbor.
   b left the children with her sister.
   c left the children with her mother.
4 Iris is going to…
   a tell her husband.
   b tell her family.
   c tell another neighbor.

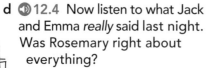

d ◀))12.4 Now listen to what Jack and Emma *really* said last night. Was Rosemary right about everything?

e Do you and your friends ever gossip? What about?

2 GRAMMAR & VOCABULARY
reported speech; *say* or *tell*?

a Compare what Emma said (direct speech) with what Rosemary says that she said (reported speech). <u>Underline</u> the words that are different in the highlighted reported speech.

Emma	I'm going to stay with my mom.
Rosemary	She said that she was going to stay with her mom.

Emma	I won't come back.
Rosemary	She told him that she wouldn't come back.

Emma	I've taken the children to my sister's.
Rosemary	She said that she'd taken them to her sister's.

b **G** p.148 Grammar Bank 12B

c ◀))12.6 Listen to some sentences in direct speech. Say them in reported speech. Begin *He said…* or *She said…*

1 ◀)) *I'm in a hurry.*
   (*She said that she was in a hurry.*

2 ◀)) *I'll write.*
   (*He said that he would write.*

d Complete the sentences with the correct form of *say* or *tell*.

1 "I have a problem," Annie _____.
2 Annie _____ us that she had a problem.
3 Lisa _____ that she was leaving her husband.
4 He _____ the teacher that he'd left his homework at home.
5 His teacher _____ that he didn't believe him.
6 Can you _____ Mark that I can't meet him tonight?
7 What did you _____ to her?
8 When I was a child, my mother used to _____ us not to _____ hello to people we didn't know.

3 SPEAKING

a Read the questions and plan your answers. One answer must be invented!

- What's your favorite food?
- Who's your favorite singer?
- What are you planning to do this summer?
- What languages can you speak?
- What did you do last Saturday?
- Have you ever spoken to a famous person?

b Work in pairs. **A** ask **B** the questions. Listen and take notes on **B**'s answers. Then change roles.

c Change partners. Tell your new partner what your first partner said. Decide together which answer you think your previous partners invented.

He told me (that)... *She said (that)...*

d Check with your first partners. Were you right?

4 PRONUNCIATION double consonants

a Look at five groups of words. Match each group to a vowel sound.

æ cat	ʌ up	fish	ɛ egg	clock

1 gossip college opposite bottle robber
2 luggage runner funny summer butterfly
3 written miss bitten different middle
4 happy married accident rabbit baggage
5 letter leggings message umbrella tennis

b ◉12.7 Listen and check. Practice saying the words.

> 🔍 **Double consonants**
> The vowel sound before a double consonant is normally short when it is the stressed syllable, e.g., *gossip* /ɑ/, *luggage* /ʌ/, *written* /ɪ/, *happy* /æ/, and *letter* /ɛ/.
>
> Double consonants are usually pronounced the same as single consonants, e.g., *pp* = /p/.

c How do you think you pronounce the words below? Check the pronunciation and meaning with a dictionary.

kettle pillow pottery supper waffle

5 READING & SPEAKING

a Read the text once. Is it a) a magazine article, b) a traditional story, or c) an extract from a novel? How do you know?

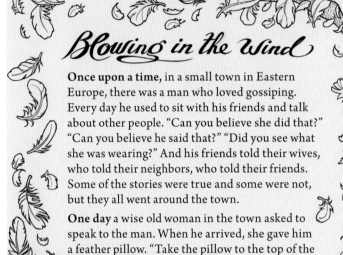

Blowing in the Wind

Once upon a time, in a small town in Eastern Europe, there was a man who loved gossiping. Every day he used to sit with his friends and talk about other people. "Can you believe she did that?" "Can you believe he said that?" "Did you see what she was wearing?" And his friends told their wives, who told their neighbors, who told their friends. Some of the stories were true and some were not, but they all went around the town.

One day a wise old woman in the town asked to speak to the man. When he arrived, she gave him a feather pillow. "Take the pillow to the top of the hill, then cut it open, and release all the feathers," she said. "But why?" he asked. "Just do as I say," she answered, "and come back tomorrow." So the man went to the top of the hill. He cut open the pillow. All the feathers flew out, and the wind carried them in all directions.

The next day he went back to see the wise woman and he told her that he had done what she wanted. "Good," she replied. "Now I want you to go back up the hill with the empty pillow and refill it with the feathers." "But that's impossible," said the man. "The feathers have blown everywhere."

b Read the story again. What do you think the moral is? Go to **Communication** Blowing in the wind **p.107**. Read the end of the story and check.

c Answer the questions with a partner. Give examples where you can.

1 Who do you think gossip more, men or women?
2 Do you think men and women gossip about different things?
3 Do older people gossip more than younger people?
4 Do you have any friends who gossip a lot? Are you careful about what you tell them?
5 Are people in your country interested in celebrity gossip? Are you?
6 Do you think gossip spreads more quickly than it used to? Why?
7 Have you ever posted gossip on social media? What was it?

Who painted that picture?

I can't remember.

1 PRONUNCIATION & VOCABULARY
review of question words

a How do you pronounce these question words? Put them in the correct row.

how   what   when   where   which   who   whose   why

witch	
house	

b ◗)12.8 Listen and check.

c Complete the questions with words from **a**. One word is used three times.

Your English class

1 _____ do you usually get to class: on foot, by car, or on public transportation?
2 _____ do you usually sit next to?
3 _____ are you going to do after this class?
4 _____ many different teachers have you had since you started learning English?
5 In your class, _____ pronunciation do you think is the best?
6 _____ often have you missed a class?
7 If you could go to an English-speaking country on vacation, _____ would you go?
8 _____ would your ideal time be to have English classes?
9 _____ do you find more difficult, speaking or listening?
10 Are you going to continue learning English? _____ (not)?

d Ask and answer the questions with a partner.

2 GRAMMAR questions without auxiliaries

a With a partner, see how many of the quiz questions you can answer from memory.

b Now try to find the answers you couldn't remember in Files 1–11.

c Look at the quiz. Answer these questions.

1 What is the subject of the verb in question 1?
2 What is the subject of the verb in question 2?
3 How are the verbs different in questions 1 and 2?
4 Which other five questions on the quiz are similar grammatically to question 1?

d **G** p.148 Grammar Bank 12C

The American English File Quiz

1 Who painted *The Milkmaid* and *Girl Reading a Letter*?

2 Where did Sam find his phone?

3 What were the couple looking at in Cartier-Bresson's photo *Couple in the Park*?

4 What kind of guided tour can you book on *TripAside*?

5 How much exercise a day is good for our health?

6 Which city came in first in the *World's Most Honest City* Reader's Digest survey?

7 What did Captain Edward Murphy give his name to?

8 Who wrote the short story *Girl*?

9 What is the most dangerous land or sea animal in North America?

10 What phobia does Nicole Kidman have?

11 Who won a Golden Globe award for her role in *Psycho*?

12 Who directed the 2016 movie *Warcraft*?

13 Who invented the saxophone?

14 Which Harry Potter character was probably inspired by one of J.K. Rowling's teachers?

15 Who did Jim Springer meet for the first time when he was 39 years old?

3 SPEAKING

Ⓒ **Communication** General knowledge quiz **A p.107 B p.112 First complete the questions. Then ask them to your partner.**

4 ▶ VIDEO LISTENING

a Have you ever been on a quiz team? Did you enjoy it?

b Watch the video *Trivia night* and answer the quiz questions in teams.

Trivia Night Answer Sheet

Round 1 Sports

1 _____
2 _____
3 _____
4 _____
5 _____

Round 2 Music

1 _____
2 _____
3 _____
4 _____
5 _____

Round 3 Geography

1 _____
2 _____
3 _____
4 _____
5 _____

Ⓖ **Go online** to watch the video and review the lesson

11&12 Review and Check

GRAMMAR

Circle a, b, or c.

1 When I was a child I ____ have long hair.
a use to   b used to   c used

2 Jack ____ like sports when he was at school.
a don't use to
b didn't used to
c didn't use to

3 I might ____ Sophie a ring for her birthday.
a buy   b to buy   c buying

4 Sue ____ come. She has to work late.
a might no   b not might   c might not

5 A I love traveling. B ____
a So do I.   b Neither do I.   c So am I.

6 A I can't do this exercise. B ____
a So can I.
b Neither can't I.
c Neither can I.

7 A I went to the movies last night.
B ____ What did you see?
a So went I.   b So I did.   c So did I.

8 I was too late – when I got to the train station, the train ____.
a has left   b had left   c left

9 When I got to the airport, I remembered that I ____ the kitchen window.
a hadn't closed
b didn't close
c haven't closed

10 Lisa told me that she ____ to marry Jason.
a has wanted   b want   c wanted

11 Kevin said he ____ back in ten minutes.
a would be   b was   c will be

12 Our grandfather ____ that he had worked in a factory when he was young.
a said us   b told   c told us

13 Who ____ in the house next door?
a lives   b live   c does live

14 Where ____ that dress?
a you bought
b bought you
c did you buy

15 How many people ____ to go on the trip?
a do want   b does want   c want

VOCABULARY

a Make nouns from the verbs.

1 invent _____   4 invite _____
2 decide _____   5 die _____
3 choose _____

b Write the school subjects.

1 _____ *Hamlet* is one of Shakespeare's greatest plays.
2 _____ 200 ÷ 8 = 25
3 _____ What's the capital of Morocco?
4 _____ There are 20,000 species of bee in the world.
5 _____ Augustus was the first Roman Emperor.

c Complete the missing words.

1 Julia and Jane are i_____ twins.
2 I live on the same street a_____ my sister.
3 Her new novel is very s_____ to her last one.
4 Dave is very attractive and his son looks just l_____ him.
5 My parents b_____ love classical music.

d Circle the correct time expression.

1 We were having a barbecue when it *suddenly / right away* started raining.
2 The doctor will see you again next week. *Eventually / Meanwhile*, you have to rest as much as possible.
3 When the phone rang I answered it *suddenly / immediately*.
4 It was a long trip, but *eventually / meanwhile* I got home.
5 She said it was important, so I did it *right away / eventually*.

e Complete the sentences with *say* or *tell*.

1 _____ me a story!
2 Did he _____ that he would come back?
3 If you see Jack, _____ hello!
4 What did they _____ to you?
5 You should _____ your teacher what happened.

PRONUNCIATION

a Practice the words and sounds.

Vowel sounds: ear, tourist, owl, boy
Consonant sounds: thumb, mother, right

b P p.166–7 Sound Bank Say more words for each sound.

c What sound in a do the pink letters have in these words?

1 math 2 sure 3 neither 4 fear 5 written

d Underline the stressed syllable.

1 in|de|ci|sive   3 i|mme|di|ate|ly   5 ac|ci|dent
2 i|den|ti|cal   4 neigh|bor

100

CAN YOU understand this text?

a Read the two stories. What do they have in common?

b Read the stories again and mark the sentences **T** (true) or **F** (false).

1 Matteo and Enrica were going to Italy for a birthday party.
2 They were late because they got lost on the way to the airport.
3 When they got to the plane, it was ready to leave.
4 They were arrested after they'd gotten on the plane.
5 Hubert bought the lottery scratch-off cards in an airport store.
6 One million dollars is the biggest prize for a scratch-off card.
7 At first, he wasn't sure if he'd really won the prize.
8 He's decided to give all the money away to other people.

▶ CAN YOU understand these people?

🔊 **12.10** Watch or listen and answer the questions.

① Brian ② Caroline ③ John ④ Morad ⑤ Kathy

1 When Brian was in school he didn't like studying ____.
   a math b history c biology
2 Caroline's French teacher inspired her to ____.
   a be a French teacher b continue learning French
   c set up a language school in Australia
3 When John has to make a decision he prefers to ____.
   a make it quickly b think about it for a long time
   c ask for advice
4 Morad has ____.
   a a twin brother b twin brothers c two brothers
5 Kathy thinks that ____.
   a men gossip more than women
   b women gossip more than men
   c men and women gossip the same amount

CAN YOU say this in English?

Check (✓) the box if you can do these things.

Can you...?

1 ☐ talk about 3 things you used to do when you were a child
2 ☐ say 2 things you might do next week
3 ☐ respond to these sentences with *so* or *neither*:
   I like pop music.   I haven't finished this exercise yet.
   I'm going out tonight.   I didn't know the answer.
4 ☐ continue these sentences with the past perfect:
   a I got to the train station, but…
   b When I saw him I was surprised because…
5 ☐ report two things that somebody said to you yesterday using *said* or *told me*
6 ☐ ask three questions without an auxiliary verb beginning with *Who, How many,* and *Which*

Stop the plane – we want to get on!

An Italian couple ran out onto the runway of Malta's international airport to stop a Ryanair jet from leaving for Italy without them, a Maltese court heard on Thursday.

Matteo Clementi, 26, and Enrica Apollonio, 23, got stuck in terrible traffic on their way to the airport on Wednesday. When they arrived, the gate was closed and they were not allowed to board their flight back to Italy. They went to the next gate, forced open a security door, and ran toward the plane. The engines were running and the stairs had been removed, but the couple tried signaling to the pilots to let them get on. However, they were not allowed to board and were arrested by security staff.

A lawyer defending them in court said that Wednesday was Enrica's 23rd birthday. She had wanted to celebrate it with her family and friends in Italy. Instead, she spent the evening in prison, and the couple was fined €2,329.

From $20 to $1,000,000 in 30 minutes

A man who found $20 on the street near San Francisco International Airport used it to play the California lottery and won $1 million, lottery spokesman Greg Parashak said on Monday.

Hubert Tang used the $20 to buy two lottery scartch-off cards at a store near the airport on Wednesday and won the top prize with one of them, Parashak told us.

Tang said, "I scratched off the ticket outside of the store. I told my friend who I was with that I didn't know if it was real, but I thought I had just won a million dollars." Tang, who works as a waiter at the airport, had not played the lottery for the last ten years. He said that he planned to continue working and had not decided how to spend the money. But he said that he might leave $20 bills in different places so that other people could find them and be lucky like him.

🔄 **Go online** to watch the video, review Files 11 & 12, and check your progress

Communication

a Read the article *How to survive meeting your partner's parents for the first time*. Then tell **B** the five tips and give more details. When you finish, decide with **B** which is the most important tip.

> ### How to survive meeting your partner's parents for the first time
>
> **1** **Do some "homework" before you go.** Ask your partner about his or her parents. Where do they work? Do you have any common interests? If you do this, it will be easy to have a conversation with them.
>
> **2** **Be ready to answer questions about yourself!** Most parents want to know about their son or daughter's future partner, for example about their ambitions. Try to make a good impression!
>
> **3** **If you are invited for a meal, eat everything!** It's also a good idea to say something positive about the meal, like "This is absolutely delicious!" Offer to help with the dishes after the meal.
>
> **4** **Be yourself and don't just agree with everything they say.** If they ask you for your opinion, be honest. However, try not to talk about controversial subjects – this isn't the moment to give your views on religion and politics!
>
> **5** **Avoid embarrassing silences.** If the conversation is dying and you can't think of what to say, ask them what your partner was like as a child. All parents love talking about their children.

Adapted from wikiHow

b **B** will tell you five tips for *How to survive a first date (and make a success of it)*. Listen and when he or she finishes, decide together which is the most important tip.

7C WHAT ARE THE RULES?
Student A

a Look at photos 1–6. Complete the rules with *have to*, *don't have to*, *must*, *must not*, or *can't* and a verb from the list.

be   pay   take   touch   turn off   wear

1 You _____ your phone.
2 Children _____.
3 You _____ a jacket.
4 You _____ the door.
5 You _____ over 18 to see this movie.
6 You _____ photos here.

b Read your rules to **B in a different order**. **B** will say which photo they go with.

c Look at photos 7–12. Listen to **B**'s rules, and say which photo they go with.

9A WOULD YOU KNOW WHAT TO DO? Student A

a Read the answers to *In the city*.

IN THE CITY

1 **The answer is b.** Dogs like to attack any part of you that is moving, usually hands or arms. It is also dangerous to turn your back on the dog. You shouldn't look the dog in its eyes because this will make it angry. Shouting "down" or "go away" at the dog will not work because dogs usually only react to their master's voice.

2 **The answer is a.** Wasps and bees will usually fly out of an open window, but don't wave your hands around because they follow movement and might try to sting you. And you must not hit the wasp or bee because this will make them very angry. Of course, as soon as you can, you should stop the car and open the doors.

b Tell **B** and **C** the correct answers, and why the other ones are wrong.

c Listen to **B** and **C** tell you about the other sections (*In the country* and *In the water*). Check your answers.

10B EARLY BIRDS Student A

a Read about Ella's day and answer the questions with short notes.

1 What time does she get up?
2 How does she wake up on time?
3 How does she feel when she wakes up?
4 Does she have anything to eat or drink before she goes to work?
5 How does she get to work?
6 What time does she start and finish work?
7 What time does she usually go to bed?
8 Would she like to change her working hours?

The alarm goes off at 2:35 a.m. I use my phone, and my partner also sets the alarm on his phone because I don't feel very secure if I just have one alarm. I get up right away. I usually feel terrible! It's always really hard to get out of bed. Luckily, I don't have to think about clothes because I always wear a white chef's jacket and a pair of jeans.

I don't have breakfast – I just get dressed and go right to work. I live very close to the shop, so I walk to work – it only takes five minutes. I start baking at 3:00 a.m. I'm always desperate for a cup of tea, and as soon as I have time I make one. I can't really function without a cup of tea. I make all the bread and cakes between 3:00 and 8:30 – that's when I open the shop.

I usually finish work at about 3:00 in the afternoon, so I'm often at work for about 12 hours. I go to bed at 8:30. Because we go to bed so early, during the week we don't go out at all. I sometimes go out on a Saturday evening, but I feel exhausted the next day.

Would I like to change my working hours? Yes. I love my job, and I don't mind getting up early, but I would like to sleep more.

> **Glossary**
> **right away** immediately
> **baking** making bread and cakes

b Use the questions and your notes to tell **B** about Ella's day.

(*Ella gets up very early, at 2:35.*

c Then listen to **B** tell you about Peter's day.

d How are Ella and Peter similar? How are they different?

10C PASSIVES QUIZ Student A

a Complete your sentences with the verb in the passive and (circle) the correct answer.

1 Until 1664, New York _____ (call)…
   a New Amsterdam b New Hampshire c New Liberty
2 The *Lord of the Rings* movies _____ (direct) by…
   a Ridley Scott b James Cameron c Peter Jackson
3 The noun that _____ (use) most frequently in conversation is…
   a money b time c work
4 Penguins _____ (find)…
   a at the South Pole b at the North Pole c in Alaska
5 The Italian flag _____ (design) by…
   a Garibaldi b Mussolini c Napoleon
6 The first cell phones _____ (sell) in…
   a 1963 b 1973 c 1983
7 The British politician Winston Churchill _____ (be born)…
   a on a train b in a toilet c under a bridge
8 The Statue of Liberty _____ (give) to the United States by….
   a Germany b the UK c France

b Read your sentences to **B. B** will tell you if you are right.

c Now listen to **B**'s sentences. Say if he / she is right.
   B's answers
   1 The smartphone was invented by IBM.
   2 *Star Wars* was created by George Lucas.
   3 The book that is stolen most often from libraries is *The Guinness Book of Records*.
   4 In the world, 16,000 babies are born every hour.
   5 Chess was invented by the Chinese.
   6 The first Skype call was made in 2003.
   7 Soccer was first played by the British.
   8 In 1962, the original London Bridge was bought by a rich American.

12A WHAT HAD HAPPENED? Student A

a Look at the odd numbered sentences (1, 3, 5, 7, 9, and 11) and think of the missing verb (⊞ = affirmative verb, ⊟ = negative verb). Don't write anything yet!

1 Diana was very angry because her husband _____ the dinner. ⊟
2 We went back to see the house where we **had lived** when we were children.
3 He couldn't catch the plane because he _____ his passport. ⊞
4 The apartment was very dirty because nobody **had cleaned** it for a long time.
5 We went back to the hotel where we _____ on our honeymoon. ⊞
6 The cat was hungry because it **hadn't eaten** anything for two days.
7 After I left the store, I suddenly remembered that I _____ for the jacket. ⊟
8 I ran to the train station, but the last train **had gone**.
9 Nicole was happy to hear that she _____ the exam. ⊞
10 I didn't want to lend Jane the book because I **hadn't read** it.
11 Jack was angry because I _____ him to my party. ⊟
12 They got to the movie theater late and the movie **had started**.

b Read your sentence 1 to **B** with the missing verb you chose. If it's not right, try again until **B** tells you "That's right." Then write the verb.

c Listen to **B** say sentence 2. If it's the same as 2 above, say "That's right." If not, say "Try again" until **B** gets it right.

d Take turns with sentences 3–12.

12A TWO MORE STORIES
Student A

a Read your story and write answers to the questions.

1 Where was the swimming pool? What kind of pool was it?
2 Why did the pool assistant shout "Get out of the water! Quickly!"
3 What had happened in the night?
4 Were any of the swimmers hurt? What happened to the shark?

In Sydney, early in the morning, some swimmers were taking a swim in an outdoor swimming pool that was very close to the ocean. The swimmers were very surprised when suddenly the pool assistant started shouting, "Get out of the water! Quickly!" The swimmers immediately got out. Then they realized that there was a shark at the other end! A large wave had carried the shark into the pool overnight. Fortunately, none of the swimmers were hurt, and the shark was caught in a net and put back into the ocean.

b Tell your story to **B**. Use your answers to help you.

(*This happened at a swimming pool in Sydney…*)

c Listen to **B** telling you his / her story.

12B BLOWING IN THE WIND
Students A+B

"Your gossip is like the feathers," said the wise woman. "You can never take back what you have said, and you don't know how far it travels and the damage it can do. From now on, I want you to think before you speak." And he did.

12C GENERAL KNOWLEDGE QUIZ Student A

a Complete your questions with the verb in parentheses in the simple past. The correct answers are in red.

1 Who _____ the battle of Waterloo in 1815? (lose)
   a the Duke of Wellington **b** Bismarck **c** Napoleon
2 Which American actor _____ in the 2015 movie *The Martian*? (star)
   a Matt Damon **b** Tom Hanks **c** Brad Pitt
3 Who _____ the songs that feature in the movie and musical *Mamma Mia*? (write)
   a The Beatles **b** Abba **c** Madonna
4 Which Formula One driver _____ his first world championship in 2008 at the age of 23? (win)
   a Fernando Alonso **b** Lewis Hamilton **c** Michael Schumacher
5 Which famous Roman _____ "I came, I saw, I conquered"? (say)
   a Augustus **b** Nero **c** Julius Caesar
6 Who _____ the world record for the 100- and 200-meter races at the Beijing Olympics in 2008? (break)
   a Usain Bolt **b** Carl Lewis **c** Michael Johnson
7 Which painter _____ off part of his ear? (cut)
   a Picasso **b** Van Gogh **c** Matisse
8 Who _____ penicillin? (discover)
   a Alexander Fleming **b** James Watson **c** Thomas Edison

b Ask **B** your questions. Give your partner one point for each correct answer.

c Answer **B**'s questions. Who got the most correct answers?

9A WOULD YOU KNOW WHAT TO DO? Student C

a Read the answers to *In the water*.

IN THE WATER

5 The answer is c. If a jellyfish stings you, you should clean the sting with vinegar because this stops the poison. If you don't have any vinegar, then use ocean water. But don't use fresh water, for example water from a tap or bottled water because this will make the sting hurt more. And you shouldn't rub the sting because this will make it worse, too. After you have washed the sting, you should clean off any tentacle parts that are on your skin. And take a painkiller!

6 The answer is a. If you are near the shore and the shark is not too close, you can probably swim to the shore without attracting its attention. For this reason, it is important to swim smoothly and not to splash or make sudden movements. Keeping still is dangerous because if the shark swims in your direction. It will see you and it will attack you. Don't shout because shouting will provoke the shark and it will attack you.

b Listen to **A** and **B** tell you about the other sections (*In the city* and *In the country*). Check your answers.

c Tell **A** and **B** the correct answers for *In the water*, and why the other ones are wrong.

7A HOW TO SURVIVE... Student B

a Read the article *How to survive a first date (and make a success of it)*.

How to survive a first date (and make a success of it)

1 **Think carefully about what to wear for the date.** It's important to dress nicely, but casually (no suits!). Don't wear too much perfume or aftershave!

2 **Choose a place that isn't too expensive (you don't know who is going to pay).** Try to go somewhere that isn't very noisy.

3 **Don't be too romantic on a first date.** For example, arriving with a red rose on a first date isn't a good idea!

4 **Remember to listen more than you talk, but don't let the conversation die.** Silence is a killer on a first date! Be natural. Don't pretend to be somebody you aren't.

5 **If you are a man,** be a gentleman and pay the check at the end of the evening. If you are a woman, offer to pay your half of the check (but don't insist!).

b **A** will tell you five tips for *How to survive meeting your partner's parents for the first time*. Listen and when he or she finishes, decide together which is the most important tip.

c Look again quickly at your article. Then tell **A** the five tips and give more details. When you finish, decide with **A** which is the most important tip.

9A WOULD YOU KNOW WHAT TO DO? Student B

a Read the answers to *In the country*.

IN THE COUNTRY

3 **The answer is c.** If you tie a bandage or a piece of material above the bite, this will stop the poison from getting to your heart too quickly. However, be careful not to tie it too tightly. You shouldn't put ice or anything cold on the bite because this will make it more difficult to get the poison out later, and never try to suck out the poison. If it gets into your mouth, it could go into your blood.

4 **The answer is a.** If you let your dog run free, the cows will go after it, but it will escape because it can run much faster than the cows. The worst thing you can do is pick up your dog because the cows will probably attack both of you. And don't shout or wave your arms because this will worry the cows and could cause them to attack.

b Listen to **A** tell you about *In the city*. Check your answers.

c Tell **A** and **C** the correct answers for *In the country*, and why the other ones are wrong.

d Listen to **C** tell you about *In the water*. Check your answers.

7C WHAT ARE THE RULES? Student B

a Look at photos 7–12. Complete the rules with *have to*, *don't have to*, *must*, *must not*, or *can't* and a verb from the list.

come   drive   pay   play   put   wear

7 You _____ anything now.
8 You _____ soccer here at night.
9 You _____ your feet on the seats.
10 You _____ to class on Mondays.
11 You _____ in one direction.
12 You _____ athletic shoes here.

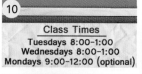

b Look at photos 1–6. Listen to **A**'s rules, and say which photo they go with.

c Read your rules to **A in a different order.** **A** will say which photo they go with.

a Read about Peter's day and answer the questions with short notes.

1 What time does he get up?
2 How does he wake up on time?
3 How does he feel when he wakes up?
4 Does he have anything to eat or drink before he goes to work?
5 How does he get to work?
6 What time does he start and finish work?
7 What time does he usually go to bed?
8 Would he like to change his working hours?

The *Peter Gordon Breakfast Show* starts at exactly 6:00, so I need to be at work at 5:30 a.m. on weekday mornings. I'm lucky because I live very close to the studio – it's only three to four minutes by car – so I get up at about 4:45. I wake up on time because I have an alarm that repeats, and I wear a Fitbit that vibrates as well. When that goes off, I know that I really have to get up!

For the first few minutes I feel a little sleepy, but then I wake up quickly. I choose my clothes the night before, and that way everything's ready. I have a cup of tea, and then I leave the house at about 5:15. I have breakfast during the radio show while I'm playing music – maybe a smoothie and some cereal. I'm a director of the radio station, so after my show I usually work in the office until late afternoon – it's a long working day!

I go to bed late, usually at about 11:00. I find it very difficult to go to bed early, it's always been a problem for me. So I only get about five or six hours of sleep – but that's enough for me. Because I get up early, I try not to go out with friends during the week. I only go to necessary events, like work events. Weekends are different!

I know I get up really early, but I don't want to change my hours because I really love my breakfast show, and I never want to give it up.

> **Glossary**
> **Fitbit** an electronic bracelet that measures your physical activity
> **smoothie** a drink made with fruit or fruit juice mixed with milk

b Listen to **A** tell you about Ella's day.

c Use the questions and your notes to tell **A** about Peter's day.

(Peter gets up at about 4:45…

d How are Ella and Peter similar? How are they different?

a Complete your sentences with the verb in the passive and circle the correct answer.

1 The smartphone _____ (invent) by…
   a Apple   b Nokia   c IBM
2 *Star Wars* was _____ (create) by…
   a George Lucas
   b Steven Spielberg
   c Stanley Kubrick
3 The book that _____ (steal) most often from libraries is…
   a *The Bible*
   b *The Guinness Book of Records*
   c *The Lord of the Rings*
4 In the world, 16,000 babies _____ (be born)…
   a every second   b every hour   c every day
5 Chess _____ (invent) by…
   a the Egyptians
   b the Indians
   c the Chinese
6 The first Skype call _____ (make) in…
   a 1993   b 2003   c 2013
7 Soccer _____ first (play) by…
   a the British   b the Romans   c the Greeks
8 In 1962, the original London Bridge _____ (buy) by…
   a a rich American
   b a museum
   c the Royal family

b Now listen to **A**'s sentences. Say if he / she is right.

   A's answers
   1 Until 1664, New York was called New Amsterdam.
   2 The *Lord of the Rings* movies were directed by Peter Jackson.
   3 The noun that is used most frequently in conversation is *time*.
   4 Penguins are found at the South Pole.
   5 The Italian flag was designed by Napoleon.
   6 The first cell phones were sold in 1983.
   7 The British politician Winston Churchill was born in a toilet.
   8 The Statue of Liberty was given to the United States by France.

c Read your sentences to **A**. **A** will tell you if you are right.

12A WHAT HAD HAPPENED? Student B

a Look at the even numbered sentences (2, 4, 6, 8, 10, and 12) and think of the missing verb (⊞ = affirmative verb, ⊟ = negative verb). Don't write anything yet!

1 Diana was very angry because her husband **hadn't cooked** the dinner.
2 We went back to see the house where we _____ when we were children. ⊞
3 He couldn't catch the plane because he **had forgotten** his passport.
4 The apartment was very dirty because nobody _____ it for a long time. ⊞
5 We went back to the hotel where we **had stayed** on our honeymoon.
6 The cat was hungry because it _____ anything for two days. ⊟
7 After I left the store, I suddenly remembered that I **hadn't paid** for the jacket.
8 I ran to the train station, but the last train _____. ⊞
9 Nicole was happy to hear that she **had passed** the exam.
10 I didn't want to lend Jane the book because I _____ it. ⊟
11 Jack was angry because I **hadn't invited** him to my party.
12 They got to the movie theater late and the movie _____. ⊞

b Listen to **A** say sentence 1. If it's the same as 1 above, say "That's right." If not, say "Try again" until **A** gets it right.

c Read your sentence 2 to **A** with the missing verb you chose. If it's not right, try again until **A** tells you "That's right." Then write in the verb.

d Take turns with sentences 3–12.

12A TWO MORE STORIES Student B

a Read your story and write answers to the questions.

1 Where was the airport?
2 Why were the airport workers surprised?
3 What had the old lady done?
4 How far did she travel on the luggage belt?

Last Monday, workers in the luggage area at Stockholm's Arlanda airport, in Sweden, got a big surprise. They were taking suitcases off the luggage belt to put them on the different planes, when suddenly they saw an old lady sitting on the belt next to her suitcase. The woman had gotten confused at the check-in desk. She had put her luggage on the belt and then had sat down on the belt herself. A spokesman at the airport said, "Unfortunately, she did not understand when she was given check-in instructions. She got on the belt together with her bag. Luckily, it wasn't a long ride – only a few feet."

b Listen to **A** telling you his / her story.

c Tell your story to **A**. Use your answers to help you.

(*This happened at an airport in Sweden…*)

12C GENERAL KNOWLEDGE QUIZ Student B

a Complete your questions with the verb in parentheses in the simple past. The correct answers are in red.

1 Who _____ President of the US eight years after his father had been president? (become)
 a Bill Clinton
 b Barack Obama
 c George Bush

2 Who _____ the part of Hermione Granger in the Harry Potter movies? (play)
 a Emma Watson
 b Carey Mulligan
 c Kate Winslet

3 Which sport _____ an Olympic sport in 2016? (become)
 a golf
 b handball
 c volleyball

4 Who _____ the Sistine Chapel? (paint)
 a Leonardo da Vinci
 b Michelangelo
 c Raphael

5 Who _____ *The Da Vinci Code*? (write)
 a Stephen King
 b John Grisham
 c Dan Brown

6 Who _____ a wooden horse to enter the city of Troy? (use)
 a The Greeks
 b The Romans
 c The Persians

7 Which famous boxer _____ to fight in the Vietnam War in 1967? (refuse)
 a Muhammad Ali
 b Joe Frazier
 c Sugar Ray Robinson

8 Who _____ the telephone? (invent)
 a Marconi
 b Bell
 c Stephens

b Answer **A**'s questions.

c Ask **A** your questions. Give your partner one point for each correct answer. Who got the most correct answers?

Writing

5 A FORMAL EMAIL

a Read the email to a language school. Check (✓) the questions that Ryo wants the school to answer.

> How much do the courses cost?
> When do the courses start and end?
> How many students are there in a class?
> Can I combine two kinds of classes?
> Can my wife stay with me?
> Where are the teachers from?

From: Ryo Yamada [yamadar998@yahoo.co.jp]
To: Beacon Intensive Language School [info@BILS.edu]
Subject: Information about courses

Dear Sir / Madam,

I am writing to ask for information about your language courses. I am especially interested in an intensive course of two or three weeks. I am 31 years old, and I work in the library at the University of Tokyo. I can read English well, but I need to improve my listening and speaking. The book I am currently studying is "pre-intermediate."

I would like to do an intensive course for three weeks next summer. Is it possible to do three hours of general English and two hours of business English every day? Could you please send me some information about dates and prices? I would also like some more information about accommodations. If possible, I would like to stay with a family, however my wife would like to visit me for a week when I am at the school. Could she stay with me in the same family?

I look forward to hearing from you.

Sincerely,

Ryo Yamada

b Look at the highlighted phrases. How would they be different in an informal email?

Formal	Informal
Dear Sir / Madam,	
I am writing	
I would like	
however	
I look forward to hearing from you.	
Sincerely,	

c Read the advertisement and then plan an email to the school. Decide how long you want to study for, what kind of course, and where you want to stay. Think of two or three questions you would like to ask.

Learn English in Boston

Come and improve your English this summer!

We run courses from two to four weeks. You can have classes from three to six hours a day or you can combine studying with cultural activities like theater trips or museum visits.

There are general English courses from beginner to advanced, as well as business English and exam preparation classes.

You can stay with a local family, or in student accommodations.

Write to us for more information. Tell us about yourself and what you are looking for, and we will suggest the perfect course for you.

Email us at info@bostonenglishfirst.net

d Write a formal email asking for information. Write two paragraphs.

Paragraph 1	Explain why you are writing. Give some personal information (your age and occupation, and your level of English).
Paragraph 2	Explain what you would like to do. Ask your questions, and ask them to send you the information.

e Check your email for mistakes (grammar, punctuation, and spelling).

 p.59

6 A BIOGRAPHY

a Read the biography of Matt Damon. Then cover the text and try to remember three things about him.

b Put the verbs in parentheses in the simple past or present perfect.

> 🔍 **Writing a biography – use of tenses**
>
> If you write a biography of a person who is dead, the verbs will all be in the **simple past**.
>
> If the person is alive, all finished actions will be in the **simple past** (such as the person's early life, e.g., *He was born, He went to college*, etc., or specific actions in their life, e.g., *He got married, He moved to another country*, etc.).
>
> However, you must use the **present perfect** for unfinished actions that started in the past and are still true now (and which might change), e.g., *He has lived in Los Angeles since his wedding.* (= he lives there now)
> *He has appeared in a lot of movies.* (= he might appear in more in the future)
>
> Use the **simple present** (or **present continuous**) to talk about the present day, e.g., *He lives in Los Angeles. He's working on a new movie.*

c You're going to write a biography of someone you know, or a famous person, who is still alive. Plan and make notes for each paragraph before you begin.

Paragraph 1	where and when they were born, their early life (simple past)
Paragraph 2	their life as a young adult (simple past)
Paragraph 3	their later life and their life now (simple past, present perfect, simple present / present continuous)

d Write the biography. Write three paragraphs using your notes.

e Check your biography for mistakes (grammar, punctuation, and spelling). Show your biography to other students in the class. Which of your classmates' biographies is the most interesting?

⟲ p.75

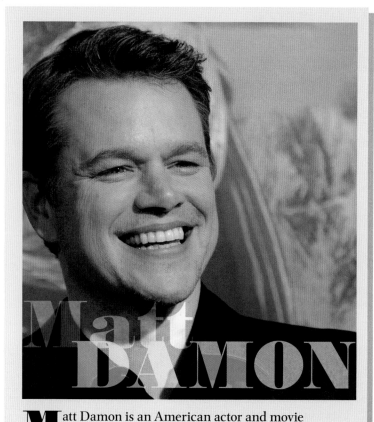

Matt Damon is an American actor and movie producer. He ¹ _was born_ (be born) in 1970 in Cambridge, Massachusetts. His father Kent worked in finance, and his mother Nancy was a college professor. His parents ² _____ (divorce) when he was two years old, and he ³ _____ (live) with his mother and brother in a large house with five other families.

Matt Damon ⁴ _____ (become) interested in acting when he was in high school, and he ⁵ _____ (appear) in several school theater productions. When he was 18, he ⁶ _____ (go) to Harvard University to study English. He ⁷ _____ (write) a movie script as part of his course - the script was for the movie *Good Will Hunting*. Matt and his friend Ben Affleck ⁸ _____ (star) in the movie and it made them famous. They both ⁹ _____ (win) an Oscar for Best Original Screenplay for their work on the script. Matt decided to become an actor and he ¹⁰ _____ (not finish) college.

Since then, Matt Damon ¹¹ _____ (become) one of the most successful actors in Hollywood. He ¹² _____ (appear) in over 70 movies, but he is most famous for playing Jason Bourne, a CIA assassin, in the Bourne movies. He ¹³ _____ (receive) many awards, and in 2015 he ¹⁴ _____ (win) a Golden Globe for Best Actor for his performance in *The Martian*. He ¹⁵ _____ (be) married to Luciana Barroso since 2005. They live in Los Angeles with their four daughters.

7 AN ARTICLE

a Read the article once. Why does the writer enjoy parkrun?

1 Because it helps her to lose weight.
2 Because she likes exercising with other people.
3 Because she likes getting up early.

b Read the article again and fill in the blanks with an adjective from the list.

faster   friendly   healthy   local   overweight   young

c What is each paragraph about? Match paragraphs 1–4 to the correct summary.

☐ She recommends the activity and explains why.
☐ She says when and why she started doing it. She gives more details about when and where she does it now.
☐ She gives basic information about the activity.
☐ She explains why she enjoys it.

d You are going to write an article with four paragraphs about an activity that you enjoy in your free time. Plan what you're going to write in each paragraph. Look at the highlighted phrases, and make a list of useful phrases connected with your activity.

e Write an article with the title "Why I love _____." Write four paragraphs.

f Check your article for mistakes (grammar, punctuation, and spelling). Show it to other students in the class. How many of them do the same activity? How many of them would like to try it?

🔄 p.79

Why I love parkrun

Rachel Farrah

1 Parkrun organizes free five kilometer runs all over the world. Every Saturday morning, in countries around the world, people meet at a park and go for a run together. After the run, you get a text message that tells you your time, so you can see that you're getting ¹_____ and in better shape.

2 I started doing parkrun three years ago. I was ²_____ and stressed, and a friend invited me to go to the ³_____ run with him. I really didn't want to go at first, but after a few weeks I felt much better. Now, I try to do it every Saturday, and I've done more than 100 runs since I started.

3 I love parkrun because of the people who do it – the atmosphere is really ⁴_____, and it's much more fun and motivating to run with other people. I know that my running friends will be in the park at the same time every weekend, and that makes me get up and get out of the house.

4 It doesn't matter if you're old or ⁵_____, male or female, fast or slow – if you want a ⁶_____ start to the weekend, you should try it! And if there isn't a parkrun in your town or city, maybe you should start one!

Listening

🔊 **7.1**

Simon When I was about 30, I got a job working as an editor in a publishing company. It was my first office job, and, um, I didn't really know what to wear, but, um, for the interview I wore a suit. In fact, I bought the suit specially for the interview. I got the job, so I thought that must be OK, so, um, on the first day, I went to work wearing a suit and a tie. I got to work early, um, I wanted to make a good impression, and I was the first person in the office, so I went in, I found my desk, with my name on it, and I sat down and there were a few papers and documents for me to read, so I started reading those. I turned on my computer, and after about ten, fifteen minutes the other people in the office started to arrive, and I noticed that nobody else was wearing a suit, and I thought, OK it's not a big problem. So, I introduced myself to the other people. I said, "Hello, how are you? Hello, nice to meet you," and the next thing someone said to me was, "My computer's really slow, do you think you know what the problem is?" and I said, "No, no, not really." So, then I introduced myself to somebody else and said, "Hello, nice to meet you," and she replied, "Hello, nice to meet you," and then she said, "Do you know how I can connect my computer to the printer?" and I said, "No, I have no idea how to do that." Anyway, I went back to work and about half an hour later I had a meeting with my boss, and she said, "How's it going?" and I said, "Yeah, it's all going well, everybody seems really nice. Just one thing, why does everybody think I can fix their computer?" and she looked at me and what I was wearing and she said, "It's your suit. Nobody in this office wears a suit, so they think you're from the IT department and you've come to help with a computer problem. They're the only ones who wear suits!" So, I never wore it again. To this day.

Claire It was my first day at work as a teacher at a language school, and they asked me to come the first week of the new school year to observe some teachers, to watch their lessons, and then I was going to start teaching the following week. But when I arrived, there they told me that one of the teachers was sick and they asked me to take the class, and it was three-year-old kids! So, I was in a class with about ten three-year-olds who were running around – my boss gave me a storybook to read to them, but the kids couldn't speak any English. I'd never taught – never been trained to teach children that small. I tried to read the book to two of them, but the others were running around shouting and hitting each other, and at the worst possible moment, just when all of them were being really noisy and not doing anything I was telling them to, my boss – the director of the school – opened the door and just looked at me. I felt terrible but then she said, "These children are too young for you, aren't they?" and I said yes, I was nearly crying. Luckily after that, she never gave me any classes with really young children, but it was the most stressful class I've ever tried to teach.

🔊 **7.8**

Host The capital city of Estonia, Tallinn, is one of the most beautiful cities on the Baltic coast. It is also one of the world's "smart cities," which means that technology plays an important role in people's lives and in business.
But some people in Tallin are using the internet for something very unusual. It's called the Bank of Happiness, but it's a very different kind of bank.

Nobody pays money into the bank, and the bank doesn't lend money to anybody. Instead, the Bank of Happiness is a forum where thousands of people from Estonia, and other countries too, connect with each other, and they offer or receive services completely free of charge.
Here's how it works: you register and you post what you are offering or what you need – it's really easy. For example, people offer to do the shopping for somebody, or walk their dog. Other people post things like "I need someone who can fix my car" or "Can anybody translate an email into French for me?" But the important thing is that nobody pays any money. Everything is free. The bank was started over five years ago by a 39-year-old Estonian woman, Airi Kivi. She is a psychologist and a family therapist, and her goal was to make people think and act with their hearts.

Airi I thought, we need something like this Bank of Happiness, where people can meet each other and help each other – do something cool. The Estonian economy was also having problems at the time. A little bit later, I thought, wow, the Bank of Happiness is perfect for this economic crisis. A lot of people are unemployed and they can use our bank. In the Bank of Happiness people don't need to pay each other back. For example, a teenager will do the shopping for his old neighbor, and maybe the neighbor can't do anything for him in return. But then perhaps the neighbor will post a comment on the site and tell people about what the teenager did, and then another person who sees this will probably do something to help the teenager. The principle of the bank is that it's not money and things that make people happy. What really makes them happy is doing things for other people.

🔊 **7.15**

Max I arrived at the airport in San Juan, Puerto Rico where I met Nilda. *Hola. Soy Max.*
Paula *Encantada. Soy Nilda.*
Max Nilda took me to my hotel, and that evening we went to eat, and it was time for my first test. I had to order a sandwich and a drink in a café, and then ask for the check. I sat down at a table, and I tried to order a soda and a chicken sandwich. *Por favor, una refresca y un emparedado de pollo.*
Waiter *En seguida.*
Max Terrific! The waiter understood me the first time. My pronunciation wasn't perfect, but I got my soda and my sandwich. I really enjoyed it. But then the more difficult part. Asking for the check... *Cuánto es?*
Waiter *Seis noventa.*
Max *Cómo?*
Waiter *Seis noventa.*
Max Six ninety. I understood! Nilda gave me eight points for the test. I was very happy with that. Next, we went out on the street. Test number two was asking for directions and understanding them. We were on a narrow street and I had to stop someone and ask him or her for the nearest drugstore, *una farmacia.* I stopped a woman. At first I didn't understand anything she said!
Passer-by *Siga todo derecho y tome la segunda calle al la izquierda. Hay una farmacia en esa calle.*
Max I asked the woman to speak more slowly.
Passer-by *Todo derecho y tome la segunda calle por la izquierda. IZQUIERDA.*

Max I got it this time, I think. The second street on the left. I followed the directions and guess what? There was a drugstore there! Seven points from Nilda.
Test number three. I wasn't looking forward to this one. I had to take a taxi to a historical place in San Juan. Nilda wrote down the name of the place on a piece of paper. It was the name of an old fort near the ocean. We stopped a taxi. *El Morro, por favor.*
Taxi driver *Qué? Adónde?*
Max He didn't understand me. I tried again, but he still didn't understand. I was desperate, so I said *fort, old, water.*
Taxi driver *Ah, El Morro.*
Max Finally! Nilda only gave me five points because I ended up using English. Still, at least I made the taxi driver understand where I wanted to go. And so to the final test. I had to leave a message in Spanish on somebody's voicemail. I had to give my name, spell it, and ask the person to call me back. Nilda gave me the number (it was one of her friends named Lourdes) and I dialed. I was feeling a little nervous at this point, because talking on the phone in a foreign language is never easy.
Lourdes *Deje su mensaje después de la señal.*
Max *Uh. Buenas noches. Soy Max. Max. M-A- X. Uh. Por favor...llámarme esta noche....Oh yes...a las 8:30, uh, gracias.* Well, my grammar wasn't correct, but I left the message. Half an hour later, at eight-thirty, Lourdes called me. Success! Nilda gave me eight points. That was the end of my four tests. Nilda was happy with me. My final score was seven. I was very happy with that. So how much can you learn in a month? Well, of course you can't learn Spanish in a month, but you can learn enough to survive if you are on vacation or on a trip. Now I want to go back to Washington, D.C., and try and learn some more. *Adiós!*

🔊 **8.1**

Hi Tracey. You know the answer to your last question, and it is "yes." You're making your life more difficult. But it's also true that having a long-term relationship with anyone is difficult, and in your case you can at least see what some of the problems are. I'm sure this man loves you and will support you in all your goals in life, but it's true that he has already done all the things you want to do. It's not his fault, but it means that he will never get as excited as you about, for example, a wedding or having another child. And everything you experience together he will probably compare to the last time he did it. You should think carefully about what kind of partner you really want: someone who can support you and show you the way in life, or someone who will discover life with you. You shouldn't make a decision in a hurry. When you are clearer about what you want, then you can decide if you're going to stay with this man or not. Good luck!

🔊 **8.5**

Annabel Hello. I'm Annabel.
Peter And I'm Peter.
Expert Hi there, Annabel and Peter. What's your problem?
Annabel We have a son, Jamie, and he's 25. He's a chef.
Peter But he still lives with us because he says it's too expensive to rent an apartment and he doesn't earn enough money.

Annabel He gives us some money every month for bills – not much, but a little – and, you know, it's nice to have him at home, but we think he needs to be more independent.

Peter Yes, absolutely.

Annabel But last week he told us that he's planning a two-week vacation to Mexico with his friends. I mean, it's true that he works full-time and we know he needs a break, but we really think…

Peter Yes, we don't think he should go on an expensive vacation when he doesn't give us much money. We think he should save his money, so that he can get his own place to live. Should we tell him that he can't go to Mexico?

🔊 8.6

Expert You know, to be honest I think you're being a little hard on him. I mean, he's only 25. It's good that he has a job and everybody needs a vacation. My advice is that you should let him go to Mexico, but when he comes back, you should sit down with him and talk to him about starting to pay rent. That way he'll understand that he needs to start planning for the future and to start thinking about renting an apartment. But I know from talking to other parents that there are a lot of young people still living at home in their 20s and 30s, and some of them don't even have jobs. So, in many ways I think you're lucky.

Annabel You see? That's just what I think…

🔊 8.7

Nick Hi there. I'm Nick.

Expert Hi, Nick. So what's your problem?

Nick Well, I've been with my girlfriend for three years. We have a really great relationship although we're very different. She's smart and popular and I'm, uh, quiet and hard-working. Anyway, now she wants to move to Chicago, because she thinks she can get a better job there, and she wants me to go to Chicago, too – you know, Chicago's much more exciting than Galena, Texas, where we live now. But I have a good job in Galena and I get a good salary. I mean the idea of moving and having a new life is like a dream, but for me that's what it is, I mean it's a dream, it isn't real. What should I do? Should I follow my heart and move to Chicago with her? Or should I stay here where I know I have a good job, but possibly lose my girlfriend?

🔊 8.8

Expert I think you should sit down together and talk about your dreams for the future, and see if they are the same dreams. If they are, and you can see a future together, then the first thing is for her to look for a job in Chicago. If she finds one, then maybe she can move there first and you can go on weekends and see how you feel about life there.

Nick Thanks a lot for that. I think that's really good advice.

🔊 8.9

Jane Hello. My name's Jane.

Expert Hi, Jane. Why are you calling?

Jane Well, a month ago my friend Susan and I decided to go on vacation together this summer, to Turkey. So we planned everything and, uh, I was really looking forward to it because Susan's an old friend and I don't see her very often. But the other day she told me that she was telling another friend of hers about our vacation, somebody I don't know, a woman called Angie, and Angie was really interested, and now Susan has invited her to come, too. Susan never asked me what I thought! I don't even know Angie, and I really don't want to go on vacation with someone I don't know. What should I do?

🔊 8.10

Expert I think your friend has been a little insensitive, and she's put you in a difficult position. You have several different options. You

could say that you aren't going if Angie goes, but then you'll put Susan in a difficult position. Or you could just cancel, and suggest taking another vacation later with just the two of you. Or you could invite someone else who you like, and then there would be four of you, which is sometimes a better number than three. But in fact, you don't know Angie and maybe you'll like her. So, I think you should try to get to know her first. If you like her, then the vacation will probably be a success. If not, then you should tell your friend you aren't going, because you don't think it will work with Angie. You know, a bad vacation is worse than no vacation.

🔊 8.14

Peter I studied math in college and usually, after studying math in college, people get a job in a bank or in IT, but when I graduated, it was the recession and it was very difficult to get a job. I was unemployed for a very long time. I was looking for jobs, and I applied for lots of different jobs, but they just answered "Sorry, we don't want you," and I was getting a little depressed. This went on for about four months, and then one day I was on a bus – I can even remember where I was sitting – and my phone rang. I said hello, and a woman said, "Hello, you applied for a job with us a few months ago. Are you still interested?" So I said, yes, absolutely, I'm very interested. So then she said "we'd like you to come for an interview…" and then at that moment we got cut off because the bus went into a tunnel. And the phone number wasn't on my phone – it just said "unknown number," and I couldn't remember what the name of the company was because I'd applied for so many jobs. So, I thought "four months of nothing and then when they call, I get cut off." Luckily they called back the next day, and in the end I had an interview, and I got the job.

Sue This happened when I was at a conference in Thailand. The conference hotel was amazing; it was in a beautiful national park called Khao Yai, north of Bangkok. We were very busy with talks and meetings most of the time, but we had one free morning, and we could choose from different trips or activities. I was interested in either a trip to see birds or a trip to see a tiger. A tiger, not tigers, because they told us that there was only one tiger in the whole park! Well, I chose the tiger trip, because I thought it would be really cool to see a tiger in the wild. But we had to leave really early in the morning, because we had to travel a long way to the part of the park where the tiger usually was – the bird trip was closer to the hotel. So, we tiger-watchers got up at 5:00 in the morning, but our guide said that we probably wouldn't see the tiger, because you know, there was only one tiger. We finally got there and we spent the whole morning looking for the tiger, but no luck. But we saw some nice birds, and it was fun, so when we got back to the conference hotel, we felt we'd had a really good morning. But then the other group got back, the ones who went to see the birds, and of course they saw lots of amazing birds, but they also saw the tiger! I guess that day it wasn't in its usual part of the park. And I thought isn't that typical – you go on the tiger trip and you don't see the tiger, but the people on the bird trip see the tiger!

🔊 9.4

Host So David, what are the five most dangerous animals in North America? Can you tell us in reverse order, I mean starting with the fifth most dangerous?

David Yes, of course. At number five is the crocodile. They can be over 15 feet long and weigh up to 1,000 pounds. Crocodiles are very common in the US state of Florida and some parts of Mexico. Crocodiles will eat anything from small animals like fish and birds to large animals like deer. They don't usually attack

people, except when people walk, play, or swim in areas where crocodiles live. It's very uncommon to die from a crocodile attack, however two to three people die each year from crocodile bites.

Host And number 4?

David The fourth most dangerous animals in North America are sharks. Sharks live in both the Atlantic and Pacific oceans, which surround North America. More than half of all the shark attacks in the world happen in the ocean near California and Florida. In fact, the place where people are most likely to be attacked by a shark is Smyrna Beach, on the eastern side of Florida, especially if you are surfing.

Host And third?

David In third place are snakes. There are a number of poisonous snakes in North America, but the most poisonous one is the coral snake. They can be about 4 feet long with black, red, and yellow bands. They don't usually attack people, except when people step on them by accident. A bite from a coral snake can be very painful, and, can occasionally kill. However, a coral snake must continue biting for a few seconds before the poison is injected into you. So if you can shake off the snake quickly, then the poison won't go into you.

Host And in second place?

David Bears. While there have only been 27 deaths from bear attacks in the 2000s in Canada and the US combined, bears are still highly dangerous. Of all the bears in North America (black bears, brown bears, and polar bears), the brown bear is the most dangerous. They can be almost 10 feet high and weigh as much as 900 pounds. They have powerful jaws, sharp teeth, and sharp claws.

Host And in first place?

David Believe it or not…deer. Deer cause about 200 deaths a year in North America, more than any other animal. These are large animals – they can weigh 220 pounds. You need to be especially careful in the fall, when the male deer can get very aggressive. They also cause frequent accidents on the road by running out in front of cars – there are about 100,000 car accidents a year which involve deer.

Host Well, David, that was certainly…

🔊 9.6

Interviewer Do you have any phobias?

Julia Yes, I'm very, very scared of spiders.

Interviewer And how long have you had this phobia?

Julia I've had it since I was about 12, so for more than 30 years.

Interviewer Did something happen to start the phobia?

Julia I remember – and it's when I think I started being frightened – I remember a very big spider in the apartment that we lived in at the time coming out from under the TV and going across the room, and me being absolutely terrified, and that's the first time I remember being scared.

Interviewer How does it affect your life?

Julia In the past it was really awful. I mean, I couldn't sit in the same room as a spider, and I always had to keep all the doors and windows shut because I was frightened that spiders might come in. But I had some therapy, and I can now sit in the same room as a spider, not for long, it still has to be moved, and I can put it in a glass now and take it outside myself, if I have to, if there's nobody else there, so it doesn't affect me as badly as it did before, but I still don't like them…

Interviewer What kind of therapy did you have? How long did it take?

Julia Probably about six weeks. I went to the therapist's office and he used a kind of hypnosis. He made me go back to that first incident with the spider and the TV and we talked about it again and again until it wasn't so frightening, and then in the last session he brought in a spider in a jar, into the room and he made me hold the jar – I couldn't put the spider on my hand, but that was a great improvement, because before I couldn't even look at a drawing of a spider in a children's book, and I certainly couldn't look at photos of spiders.

Interviewer Wow! Amazing.

Interviewer Do you have any phobias?

Chloe Um, yes, I have a phobia of buttons.

Interviewer Buttons on clothes?

Chloe Yes. I don't like touching them.

Interviewer And how long have you had the phobia?

Chloe All my life, I think. For as long as I can remember.

Interviewer Do you know what happened to start the phobia?

Chloe I don't know exactly, but my mom has told me that when I was very little, about six or seven months old, she tried to dress me in a sweater, a wool sweater with buttons that my grandmother had made for me, and apparently I screamed and screamed until she took it off again.

Interviewer OK. And how does the phobia affect your life?

Chloe It really affects the kind of clothes I can buy, especially in the winter when I need a coat – there aren't many coats that don't have buttons. But it's better than it was, when I was younger I refused to wear anything that had buttons, so, for example, my mother had to adapt my school clothes so that there were no buttons.

Interviewer Have you had any therapy?

Chloe No, no. I haven't had any therapy. It seems like such a silly thing to be afraid of.

Interviewer What about if other people are wearing clothes with buttons on, is that OK?

Chloe Well, if the buttons aren't touching me that's fine, but I don't like hugging people that have buttons on their clothes.

🔊 **9.16**

Host Good evening, and welcome to *Family*, the show where we discuss issues concerning parents and children. Last week, we talked about children following their parents into the same job, and whether children of celebrities have an easier life than other children. Today, we're going to look at a celebrity son who did something different, and has been successful without the help of his famous father. Duncan Jones may not be a name you recognize if you're not a serious movie fan. Duncan Jones is his real name, but when he was very young, he was called Zowie Bowie. His father was the famous singer David Bowie, whose real surname was Jones. Zowie was actually Duncan's middle name.

Duncan was born in the UK in 1971. When he was nine his parents divorced, and Duncan stayed with his father. He continued to visit his mother, David Bowie's first wife Angie, until he was 13, but their relationship wasn't a happy one and he hasn't seen her since then.

When he was a child, Duncan wasn't interested in music. His father tried and tried to get him to learn an instrument, the drums, the saxophone, and the piano, but Duncan just wasn't interested – he was more interested in sports, and in movies. So, his father bought him a little 8 mm video camera, and he used it to make movies with his Star Wars toys. After he graduated from high school, Duncan went to the London Film School and studied to be a movie director.

In the early years of his career, Duncan directed TV commercials, for example, for the fashion label French Connection, and Heinz ketchup, and he also worked on video games.

In 2006 he made his first movie, called *Moon*, a science fiction drama, which was a great success. He won many awards for the movie, including the prize for best new British director.

Since then he has made many more successful movies, including *Source Code*, a science fiction thriller starring Jake Gyllenhaal, and *Warcraft*, based on the game World of Warcraft.

Duncan has said that one of the reasons why he went into movie directing was that he wanted to be behind the camera, not in front of it. As a child there were often paparazzi around, which he hated. Even now, as a successful movie director, he doesn't like being photographed. Although, as he says, "I've never needed to use my father's name," Duncan was very close to his father all his life and was with him when he died, in January 2016. He said of him "He was a wonderful father who encouraged me to be creative, but different."

🔊 **10.7**

Tim Powell isn't a morning person. Which is surprising, because on weekdays he gets up very early. While most of us are still asleep, Powell wakes up at 5:45, exercises for 30 minutes at his home gym, and has a big breakfast. Then he gets ready for work and drives to the office. When he gets to the building where he works, he goes for a walk around a local park, and then he goes inside to start work at 9. And on Thursdays he gets up even earlier, at 5:20 a.m., to study German.

Powell is a lawyer. He works 70 hours a week, and he says that getting up early helps him to do more during the day. He isn't the only one – many busy, successful people get up very early.

🔊 **10.8**

Experts agree that getting up early is a big help if you have a lot of things to do. There are three main reasons for this. The first reason why it's good to get up early is that the early morning is quiet. Nobody calls you at 6:00 a.m. There aren't any important emails or messages to answer. There aren't any meetings. There aren't any people. The morning is your time.

The second reason is that if you get up early, you go to bed early. Most people don't do anything useful in the evenings. People who go to bed late spend many hours watching TV, seeing their friends, and spending time on social media. So, if you want to do a lot, it's better to go to bed early, and have shorter evenings and longer mornings.

The third reason is that it's better to do things in the morning, when you have energy. Most people are tired after a day at work or school. And when you're tired, the last thing you want to do is to exercise, or to study, or to practice a musical instrument.

And if you find it impossible to get up early? Set your alarm five minutes earlier than you usually get up. And the next day, set it five minutes earlier again. After three weeks, you'll have nearly two hours that you never had before!

🔊 **11.7**

1 **Interviewer** Did you like school?

A I didn't hate school, but I don't think I liked it very much. I used to enjoy PE, I used to enjoy playing sports. Um, I liked English but there were a lot of subjects I didn't like. I didn't like math very much, history was boring, and I found science difficult. I had a small group of friends, not many, but a close group of friends and I used to spend time with them talking about sports, talking about music, so it wasn't too bad, but I didn't like it very much. I've never been back to school, I've never been to a school reunion, or anything like that.

2 **Interviewer** Did you like school?

B No, not really. I didn't like it at all.

Interviewer Why not?

B It was a boys' school and I got bored with just being with boys all the time. And I didn't really like any of the subjects.

3 **Interviewer** Did you like school?

C Well, yes and no. Some things I really loved, some things I thought "this isn't much fun," but I used to enjoy a lot of subjects.

Interviewer Like what?

C I liked English and I liked math.

Interviewer And what didn't you enjoy?

C I hated geography. And I hated PE. The PE teacher once caught me reading a book on the soccer field, and I was punished for that.

4 **Interviewer** Did you like school?

D I didn't like it, I absolutely loved it! I liked all the subjects, especially English and history. I remember one time when I was about six or seven, I got sick during spring break and I was really, really sad, and my mom thought I was sad because I was sick during vacation, but in fact, I was terrified that I'd never get better and I'd never go back to school.

5 **Interviewer** Did you like school?

E Uh, sometimes. Yeah, most of the time.

Interviewer What did you like about it?

E Well, I had some good friends, and I liked learning things, but there were some subjects that I didn't like very much, and I hated PE. I used to invent a lot of excuses, like saying that I was sick, because I didn't want to do it.

6 **Interviewer** Did you like school?

F Yes, definitely, I really enjoyed school. Elementary school was all fun and we had great teachers. I always really looked forward to getting back to school. High school was harder work and we used to have lots of exams and tests, but we had really inspiring teachers. My favorites were in math and biology. And overall, yeah, I really liked it.

🔊 **11.14**

Buying jeans isn't as easy as it used to be. Years ago, there was only one kind of jeans – probably Levis. Nowadays, there are hundreds – different styles, different colors, different lengths, with buttons, with zippers. There are so many options that you feel the perfect pair must be waiting for you somewhere…

And it isn't just jeans. In big supermarkets, we have to choose between thousands of products – my local supermarket has 35 different kinds of milk! When we're buying clothes or electrical gadgets, ordering a coffee in a café, looking for a hotel on a travel website, deciding which TV channel to watch, or even choosing a future partner on a dating website, we constantly have to choose from hundreds of possibilities.

People often think that being able to choose from a lot of options is a good thing.

However, university researchers have discovered that too much choice is making us feel unhappy and dissatisfied. The problem is that we have so many options that we get stressed every time we have to make a decision because we're worried about making the wrong one. Then when we choose one thing, we feel bad because we think we are missing other opportunities, and this makes us dissatisfied with what we've chosen.

Research also shows that we feel happier when we have less choice. In a study, Professor Mark Lepper at Stanford University found that people who tried six kinds of jam and then chose one felt happier with their choice than those who were offered 24 jams to taste.

But if all this choice is bad for us, what can we do about it? Professor Lepper suggests that we should try to relax when we have to decide what to buy. "Don't take these choices too seriously or it will become stressful," he says. "If you pick a sofa from IKEA in 30 seconds, you'll feel better than if you spend hours researching sofas – because you won't know what you're missing."

🔊 **11.16**

I went on the Twin Strangers website. All you have to do is pay $3.95, upload a photo of your face, and then describe it, your nose, mouth, and eyes. I looked in a mirror and decided that I have an oval face, blue eyes and, unfortunately, thin lips. Immediately, I got a lot of photos of possible matches. My first reaction was "they all look totally different from me." Then something interesting began to happen. Some of the people started to look familiar, like people in my family. I found one woman who looked just like my brother. I started to wonder. Was there something there?

I called my husband to come and take a look at all these "twins." His first reaction was the same as mine, but then he went quiet. He pointed to one woman who, at first sight, looks completely different from me, but whose picture I had stopped at several times. He said, "She has the same mouth as you. In fact, she's a little like you." And he was right.

I decided to change my profile a little. Many people tell me I look younger than I really am, so I put my age as ten years younger, and then searched again. The result was surprising. Suddenly, there seemed to be a number of women a little like me. Especially one. I put her picture on my Facebook page and asked my friends what they thought. The first person to answer was my brother. Yes, he wrote. She looks like you and our sister.

It's a strange feeling. I keep looking at her picture. We're very similar, but not identical, for example, she has brown eyes, but mine are blue. But there's something there. Not just the blonde hair and the thin lips. There's something in her eyes that I recognize. It's a very strange feeling, but I'm really happy that I found her. I sent her a message through the website, but she hasn't replied yet. I'm going to keep trying. I want to know who she is.

 12.3

Iris Hello, Rosemary. How are you this morning?

Rosemary Hello, Iris. I'm fine thanks, but you'll never guess what's happened. Jack and Emma have broken up!

Iris No! Jack and Emma, from next door? That can't be true. I saw them last week, and they looked really happy.

Rosemary No, it's definitely true. I heard them shouting. They were having a terrible argument.

Iris No! When?

Rosemary Last night. After he came home from work.

Iris What did they say?

Rosemary Well, I wasn't really listening…

Iris Of course not.

Rosemary But I couldn't help hearing. She was talking so loudly, and of course, the walls are very thin…

Iris So what did they say?

Rosemary Well, she said that she was going to stay with her mother! She told him that she wouldn't come back.

Iris Ooh, how awful. What about the children?

Rosemary She said she'd taken them to her sister's. I suppose she'll take them with her in the end. And anyway, then five minutes later I saw her leaving the house with a suitcase!

Iris No! Why do you think she's leaving him? Is he seeing another woman?

Rosemary I don't know. Ooh, here's my bus.

Iris I have to go and tell Mrs. Jones from across the street. She always thought there was something… something strange about him.

 12.4

Jack Hi, Emma. I'm back. Where are you?

Emma I'm upstairs in the bedroom. I'm packing.

Jack Why? Where are you going?

Emma I'm going to stay with my mom.

Jack Your mom? Why?

Emma She's had an accident. She fell on the street yesterday and she's broken her leg.

Jack How awful. Poor thing. Can I help you with anything?

Emma Actually, yes. Could you get my small suitcase in the closet?

Jack How long do you think you'll have to stay?

Emma I won't come back until the weekend, I don't think. I'll have to make sure she's OK. I've taken the children to my sister's for the night, and she'll take them to school tomorrow morning. Can you pick them up after school?

Jack Of course I can, honey. Now, don't worry about anything. We'll be absolutely fine, and here's your suitcase.

Emma Thanks, dear. The taxi'll be here in five minutes.

 Go online to listen to the audio and see all the Listening scripts

7A uses of the infinitive

1 You need **to be** on time.
   Try **not to talk** too much.   🔊 7.3
2 It'll be nice **to meet** new people.
   It's important **not to be** late.
3 I don't know where **to go** or what **to do**.
4 **A** Why did you wear a suit?
   B To make a good impression.
   I wore a suit **to make** a good impression.

- The infinitive is the base form of the verb + *to*. It can be affirmative (e.g., *to be*) or negative (e.g., *not to be*).

- We use the infinitive:
  1 after some verbs, e.g., *want, need, would like*, etc. See **Verb forms** p.158.
  2 after adjectives.
  3 after questions words, e.g., *what, where, when*, etc.
  4 to say why you do / did something.
     I came to this school **to learn** *English.* **NOT** ~~for learn English.~~

🔍 **Base form**
Remember that we use the base form after auxiliary verbs (*do / does / didn't*) and after most modal verbs (*can, could, will, would*, etc.), e.g., **Do** *you* **live** *near here?* **Can** *you* **help** *me?* **I** **won't forget**. *What* **would** *you* **do**?

7B uses of the gerund (verb + -ing)

1 **Eating** outside in the summer makes me feel good.   🔊 7.7
   Happiness is **getting up** late and **not going** to work.
2 I love **having** breakfast in bed.
   I hate **not getting** to the airport early.
3 I'm thinking of **buying** a new car.
   Jim left without **saying** goodbye.

- The gerund is the base form of the verb + *-ing*. It can be affirmative (e.g., *going*) or negative (e.g., *not going*).
- We use the gerund:
  1 as a noun, e.g., as the subject or object of a sentence.
  2 after some verbs, e.g., *like, love, hate, enjoy*, etc. See **Verb forms** p.158.
  3 after prepositions.
- Remember the spelling rules for the *-ing* form. See **1C** p.126.

7C *have to, don't have to, must, must not, can't*

have to, don't have to

⊞ I **have to** speak English at work.   🔊 7.13
   She **has to** get up at seven every day.
⊟ We **don't have to** wear a uniform at this school.
   He **doesn't have to** work on Saturdays.
❓ **Do** I **have to** buy a grammar book?
   What time **does** she **have to** get up in the morning?

- We use *have to* + verb (base form) to talk about rules and obligations.
- We use *don't have to* + verb (base form) to say that there is no obligation, or that something is not necessary.
- We use *do / does* to make questions and negatives.
  Do *I have to go?* **NOT** ~~Have I to go?~~
- We don't contract *have* or *has*.
  I **have to** *go.* **NOT** ~~I've to go.~~

must / must not / can't

⊞ You **must** do your homework tonight.   🔊 7.14
   She **must** clean up her room before she goes out.
⊟ You **must not** leave your bags here.
   You **can't** bring food into the library.

- We use *must* + verb (base form) to talk about rules and obligations.

- Use *can't / must not* + base form to say something is prohibited or to state a rule.
- The words *can't* and *must not* have similar meanings, but *can't* is more common in speaking. You can also use *cannot*.
- The verbs *must / must not* are the same for all persons.
- The verb *must* is not often used in questions (*have to* is more common).

🔍 **must and have to**
Must and *have to* are very similar, but *have to* is more common, especially in speaking. *Must* is often used in official forms, notices, and signs.

must not and don't have to
Must not and *don't have to* have completely different meanings. Compare:
You **must not** *go.* = It's prohibited. Don't go.
You **don't have to** *go.* = You can go if you want to, but it's not obligatory / necessary.

Impersonal you
We often use *have to* and *must* with impersonal *you* (*you* = people in general), e.g.,
You **have to** *wear a seatbelt in a car.*
You **must not / can't** *take photos in the museum.*

7A

a Match the sentence halves.

You need to be ready *B*

1 I know you're tired, but try ▢
2 In my job it's important ▢
3 I don't know where ▢
4 We were late, so Tomo offered ▢
5 When you give a presentation it's normal ▢

A to drive us to the train station.
B to show your ID at the gate.
C to feel nervous.
D to dress formally.
E to park.
F to stay awake for the party.

b Complete the sentences with an affirmative or negative infinitive.

| not be   do   not drive   ~~have~~   learn   look for |
| not make   meet   pay |

I'm planning *to have* a party next week.

1 **A** Hi, I'm Ji Su. **B** I'm Rosaria. Nice _____ you.
2 What do you want _____ tonight? Stay in or go out?
3 Let's meet outside the restaurant. I promise _____ late.
4 Try _____ a noise. Your father's asleep.
5 I'd really like _____ a new language.
6 Be careful _____ too fast – the roads are icy.
7 My brother has decided _____ a new job.
8 The museum is free. You don't need _____ to go in.

⬅ p.55

7B

a Complete the sentences with a verb from the list in the *-ing* form.

| ~~do~~   not know   message   practice   remember |
| study   swim   teach   travel |

I really enjoy *doing* yoga. It makes me feel great!

1 One thing that always makes me happy is _____ in the ocean.
2 You can't learn to play a musical instrument well without _____ regularly.
3 My mother's very bad at _____ names.
4 _____ teenagers is very hard work.
5 My sister spends hours _____ her friends.
6 I hate _____ the answer when somebody asks me a question.
7 _____ by train is usually cheaper than by plane.
8 My brother wants to go on _____ French for as long as he can. He'd like to speak it really fluently!

b Put the verbs in the *-ing* form or base form.

I like *listening* to the radio in the mornings. (listen)

1 _____ Pilates is good for your health. (do)
2 We offered _____ for the meal. (pay)
3 We won't take the car. It's so expensive _____. (park)
4 I'm not very good at _____ directions. (give)
5 You can borrow the car if you remember _____ some gas. (get)
6 Has it stopped _____ yet? (rain)
7 I don't mind _____, but I don't like _____ the dishes. (cook, do)
8 I hate _____ in the dark during the winter. (get up)

⬅ p.56

7C

a Complete the sentences with the correct form of *have to*.

I *don't have to* go to school on Saturdays.

1 Janice _____ study very hard – she has exams soon.
2 You _____ buy a ticket before you get on the bus. It costs $12 and the machine is over there.
3 _____ your sister _____ go to Los Angeles for her job interview?
4 Mike _____ wear a really ugly uniform at his new school. He hates it.
5 We _____ get up early tomorrow. Our flight leaves at 6:30.
6 Harry _____ work today – he has a day off.
7 Can you wait a moment? I _____ make a phone call.
8 _____ we _____ go to bed? It's only ten o'clock!

b Circle the correct form. Check (✓) if both are possible.

We *don't have to* / *must not* go to school next week. It's a holiday.

1 You *don't have to* / *must not* cross the road when the traffic lights are red.
2 What *do I have to* / *must I* do when I finish this exercise?
3 The concert is free. You *don't have to* / *can't* pay.
4 We're late for the meeting. We *have to* / *must* go now.
5 You *don't have to* / *must not* leave the door open – the dog will get out.
6 I *have to* / *must* pay Jane back the money she lent me.
7 In the US, you *have to* / *must* drive on the right.
8 You *don't have to* / *can't* be tall to be good at soccer.

⬅ p.59

 Go online to review the grammar for each lesson

8A *should / shouldn't*

1 You **should** leave your boyfriend.   8.2
  She's very stressed. She **shouldn't** work so hard.
  You **shouldn't** drink coffee in the evening. It'll keep you awake.
2 I think you **should** get a new job.
  I don't think you **should** speak to him.

1 We use *should / shouldn't* + verb (base form) to give somebody advice or say what we think is the right thing to do; *should / shouldn't* is the same for all persons.
2 We often use *I think you should…* or *I don't think you should…* **NOT** ~~I think you shouldn't…~~

> 🔍 *ought to*
> You can also use *ought to / ought not to* instead of *should / shouldn't*, e.g.,
> You **ought to** leave your boyfriend.
> She **ought not to** work so hard.

8B first conditional: *if* + present, *will / won't* + infinitive

1 If we get to the airport early, the flight **will be** delayed.   8.12
  If you **tell** her the truth, she **won't believe** you.
  What **will** you **do** if you **don't find** a job?
2 If you **don't go**, she **won't be** very happy.
  She **won't be** very happy if you **don't go**.
3 If you **miss** the last bus, **get** a taxi.
  If you **miss** the last bus, you **can get** a taxi.

1 We use *if* + present to talk about a possible situation and *will / won't* + base form to talk about the consequence.
2 The *if*-clause can come first or second. If the *if*-clause comes first, we usually put a comma before the next clause.
3 We can also use the imperative or *can* + base form instead of *will* + base form in the other clause.

8C possessive pronouns

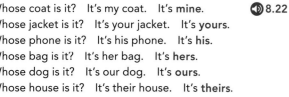

Whose coat is it?   It's my coat.   It's **mine**.   8.22
Whose jacket is it?   It's your jacket.   It's **yours**.
Whose phone is it?   It's his phone.   It's **his**.
Whose bag is it?   It's her bag.   It's **hers**.
Whose dog is it?   It's our dog.   It's **ours**.
Whose house is it?   It's their house.   It's **theirs**.

- We use possessive pronouns to talk about possession.
  *Is it **yours**? Yes, it's **mine**.*
- We use *Whose* to <u>ask</u> about possession.
  ***Whose** book is it? **Whose** is that bag?*
- We don't use possessive pronouns with a noun.
  NOT ~~It's mine book.~~
- We don't use *the* with possessive pronouns, e.g.,
  *Is this **yours**?* **NOT** ~~Is this the yours?~~

pronouns and possessive adjectives overview

subject pronouns		object pronouns		possessive adjectives		possessive pronouns
I			me.		my	mine.
You			you.		your	yours.
He			him.		his	his.
She	can come.	She loves	her.	This is	her	seat. It's	hers.
It			it.		its	its.
We			us.		our	ours.
They			them.		their	theirs.

8A

a Complete with *should* or *shouldn't*.

You *should* lose some weight.
1 You _____ work really long hours every day.
2 You _____ stop smoking.
3 You _____ eat more fruit and vegetables.
4 You _____ put so much sugar in your coffee.
5 You _____ start exercising.
6 You _____ drink less soda.
7 You _____ drink more water.
8 You _____ go to bed so late.

b Complete the sentences with *should* or *shouldn't* + a verb from the list.

be   buy   book   drive   ~~leave~~
relax   spend   study   wear

We *should leave* now. It's getting late.
1 You _____ a scarf. It's really cold today.
2 I _____ this afternoon. I have an exam tomorrow.
3 You _____ a vacation. You need a break.
4 You look really sick. You _____ at work.
5 She _____ more. She's very stressed right now.
6 You _____ so fast – this road's very dangerous.
7 Parents _____ more time with their children.
8 You _____ him an iPad – he's only seven years old.

⬅ p.62

8B

a Match the sentence halves.

If you leave now,   C
1 The hotel will be cheaper ▢
2 If you don't hear from me this afternoon, ▢
3 You'll learn more quickly ▢
4 If you get that new job, ▢
5 You won't pass your driver's test ▢
6 If I lend you this book, ▢

A if you don't take enough lessons.
B will you remember to give it back?
C ~~you'll catch the 8:00 train.~~
D if you book it early.
E if you come to every class.
F will you earn more money?
G call me this evening.

b Complete the sentences with the correct form of the verbs.

If we *start* walking, the bus *will come*. (start, come)
1 If you _____ me what really happened, I _____ anybody else. (tell, not tell)
2 If I _____ it down, I _____ it. (not write, not remember)
3 _____ you _____ me if you _____ any news? (call, get)
4 She _____ you if you _____ her nicely. (help, ask)
5 I _____ you if I _____ from Alex. (call, hear)
6 You _____ your friends if you _____ to Paris. (miss, move)
7 If you _____ carefully, you _____ everything. (listen, understand)
8 Your boss _____ happy if you _____ late for work today. (not be, be)
9 I _____ you home if you _____ me directions. (drive, give)
10 If you _____ an umbrella, it _____! (not take, rain)

⬅ p.64

8C

a Circle the correct form.

Whose car is that? It's *her* /(*hers*).
1 This isn't *my* / *mine* pen, it's Susan's.
2 I think this book is *your* / *yours*.
3 This isn't your suitcase, it's *ours* / *our*.
4 Where's Mary? I think these are *her* / *hers* gloves.
5 These keys are *mine* / *the mine*.
6 They showed us all *theirs* / *their* vacation photographs.
7 These seats are *theirs* / *their*, not ours.
8 Is this *yours* / *your* bag?
9 This isn't my jacket. It's *her* / *hers*.

b Complete the sentences with a pronoun or a possessive adjective.

This isn't my coffee, it's yours. Where's *mine* ?
1 **A** Is that Sue's car?
  B No, it's her boyfriend's. _____ is a white Ford.
2 Maya has a new boyfriend, but I haven't met _____ yet.
3 Look. Here's a photo of Alex and Kim with _____ new baby.
4 We've finished paying for our house, so it's _____ now.
5 These are your tickets. Can you give Maria and Marta _____?
6 We're lost. Can you tell _____ how to get to the train station?
7 Would you like to see _____ garden? We have some beautiful flowers.
8 New York City is famous for _____ tall buildings.

⬅ p.67

🔄 **Go online** to review the grammar for each lesson

9A second conditional: *if* + past, *would* / *wouldn't* + base form

> 1 If a cow **attacked** me, **I'd run** away. 🔊 9.5
>   If she **didn't have** a dog, she **wouldn't exercise**.
>   **Would** you **go** for a swim **if** there **were** sharks in the ocean?
> 2 If I **had** more time, **I'd exercise** more.
>   **I'd exercise** more if I **had** more time.
> 3 If we **went** by car, we **could stop** at places on the way.

1 We use *if* + past to talk about an imaginary or hypothetical future situation and *would* / *wouldn't* + base form to talk about the consequence.

- *would* + base form is sometimes known as the conditional tense. We also use it without an *if*-clause to talk about imaginary or hypothetical situations e.g., *I'd never have a cat as a pet. They'd be happier in a bigger house.*
- *would* / *wouldn't* = is the same for all persons. Contractions: *'d* = *would* (*I'd, you'd, he'd,* etc.); *wouldn't* = *would not.*

2 In a second conditional, the *if*-clause can come first or second. If the *if*-clause comes first, we usually put a comma before the next clause.

3 We can also use *could* + base form instead of *would* + base form in the other clause.

> 🔍 **be in second conditionals**
> With the verb *be* we can use *were* (instead of *was*) after *I* / *he* / *she* / *it*, e.g.,
> *If Jack was / were here, he'd know what to do.*
> Use *were* (not *was*) in the expression *If I were you,…*
> We often use this expression for advice, e.g.,
> *If I were you, I wouldn't take that job.*

first or second conditional?

Compare the first and second conditionals:

- We use the **first conditional** for **possible** future situations.
  *If I **don't have to** work tomorrow, I**'ll help** you.*
  (= It's a possibility. Maybe I will help you.)
- We use the **second conditional** for **imaginary** or **hypothetical** situations.
  *If I **didn't have to** work tomorrow, I**'d help** you.*
  (= It's a hypothetical situation. I have to work, so I can't help you.)

9B present perfect + *for* and *since*

> A Where do you live now? 🔊 9.7
> B In Tokyo.
> A **How long have** you **lived** there?
> B **I've lived** there **for** 20 years.
>
> A Where do you work?
> B In an elementary school.
> A **How long have** you **worked** there?
> B **I've worked** there **since** 2015.

- We use the present perfect + *for* and *since* to talk about actions and states that started in the past and are still true now.
  *I**'ve lived** in Tokyo **for** twenty years.* = I came to live in Tokyo twenty years ago, and I live in Tokyo now.
  We don't use the simple present in this type of sentence, e.g.,
  NOT *I live in Tokyo for twenty years.*
- We use *How long…?* to ask questions about the duration of an action or a state, e.g., *How long have you been married?*

for or since?

- We use *for* + a period of time, for example, **for** *two weeks,* **for** *ten years,* etc.
  *I've had this car **for** three months.*
- We use *since* with the beginning of a period of time, for example, **since** *2014,* **since** *last June,* etc.
  *I've been afraid of spiders **since** I was a child.*

9C present perfect or simple past? (2)

> 1 A How long **was** Janet Leigh married to Tony Curtis? 🔊 9.15
>   B She **was** married to him **for** 11 years.
>   A How many books **did** she **write**?
>   B She **wrote** four books.
> 2 A How long **has** Jamie Lee Curtis **been** married?
>   B She**'s been** married **since** 1984.
>   A What kind of books **has** she **written**?
>   B She**'s written** children's books.

- We can use *for* with the simple past for a finished period of time in the past.
2 We use the **present perfect** with *for* and *since* to talk about an unfinished period of time, from the past until now. Jamie Lee Curtis is still alive and still married.
- Compare the simple past and the present perfect.
  *Jack **was** married for ten years.* = Jack is not married now. He's divorced or dead.
  *Jack **has been** married for ten years.* = Jack is married now. He got married ten years ago.

1 We use the **simple past** to talk about a <u>finished</u> period of time in the past. Janet Leigh and Tony Curtis are dead, so **NOT** *She has been married to him for 11 years.*

9A

a Match the sentence halves.

You'd feel much better *A*

1 I'd enjoy the weekend more ▢
2 If you didn't have to study for your exams, ▢
3 Would you really wear a suit ▢
4 If we took a taxi, ▢
5 I wouldn't work ▢
6 If I went to live in Tokyo, ▢

A if you exercised.
B would you come to visit me?
C if I bought one for you?
D we could go out tonight.
E if I didn't have to work on Saturday.
F we would get there sooner.
G if I didn't need the money.

b Complete the sentences with the correct form of the verb to make second conditional sentences.

If I *found* a good job, I *'d move* to the US. (find, move)

1 We _____ a dog if we _____ a yard. (get, have)
2 If you _____ Indian food, I'm sure you _____it. (try, like)
3 I _____ it if I _____ it. (not buy, not like)
4 If we _____ a car, we _____ drive to the mountains. (rent, can)
5 We _____ our children more often if they _____ closer. (see, live)
6 I _____ to that restaurant if I _____ you – it's very expensive. (not go, be)
7 You _____ more if you _____ more homework. (learn, do)
8 I _____ to work if the traffic _____ so bad. (bike, not be)
9 _____ you _____ abroad if you _____ a well-paid job? (work, find)
10 I love living here. I _____ happy if I _____ leave. (not be, have to)

⬅ p.71

9B

a Write questions with *How long* and the present perfect.

/ you / be married   *How long have you been married* ?
1 / you / be afraid of flying _____?
2 / your sister / have her new car _____?
3 / they / live in this town _____?
4 / your dad / be a teacher _____?
5 / you / know your boyfriend _____?
6 / Spain / be in the EU _____?
7 / you / have / your cat _____?
8 / Dan / be in this class _____?

b Answer the questions in **a**. Use the present perfect + *for* or *since*.

I *'ve been married for* 20 years.

1 I _____ I was about 15.
2 She _____ three weeks.
3 They _____ a long time.
4 He _____ more than 20 years.
5 I _____ May.
6 It _____ 1986.
7 We _____ about two years.
8 He _____ last month.

⬅ p.73

9C

a Circle the correct form.

She was / She's been sick since May.

1 *Martin left / Martin has left* school two years ago.
2 *I lived / I've lived* in Vancouver for two years, but then I moved to Toronto.
3 *Anna was / Anna's been* in this company since April.
4 *My sister had / My sister has had* her baby yesterday!
5 I work in a travel agency. *I worked / I've worked* there for 20 years.
6 *The city changed / The city has changed* a lot since I was a child.
7 They're divorced now. *They were / They have been* only married for three years.
8 *I met / I've met* Sandra when I *was / have been* on vacation in Thailand.

b Complete with the present perfect or simple past.

1 **A** Where does your brother live?
   B In San Diego.
   A How long _____ there? (he / live)
   B Only for six months. He _____ there last September. (move)
2 **A** When _____? (Picasso / die)
   B In 1977, I think. In Paris.
   A How long _____ in France? (he / live).
   B For a long time. He _____ Spain when he was 25. (leave)
3 **A** My brother and his wife get along very well.
   B How long _____ married? (they / be)
   A They _____ married since 1995. They _____ in college. (be, meet)
   B Really? What college _____ to? (they / go)

⬅ p.75

🔵 **Go online** to review the grammar for each lesson

10A expressing movement

The ball **went over** the goalkeeper's head and **into** the goal.

He **drove out of** the garage and **along** the street.

I **ran over** the bridge and **across** the park.

- To express movement, we use a verb of movement, e.g., *go, come, run, walk,* etc., and a preposition (or adverb) of movement, e.g., *up, down, away,* etc.

🔍 **come** or **go**?
We use *come* for movement toward you, and *go* for movement away from you.

🔍 **in** or **into**? **out** or **out of**?
We use *into* / *out of* + noun.
*Come **into** the living room.*
*He went **out of** the house.*
We use *in* / *out* if there isn't a noun.
*Come **in**.*
*He went **out**.*

10B word order of phrasal verbs

1 What time do you **get up**?
  I don't usually **go out** during the week.
2 **Put on** your coat. **Put** your coat **on**. **Put** it **on**!
  Turn off the TV. **Turn** the TV **off**. **Turn** it **off**.
3 I'm **looking for** my glasses.
  A Have you found your glasses?
  B No, I'm still **looking for** them.

- A phrasal verb = verb + particle (preposition or adverb), e.g., *get up, go out, turn on, look for.*
  1 Some phrasal verbs don't have an object, e.g., *get up, go out.*
  2 Some phrasal verbs have an object and are separable. With these phrasal verbs we can put the particle (*on, off,* etc.) before <u>or</u> after the object.
- When the object is a pronoun (*me, it, him,* etc.) it <u>always</u> goes between the verb and particle.
  Here's your coat. Put it on. **NOT** ~~Put on it.~~
  3 Some phrasal verbs have an object and are inseparable, e.g., *look for.* With these phrasal verbs the verb (e.g., *look*) and the particle (e.g., *for*) are never separated.
  *I'm **looking for** my glasses.* **NOT** ~~I'm looking my glasses for.~~
- See **Phrasal verbs** p.163.

10C the passive: *be* + past participle

Present: *am / is / are* + past participle 🔊 10.14
+ 20 billion pieces of Lego **are produced** every year.
− CDs **aren't used** very much nowadays.
? Is Spanish **spoken** in New Mexico?

Past: *was / were* + past participle
+ The hot-air balloon **was invented** by two Frenchmen.
− Stamps **weren't invented** until 1840.
? When **was** the watch **invented**?

- We can often say things in two ways, in the active or in the passive.
  *Alfred Nobel **invented** dynamite.* (**active**)
  *Dynamite **was invented** by Alfred Nobel.* (**passive**)
- In the **active** sentence, the focus is more on **Alfred Nobel**.
- In the **passive** sentence, the focus is more on **dynamite**.
- We often use the passive when it isn't known or isn't important who does or did the action.
  *My car **was stolen** last week.*
  *Volvo cars **are made** in Sweden.*
- We use *by* to say who did the action.
  *The Lord of the Rings was written **by** Tolkien.*

10A

a Circle the correct word.

I lost my cell phone signal when we went *across /* *through* a tunnel.

1 We ran *to / down* the ocean, and jumped *into / out of* the water.
2 If you go *over / past* the bank, you'll see the supermarket on the right.
3 James walked *along / across* the street until he came to a big house.
4 Look! We're flying *on / over* the mountains now.
5 The dog started to run *toward / to* me, but then it suddenly stopped.
6 We biked *over / out of* the bridge and *in / into* the park.
7 In the 800-meter race, the runners run *around / across* the track twice.
8 The cat suddenly ran *across / through* the road.

b Complete the sentences with the correct word.

Alex jumped *into* his car and drove away.

1 When I was walking under the bridge, a train went _____ it.
2 Come _____. The door's open.
3 This is the first floor. Go _____ the stairs – the office is on the second floor.
4 He walked _____ the café and ordered some lunch.
5 Go _____ of the building and turn left.
6 Go _____! I don't want to talk to you.
7 I bike _____ a big hill on my way home. I go really fast!

p.78

10B

a Circle the correct form. If both are correct, check (✓) the box.

Turn off your cell phone / *Turn your cell phone off* before the movie starts. ✓

1 Tonight I have to look *my little sister after / look after my little sister.*
2 Let's *go out this evening / go this evening out.*
3 I'll *drop off the children / drop the children off* at school.
4 My brother is *looking for a new job / looking a new job for.*
5 You should *throw away those old jeans / throw those old jeans away.*
6 I don't like shopping for clothes online – I prefer to *try them on / try on them* before I buy them.
7 *Take off your shoes / Take your shoes off* before you come in.
8 We're meeting my mother tomorrow – I think you'll really *get along with her / get along her with.*
9 If the jacket doesn't fit, *take back it / take it back* to the store.
10 What time do you *get up in the morning / get in the morning up?*

b Complete the sentences with *it* or *them* and a word from the list.

back   on (x2)   out   up (x2)

I can't hear the radio. Turn *it up*.

1 Your clothes are all over the floor. Pick _____.
2 Here's your coat. Put _____.
3 **A** What does this word mean?
   B Look _____.
4 To get your passport there are three forms. Please fill _____ now.
5 You remember that money I lent you? When can you give _____?
6 **A** Is the game on TV?
   B I don't know. Turn _____ and see.

p.81

10C

a Complete with the present or past passive.

The Eiffel Tower *was completed* in 1889. (complete)

1 Many of the things we use every day _____ by women. (invent)
2 In the US, most children _____ in public schools. (educate)
3 DNA _____ by Watson and Crick in 1953. (discover)
4 This morning I _____ by the neighbor's dog. (wake up)
5 Baseball _____ in the summer in the US. (play)
6 The songs on this album _____ last year. (write)
7 Millions of toys _____ in China every year. (make)
8 Carols are songs that _____ at Christmas. (sing)
9 These birds _____ in Canada. (not usually see)
10 The London Eye _____ on December 31, 1999, to celebrate the new millennium. (open)

b Rewrite the sentences in the passive, beginning with the highlighted words.

Shakespeare wrote *Hamlet* in 1603.
Hamlet was written by Shakespeare in 1603.

1 Christopher Wren designed St. Paul's Cathedral.
2 A small Italian company produces this olive oil.
3 The Russians discovered Antarctica in 1820.
4 Spielberg didn't direct the *Star Wars* movies.
5 Van Gogh painted *Sunflowers* in 1888.
6 The Chinese didn't invent glass.
7 J.K. Rowling wrote the *Harry Potter* books.
8 They make Hyundai cars in South Korea.

p.83

 Go online to review the grammar for each lesson   145

11A *used to / didn't use to*

⊞ When I was a child, I **used to** play on the street.
My brother **used to** have very long hair when he
was a student.

🔊 11.4

⊟ Nick **didn't use to** go out much, but now he goes out
every night.
I **didn't use to** like vegetables, but now I love them.

⍰ **A** Did you **use to** wear a uniform at school? **B** Yes, I did.
A Did you **use to** like your teachers? **B** No, I didn't.

- We use *used to / didn't use to* + verb to talk about things
that happened repeatedly or were true for a long period of
time in the past, but are usually <u>not</u> true now, e.g., things
that happened when you were a child.
- *used to / didn't use to* is the same for all persons.

> **!** Be careful with negatives and questions:
> *I didn't use to like math.* **NOT** ~~I didn't used to like math.~~
> *Did you use to like math?* **NOT** ~~Did you used to like math?~~

- Instead of *used to*, you can use the simple past with an
adverb of frequency.
When I was a child, I often played on the street.

> 🔍 **used to or usually?**
> *used to* is only for talking about the past.
> For habits in the present, we use *usually* + simple present,
> **NOT** ~~use to.~~
> *I usually cook in the evenings.*
> **NOT** ~~I use to cook in the evenings.~~

11B *might / might not* (possibility)

We **might** have a picnic tomorrow, but it depends on the weather.
Karen **might** come with us tomorrow, but she's not sure yet.
I **might not** take my laptop on vacation. I haven't decided yet.
We **might not** see the boss today. I think she's away.

🔊 11.10

> 🔍 **may / may not**
> We can also use *may* instead of *might* for
> possibility, e.g.,
> *We **may** have a picnic tomorrow.*
> *I **may not** take my laptop on vacation.*

- We use *might / might not* + verb (base form) to say that perhaps
somebody will or won't do something.
- *We might have a picnic tomorrow.* = Perhaps we will have a picnic tomorrow.
- *might / might not* is the same for all persons.
- *might not* is not usually contracted.

11C *so, neither* + auxiliaries

1 **A** I love classical music.
  B So do I.
  A I went to a classical concert last night.
  B So did I.
2 **A** I'm not married.
  B Neither am I.
  A I don't want to get married.
  B Neither do I.

🔊 11.19

simple present	**A** I don't like classical music.	**B** Neither do I.
present continuous	**A** I'm having a great time.	**B** So am I.
can / can't	**A** I can swim.	**B** So can I.
simple past	**A** I didn't like the movie.	**B** Neither did I.
	A I was very tired.	**B** So was I.
would / wouldn't	**A** I wouldn't like to go there.	**B** Neither would I.
present perfect	**A** I've been to Brazil.	**B** So have I.

> **!** Be careful with the word order.
> *So do I / Neither do I.* **NOT** ~~So I do / Neither I do.~~

- We use *So do I, Neither do I*, etc., to say that we
have something in common with somebody.
  1 Use *So* + auxiliary + *I* to respond to
  affirmative sentences.
  2 Use *Neither* + auxiliary + *I* to respond to
  negative sentences.
- The auxiliary we use after *So...* and *Neither...*
depends on the tense of the verb that the other
speaker uses.

> 🔍 **neither and nor**
> We can also use *nor* instead of *neither*, e.g.,
> **A** *I didn't like the movie.* **B** *Nor / Neither did I.*
> *Neither* is usually pronounced /ˈniðər/, but can also be pronounced /ˈnaɪðər/.

11A

a Look at how Alex has changed. Write six sentences about how he was before with *He used to* or *He didn't use to.*

Then

Now

He used to be slim.

1 _____ long hair.
2 _____ glasses.
3 _____ a beard.
4 _____ soccer.
5 _____ a tie.

b Make sentences with *used to, didn't use to,* or *did...use to?*

? / you / have long hair   *Did you use to have long hair?*

1 ⊞ Angie / hate math, but she loves it now
2 ? / you / work when you lived in Cairo
3 ⊟ I / like reading when I was a child
4 ? What / you / do on summer vacation when you were young
5 ⊟ Americans / put a lot of ice in drinks
6 ⊞ This restaurant / be a movie theater in the 1960s
7 ? / your sister / eat meat, or has she always been a vegetarian
8 ⊟ I / be interested in tennis, but now I always watch it
9 ? / you / have a car when you were a student
10 ⊞ Telegrams / be the quickest way to send important messages

← p.87

11B

a Match the sentences.

Take some sunscreen. *D*

1 Let's buy a lottery ticket. ▢
2 Can you call the restaurant? ▢
3 Don't finish the milk. ▢
4 Let's use a map. ▢
5 You should try the shirt on. ▢
6 Don't wait for me tonight. ▢
7 Be careful with that knife! ▢
8 Ask how much it costs. ▢

A Someone might want some for breakfast.
B It may not be your size.
C We might get lost.
D It might be really sunny.
E We may not have enough money.
F You might cut yourself.
G It may be closed on Sundays.
H We might win.
I I may finish work late.

b Complete the sentences with *might* + a verb phrase from the list.

be cold   be in a meeting   be sick
go to the movies   not have time
not like it   have the pasta

I'm not sure what to do tonight.
I *might go to the movies*.
1 Kim isn't at school today. She _____.
2 His phone is turned off. He _____.
3 It's an unusual book. You _____.
4 I don't know if I'll finish this today.
   I _____.
5 I'm not sure what to order. I _____.
6 Take a warm jacket. It _____ later.

← p.88

11C

a Complete B's answers with an auxiliary verb.

A I love chocolate ice cream.   **B** So *do* I.
1 **A** I'm really thirsty.   **B** So _____ I.
2 **A** I didn't go out last night.   **B** Neither _____ I.
3 **A** I was born in Seoul.   **B** So _____ I.
4 **A** I don't eat meat.   **B** Neither _____ I.
5 **A** I've been to Istanbul.   **B** So _____ I.
6 **A** I can't sing.   **B** Neither _____ I.
7 **A** I'd like to go to Bali.   **B** So _____ I.
8 **A** I saw a great movie last week.   **B** So _____ I.
9 **A** I wouldn't like to be famous.   **B** Neither _____ I.
10 **A** I can play chess.   **B** So _____ I.

b Respond to **A**. Say you are the same. Use *So...I* or *Neither...I.*

A I don't like Indian food.   *Neither do I.*
1 **A** I live near the river. _____
2 **A** I'm not afraid of snakes. _____
3 **A** I went to bed late last night. _____
4 **A** I haven't been to Canada. _____
5 **A** I don't have any pets. _____
6 **A** I can speak three languages. _____
7 **A** I'll have the chicken with rice. _____
8 **A** I'm waiting for Maria. _____

← p.91

 Go online to review the grammar for each lesson

12A past perfect

⊞ When I woke up, the yard was all white. 🔊12.1
It **had snowed** during the night.
I suddenly realized that I**'d left** my cell phone in
the taxi.

⊟ We got home just in time – the game
hadn't started.
When she got to class, she realized that she
hadn't brought her book.

❓ **A** I went to New York City last weekend. I really
loved it.
B Had you **been** there before?
A No, I **hadn't**.

- We use the past perfect when we are already talking about the past and
want to talk about an earlier past action.
- *When I woke up the yard was all white. It **had snowed** during the night.*
= It snowed <u>before</u> I woke up.
- We make the past perfect with *had / hadn't* + the past participle.
- The form of the past perfect is the same for all persons.
- *had* is sometimes contracted to *'d*.

> 🔎 **had or would?**
> Be careful, *'d* can be *had* or *would*.
> *I didn't know that you**'d** found a new job.* (*'d = had*)
> *If you went by taxi, you**'d** get there much quicker.* (*'d = would*)

12B reported (or indirect) speech

- Pronouns often change in reported speech, e.g.,
I changes to *he* or *she*.
*"I'm tired." **She** told me (that) she was tired.*
- Verb tenses change like this:

direct speech	reported speech
"I can help you." (simple present)	He said (that) he could help me. (simple past)
"I'm driving." (present continuous)	She said (that) she was driving. (past continuous)
"I'll call you." (will)	He told me (that) he would call me. (would)
"I met a girl at a party." (simple past)	John told me (that) he had met a girl at a party. (past perfect)
"I've broken my arm." (present perfect)	Sara said (that) she had broken her arm. (past perfect)

direct speech	reported speech 🔊12.5
"I love you."	He said (that) he loved me.
"I've just arrived."	She said (that) she had just arrived.
"We'll come at eight."	He told me (that) they would come at eight.
"I don't want to go to the party."	Jack told Anna (that) he didn't want to go to the party.

- We use reported speech to tell somebody what another person said.
- We often introduce reported speech with *said* or *told* (+ person).
- After *said* or *told* **that** is optional, e.g., *He said (**that**) he loved me.*

> 🔎 **say or tell?**
> We use *say* or *tell* in reported speech. They mean
> the same thing, but they are used differently.
> We use *say* <u>without</u> an object or pronoun.
> *He **said** (that) he loved me.*
> **NOT** ~~He said me (that) he loved me.~~
> We use *tell* <u>with</u> an object or pronoun.
> *He **told** me (that) he loved me*
> **NOT** ~~He told (that) he loved me.~~

12C questions without auxiliaries

subject	verb	🔊12.9
Who	painted	*The Milkmaid*?
Which city	has	the most honest people?
How many people	live	near the school?
Who	wants	a cup of coffee?

- When the question word (*Who?, What?, Which?, How many?*,
etc.) is the subject of the verb in the question, we don't use
an auxiliary verb (*do / does / did*).
Who painted *The Milkmaid*? **NOT** ~~Who did paint…?~~
- In most other questions in the present and simple past, we
use the auxiliary verb *do / does / did* + the base form.
*What music **do** you like?* **NOT** ~~What music you like?~~
- See **1A** p.126.

12A

a Match the sentence halves.

I couldn't get into my house because C

1 When our friends arrived, ☐
2 I took the jacket back to the store because ☐
3 Jill didn't come with us because ☐
4 I turned on the TV news ☐
5 He was nervous because ☐
6 When I got to the supermarket checkout, ☐

A she'd made other plans.
B I realized that I'd left my wallet at home.
C~~I'd lost my keys.~~
D I'd bought the wrong size.
E it was the first time he'd flown.
F to see what had happened.
G we hadn't finished cooking the dinner.

b Complete the sentences. Put the verbs in the simple past or past perfect.

We _didn't get_ a table in the restaurant because we _hadn't made_ a reservation. (not get, not make)

1 Caroline _____ a lot, and I _____ her. (change, not recognize)
2 My friend _____ to tell me that I _____ my coat in his car. (call, leave)
3 When I _____ the radio, the news _____. (turn on, already finish)
4 She _____ me the DVD because she _____ it yet. (not lend, not watch)
5 The store _____ by the time we _____. (close, arrive)
6 When we _____ home, we saw that somebody _____ the kitchen window. (get, break)
7 When we _____ in the morning, we _____ that it _____ during the night. (get up, see, snow)

← p.95

12B

a Write the sentences in reported speech.

"I love you." He told her that he _loved her_.
1 "I'm hungry." Ana said that she _____.
2 "I'll call the doctor." He said he _____.
3 "I've bought a new phone." Paul told us that he _____.
4 "I live downtown." She said that she _____.
5 "We can't do it!" They said that they _____.
6 "I saw a great movie at the movie theater." Julie said that she _____.
7 "I don't like dogs." Ben told her he _____.

b Write the sentences in direct speech.

He told her that he was a doctor.
He said: "_I'm a doctor_."

1 She said that she was studying Japanese.
   She said: "_____."
2 Tony told me that his car had broken down.
   Tony said: "_____."
3 Yoshi said that he would send me an email.
   Yoshi said: "_____."
4 Bella and Eberto said they were in a hurry.
   Bella and Eberto said:
   "_____."
5 He said he hadn't finished his essay yet.
   He said: "_____."
6 She told us that she wouldn't arrive on time.
   She said: "_____."
7 David said he had just arrived in Lima.
   David said: "_____."

 p.96

12C

a (Circle) the correct question form.

What _you did_ / (_did you do_) last night?
1 What _happened_ / _did happen_ to you?
2 What _means this word_ / _does this word mean_?
3 How many people _came_ / _did come_ to the meeting?
4 Which bus _goes_ / _does go_ to town?
5 Which movie _won_ / _did win_ the most Academy Awards this year?
6 What _said the teacher_ / _did the teacher_ say?
7 Who _made_ / _did make_ this cake? It's delicious!

b Write the questions. Do you know the answers?

How many Formula 1 championships
did Michael Schumacher win? (Michael Schumacher / win)

1 When _____ president of the US? (Barack Obama / become)
2 Which US state _____ with the letter "H"? (start)
3 Which books _____? (George R.R. Martin / write)
4 Who _____ the soccer World Cup in Russia in 2018? (win)
5 Which sport _____ the lightest ball? (use)
6 Where _____? (the 2016 Olympics / take place)
7 Which company _____? (Steve Jobs / start)

 p.98

Go online to review the grammar for each lesson

Verb forms

1 VERBS + INFINITIVE

a Complete the **to + verb** column with *to* + a verb from the list.

be   bring   buy   catch   drive   find   get <u>married</u>   go (x2)   help   pay   rain   see   turn off

			to + verb
1	de<u>cide</u>	We've decided ▊ to France for our vacation.	*to go*
2	for<u>get</u>	Don't forget ▊ all the lights.	
3	hope	We hope ▊ you again soon.	
4	learn	I'm learning ▊. My test is next month.	
5	need	I need ▊ to the supermarket. I don't have any milk.	
6	<u>offer</u>	He offered ▊ me with my suitcase.	
7	plan	They're planning ▊ soon.	
8	pre<u>tend</u>	He pretended ▊ sick, but he wasn't really.	
9	<u>prom</u>ise	He's promised ▊ me back when he gets a job.	
10	re<u>member</u>	Remember ▊ your dictionaries to class tomorrow.	
11	start	It was very cloudy and it started ▊.	
12	try	I'm trying ▊ a job, but it's very hard.	
13	want	I want ▊ the six o'clock train.	
14	would like	I'd like ▊ a new car next month.	

b ◖))7.2 Listen and check.

ACTIVATION Cover the **to + verb** column. Say the sentences.

◖ p.55

2 VERBS + GERUND (VERB + -*ING*)

a Complete the **gerund** column with a verb from the list in the gerund.

be   cook   do   have   make   rain   ~~read~~   talk   clean up   wake up   work

			gerund
1	en<u>joy</u>	I enjoy ▊ in bed.	*reading*
2	<u>finish</u>	Have you finished ▊ your room?	
3	go on	I want to go on ▊ until I'm 70.	
4	hate	I hate ▊ late when I'm meeting someone.	
5	like	I like ▊ breakfast in a café.	
6	love	I love ▊ early on a sunny morning.	
7	mind	I don't mind ▊ the ironing. It's very relaxing.	
8	spend (time)	She spends hours ▊ on the phone.	
9	start*	It started ▊ at 5:30 in the morning.	
10	stop	Please stop ▊ so much noise. I can't think.	
11	feel like	I don't feel like ▊ today. Let's go out for lunch.	

* *start* can be used with a gerund or infinitive, e.g., *It started raining. It started to rain.*

b ◖))7.6 Listen and check.

ACTIVATION Cover the **gerund** column. Say the sentences.

◖ p.56

158

get

> 🔍 **get**
> **get** is one of the most common verbs in English. It has several different meanings, e.g., *arrive*, *become*, and can also be used with many prepositions or adverbs with different meanings, e.g., *get up*, *get on with*.

a Match the phrases and pictures.

get = become (+ adjective / past participle)
- [ ] get <u>a</u>ngry
- [ ] get di<u>vo</u>rced
- [ ] get in shape
- [ ] get lost
- [ ] get <u>m</u>arried
- [1] get <u>ner</u>vous
- [ ] get <u>rea</u>dy

get = become (+ comparative)
- [ ] get <u>be</u>tter / get worse
- [ ] get <u>col</u>der

get = buy / obtain
- [ ] get a job
- [ ] get a <u>news</u>paper
- [ ] get a <u>ti</u>cket

get + preposition (phrasal verbs)
- [ ] get along (well) with somebody
- [ ] get <u>in</u>to (out of) a car
- [ ] get on (off) a bus
- [ ] get up

get (to) = arrive
- [ ] get home
- [ ] get to school
- [ ] get to work

get = receive
- [ ] get an <u>e</u>mail (a text message)
- [ ] get a <u>pre</u>sent
- [ ] get a prize

b 🔊 **8.11** Listen and check.

ACTIVATION Cover the phrases and look at the pictures. Test yourself or a partner.

⬅ p.63

🖱 **Go online** to review the vocabulary for each lesson

Confusing verbs

a Match the verbs and photos.

2 **wear** /wɛr/ jewelry clothes	**carry** /'kæri/ a bag a baby
win /wɪn/ a game a medal a prize	**earn** /ərn/ a salary money
know /noʊ/ somebody well something	**meet** /mit/ somebody for the first time at 11 o'clock
1 **hope** /hoʊp/ that something good will happen to do something	**wait** /weɪt/ for a bus for a long time
watch /wɑtʃ/ TV a game	**look at** /lʊk æt/ a photo a view
look /lʊk/ happy about 25 years old	**look like** /lʊk laɪk/ your mother a model
miss /mɪs/ the bus a class	**lose** /luz/ a game your glasses
bring /brɪŋ/ your dictionary (to class) something back from vacation	**take** /teɪk/ an umbrella (with you) your children to school
look for /lʊk fɔr/ your glasses a job	**find** /faɪnd/ your glasses a job
say /seɪ/ sorry hello something to somebody	**tell** /tɛl/ a joke a lie somebody something
lend /lɛnd/ money to somebody	**borrow** /'bɑroʊ/ money from somebody
hear /hɪr/ a noise the doorbell	**listen to** /'lɪsn tə/ music the radio

b 🔊 **8.15** Listen and check.

ACTIVATION Work with a partner. **A** say a verb, **B** say a possible continuation.

A *Wait...* ⟩ ⟨ B *for a bus*

🔎 *hope* **and** *expect*

hope = to want something to happen and think it will happen, always for positive things, e.g., *I hope I'll pass the exam.*

expect = to think something will happen, usually for a reason (not necessarily a positive thing), e.g., *I expect I'll fail because I haven't worked very hard.*

bring **and** *take*

Please bring your dictionaries to class tomorrow = movement towards here

Don't forget to take all your things when you leave = movement away from here

← p.65

Animals

a Match the words and photos.

Insects
- [ ] bee /bi/
- [ ] butterfly /'bʌtərflaɪ/
- [ ] fly /flaɪ/
- [1] mosquito /mə'skitoʊ/
- [ ] spider /'spaɪdər/
- [ ] wasp /wɑsp/

Farm animals
- [ ] bull /bʊl/
- [ ] chicken /'tʃɪkən/
- [ ] cow /kaʊ/
- [ ] goat /goʊt/
- [ ] horse /hɔrs/
- [ ] pig /pɪg/
- [ ] sheep /ʃip/

Wild animals
- [ ] bat /bæt/
- [ ] bear /bɛr/
- [ ] bird /bərd/
- [ ] camel /'kæml/
- [ ] crocodile /'krɑkədaɪl/
- [ ] deer /dɪr/ (plural deer **NOT** deers)
- [ ] elephant /'ɛləfənt/
- [ ] giraffe /dʒə'ræf/
- [ ] kangaroo /kæŋgə'ru/
- [ ] lion /'laɪən/
- [ ] monkey /'mʌŋki/
- [ ] mouse /maʊs/ (plural mice)
- [ ] rabbit /'ræbət/
- [ ] rat /'ræt/
- [ ] snake /sneɪk/
- [ ] tiger /'taɪgər/

Sea animals
- [ ] dolphin /'dɑlfən/
- [ ] jellyfish /'dʒɛlifɪʃ/
- [ ] shark /ʃɑrk/
- [ ] whale /weɪl/

> 🔍 **bite** and **sting**
> Some insects *sting* (= inject venom into your skin), e.g., bees and wasps, and also some sea animals, e.g., jellyfish.
> Other insects *bite*, e.g., mosquitoes and spiders, and also snakes and all animals with teeth.

b ◀)) 9.2 Listen and check.

ACTIVATION Cover the words and look at the photos. Test yourself or a partner.

◀ p.70

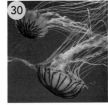

Expressing movement

a Match the words and pictures.

- [ ] **under** the bridge /ˈʌndər/
- [ ] **along** the street /əˈlɔŋ/
- [ ] **around** the lake /əˈraʊnd/
- [ ] **through** the tunnel /θru/
- [ ] **into** the store /ˈɪntu/
- [ ] **across** the road /əˈkrɔs/
- [ ] **over** the bridge /ˈoʊvər/
- [ ] **up** the steps /ʌp/
- [ ] **past** the church /pæst/
- [ ] **toward** the lake /ˈtoʊərd/
- [1] **down** the steps /daʊn/
- [ ] **out of** the store /ˈaʊt əv/

🔍 ***across* or *through***

We use *across* to talk about movement from one side to the other of something that has "sides," like a square, a street, or a river, e.g., *He swam **across** the river.*

We use *through* to talk about movement from one side to the other but "in something," e.g., a forest, a tunnel, a crowd, e.g., *We walked **through** the crowds and reached the empty streets on the other side.*

b 🔊 **10.3** Listen and check.

🔍 ***away* and *back***

We use *away* to express movement to another place, e.g., ***Go away!** I don't want to speak to you. The man **ran away** when he saw the police officer.*

We use *back* to express movement to the place where something or somebody was before, e.g., *After dinner we **went back** to our hotel. Their dog ran away and never **came back.***

ACTIVATION Cover the words and look at the pictures. Where did the woman and her dog go?

They went down the steps…

⤺ p.78

162

Phrasal verbs

a Match the sentences and pictures.

    The match will be over at about 5:30.
    My alarm goes off at six o'clock every morning.
    We set off for the airport at 6:30.
    I want to give up chocolate.
1   Don't throw away that letter!
    Turn down the music! It's very loud.
    Turn up the TV! I can't hear.
    He looked up the words in a dictionary.
    Could you fill out this form?
    I want to find out about hotels in Madrid.
    It's bedtime – go and put on your pajamas.
    Could you take off your boots, please?
    My sister's looking after Jimmy for me today.
    I'm really looking forward to vacation!

ACTIVATION

a Cover the sentences and look at the pictures. Remember the phrasal verbs.

b Look at these phrasal verbs from Files 1–10. Can you remember what they mean?

check in (for a flight)
come on
get up
go away (for the weekend)
go back (to work)
go out (at night)
sit down
stand up
wake up
call back (later)
drop off (somebody at the airport)
give back (something you've borrowed)
pay back (money you've borrowed)
pick up (something on the floor, somebody from the airport)
put away (e.g., clothes in a closet)
send back (something you don't want)
take back (something to a store)
take out (the garbage)
try on (clothes)
turn off (the TV)
turn on (the TV)
write down (the words)
go on (doing something)
get on / off (a bus)
get along with (a person)
look for (something you've lost)
look around (a store, city, museum)
run out of (gas, printer ink)

> 🔍 **Type 1 = no object**
> The verb and the particle (*on, up,* etc.) are **never separated**.
> *I get up at 7:30.*
>
> **Type 2 = + object**
> The verb and the particle (*on, up,* etc.) **can be separated**.
> *Turn the TV on.* OR *Turn on the TV.*
>
> **Type 3 = + object**
> The verb and the particle (*on, up,* etc.) are **never separated**.
> *Look for your keys.* **NOT** ~~Look your keys for.~~

◀ p.80

b 🔊 **10.5** Listen and check.

Irregular verbs

Present	Simple Past	Past participle
be /bi/	was /wəz/ were /wər/	been /bɪn/
become /bɪˈkʌm/	became /bɪˈkeɪm/	become
begin /bɪˈgɪn/	began /bɪˈgæn/	begun /bɪˈgʌn/
break /breɪk/	broke /broʊk/	broken /ˈbroʊkən/
bring /brɪŋ/	brought /brɔt/	brought
build /bɪld/	built /bɪlt/	built
buy /baɪ/	bought /bɔt/	bought
can /kæn/	could /kʊd/	–
catch /kætʃ/	caught /kɔt/	caught
choose /tʃuz/	chose /tʃoʊz/	chosen /ˈtʃoʊzn/
come /kʌm/	came /keɪm/	come
cost /kɔst/	cost	cost
cut /kʌt/	cut	cut
do /du/	did /dɪd/	done /dʌn/
dream /drim/	dreamt /drɛmt/ (also dreamed)	dreamt /drɛmt/ (also dreamed)
drink /drɪŋk/	drank /dræŋk/	drunk /drʌŋk/
drive /draɪv/	drove /droʊv/	driven /ˈdrɪvn/
eat /it/	ate /eɪt/	eaten /ˈitn/
fall /fɔl/	fell /fɛl/	fallen /ˈfɔlən/
feel /fil/	felt /fɛlt/	felt
find /faɪnd/	found /faʊnd/	found
fly /flaɪ/	flew /flu/	flown /floʊn/
forget /fərˈgɛt/	forgot /fərˈgɑt/	forgotten /fərˈgɑtn/
get /gɛt/	got /gɑt/	gotten /ˈgɑtn/
give /gɪv/	gave /geɪv/	given /ˈgɪvn/
go /goʊ/	went /wɛnt/	gone /gɑn/
grow /groʊ/	grew /gru/	grown /groʊn/
have /hæv/	had /hæd/	had
hear /hɪr/	heard /hərd/	heard
hit /hɪt/	hit	hit
keep /kip/	kept /kɛpt/	kept
know /noʊ/	knew /nu/	known /noʊn/

Present	Simple past	Past participle
learn /lərn/	learned /lərnd/	learned
leave /liv/	left /lɛft/	left
lend /lɛnd/	lent /lɛnt/	lent
let /lɛt/	let	let
lose /luz/	lost /lɔst/	lost
make /meɪk/	made /meɪd/	made
meet /mit/	met /mɛt/	met
pay /peɪ/	paid /peɪd/	paid
put /pʊt/	put	put
read /rid/	read /rɛd/	read /rɛd/
ring /rɪŋ/	rang /ræŋ/	rung /rʌŋ/
run /rʌn/	ran /ræn/	run
say /seɪ/	said /sɛd/	said
see /si/	saw /sɔ/	seen /sin/
sell /sɛl/	sold /soʊld/	sold
send /sɛnd/	sent /sɛnt/	sent
shut /ʃʌt/	shut	shut
sing /sɪŋ/	sang /sæŋ/	sung /sʌŋ/
sit /sɪt/	sat /sæt/	sat
sleep /slip/	slept /slɛpt/	slept
speak /spik/	spoke /spoʊk/	spoken /ˈspoʊkən/
spend /spɛnd/	spent /spɛnt/	spent
stand /stænd/	stood /stʊd/	stood
steal /stil/	stole /stoʊl/	stolen /ˈstoʊlən/
swim /swɪm/	swam /swæm/	swum /swʌm/
take /teɪk/	took /tʊk/	taken /ˈteɪkən/
teach /titʃ/	taught /tɔt/	taught
tell /tɛl/	told /toʊld/	told
think /θɪŋk/	thought /θɔt/	thought
throw /θroʊ/	threw /θru/	thrown /θroʊn/
understand /ˌʌndərˈstænd/	understood /ˌʌndərˈstʊd/	understood
wake /weɪk/	woke /woʊk/	woken /ˈwoʊkən/
wear /wɛr/	wore /wɔr/	worn /wɔrn/
win /wɪn/	won /wʌn/	won
write /raɪt/	wrote /roʊt/	written /ˈrɪtn/

Appendix

have got

I**'ve got** a brother and two sisters.
I **haven't got** any pets.
She**'s got** a beautiful house.
He **hasn't got** many friends.
Have they **got** any children? No, they **haven't**.
Has the hotel **got** a swimming pool? Yes, it **has**.

🔊 7.24

full form	contraction	negative	
I have got	I've got	I haven't got	
You have got	You've got	You haven't got	
He / She / It has got	He / She / It's got	He / She / It hasn't got	a car.
We have got	We've got	We haven't got	
You have got	You've got	You haven't got	
They have got	They've got	They haven't got	

?		✓		✗	
Have I got		I have.		I haven't.	
Have you got		you have.		you haven't.	
Has he / she / it got	a car? Yes,	he / she / it has.	No,	he / she / it hasn't.	
Have we got		we have.		we haven't.	
Have you got		you have.		you haven't.	
Have they got		they have.		they haven't.	

- You can use *have got* instead of *have* for possession in the present.
  I've got a bike. = I have a bike.
  Have you got a car? = Do you have a car?
- We also use *have got* to talk about family and sicknesses, and to describe people.
  I've got two sisters.
  He's got a cold.
  She's got long, brown hair.
- *have got* is not used in the past. For past possession use *had*.
  I had a pet cat when I was a child.
  Did you have a pet?
- *I have… / Do you have…?* is more common than *I've got / Have you got…?* in conversations in the US.

a Write ⊞, ⊟, and ? sentences with the correct form of *have got*.

they / big house
⊞ *They've got a big house.*

1 she / any brothers
⊟ _____

2 you / big apartment
? _____

3 we / a lot of work today
⊟ _____

4 your sister / a boyfriend
? _____

5 Roger and Val / a beautiful yard
⊞ _____

6 I / a really good teacher
⊞ _____

7 My brother / a job right now
⊟ _____

8 they / the same color eyes
⊞ _____

9 we / a meeting today
? _____

10 he / many friends at work
⊟ _____

b Complete the sentences with the correct form of *have got*.

They love animals. They*'ve got* two dogs and five cats.

1 I hope it doesn't rain – I _____ my umbrella today.

2 _____ your phone _____ a good camera?

3 I _____ a new iPad. Do you want to see it ?

4 Sorry kids, I _____ enough money to buy candy.

5 Jane _____ 50 pairs of shoes – can you believe it?

6 I can't call him now – I _____ any service on my phone.

7 _____ you _____ your keys? I can't find mine.

8 Maria's so lucky – she _____ beautiful, curly hair.

9 One more question, Mr. Jones. _____ you _____ any experience?

10 We might have problems getting there because we _____ an exact address.

⬅ p.61

Vowel sounds

		usual spelling		! but also
tree		ee	feel sheep	people machine
		ea	teach eat	key niece
		e	she we	receipt
fish		i	thin slim	English women
			history kiss	busy decide
			if since	repeat gym
ear		eer	cheer	serious
			engineer	
		ere	here we're	
		ear	beard earrings	
cat		a	cap hat	
			back catch	
			carry match	
egg		e	spell lend	friendly weather
			west send	sweater any
			very red	said
chair		air	airport stairs	their there
			pair hair	wear bear
		are	square careful	
clock		o	top rock	yacht quality
			socks college	
			hot box	
		a	father	
saw		al	walk talk	bought thought
		aw	awful draw	abroad August
		augh	caught	
			daughter	
horse		or	boring north	four board
		ore	more score	
		oor	door floor	
boot		oo	school choose	do suit juice
		u*	use polluted	shoe lose
		ew	few knew	through
bull		u	pull push	would should
		oo	good book	woman
			look cook	

		usual spelling		! but also
tourist		A very unusual sound.		
		Europe furious sure plural		
up		u	sunny must	come does
			funny run	someone enough
			lucky cut	young touch
computer		Many different spellings.		
		/ə/ is always unstressed.		
		nervous arrive polite agree		
		suggest terrible problem		
bird		er	person verb	earn work
		ir	dirty shirt	world worse
		ur	curly turn	
owl		ou	shout round	
			account blouse	
		ow	crowded down	
phone		o*	open hope	snow throw
			won't so	although
		oa	coat goal	
car		ar	far large	heart
			scarf dark	
train		a*	change wake	break steak
		ai	rain fail	great overweight
		ay	away pay	they
			gray	
boy		oi	coin noisy	
			point	
		oy	toy enjoy	
bike		i*	quiet item	buy eyes
		y	shy why	height
		igh	might sights	

* especially before consonant + e

☐ vowels   ☐ vowels followed by /r/   ☐ diphthongs

Consonant sounds

		usual spelling	! but also
	parrot	**p** promise possible copy flip-flops **pp** opposite appearance	
	bag	**b** belt body probably job cab **bb** rabbit robbed	
	key	**c** camping across **k** skirt kind **ck** checkout pick	school stomach chemistry account
	girl	**g** grow goat forget begin **gg** foggy leggings	guest spaghetti
	flower	**f** find afraid safe **ph** elephant nephew **ff** off different	enough laugh
	vase	**v** video visit love invent over river	of
	tie	**t** try tell start late **tt** better sitting	walked dressed
	dog	**d** did dead hard told **dd** address middle	loved tired
	snake	**s** stops faster **ss** miss message **ce/ci** place circle **c** cent city cycle (before e, i, y)	science answer psychology
	zebra	**z** zoo lazy freezing **s, se** reason lose has toes	
	shower	**sh** shut shoes wash finish **ti (+ vowel)** patient information **ci + a** special musician	sugar sure machine mustache
	television	An unusual sound. Asia decision confusion usually garage	

		usual spelling	! but also
	thumb	**th** thing throw healthy south math both	
	mother	**th** neither the clothes sunbathe that with	
	chess	**ch** chicken child beach **tch** catch match **t (+ ure)** picture future	question
	jazz	**j** jacket just June enjoy **dge** bridge judge	generous teenager giraffe age
	leg	**l** little less plan incredible **ll** will silly	
	right	**r** really rest practice try **rr** borrowed married **re** we're here	written wrong
	witch	**w** website twins worried win **wh** why which whale	one once question
	yacht	**y** yet year young yoga **before u** useful uniform	
	monkey	**m** mountain modern remember email **mm** summer swimming	column comb
	nose	**n** need necklace none any **nn** funny dinner	know knock
	singer	**ng** angry ring along thing bring going	think thank
	house	**h** hat hate ahead perhaps hire helpful	who whose whole

☐ voiced   ☐ unvoiced

 Go online to watch the Sound Bank videos

167

American English File ②

Third Edition

MULTI-PACK **B**

Student Book | Workbook

Christina Latham-Koenig
Clive Oxenden
Jerry Lambert

Paul Seligson

Paul Seligson and Clive Oxenden
are the original co-authors of
English File 1 and *English File 2*

OXFORD
UNIVERSITY PRESS

Contents

How to use your Workbook and Online Practice

American English File *Third Edition*

Student Book

Use your Student Book in class with your teacher.

ACTIVITIES AUDIO VIDEO RESOURCES

Go to **americanenglishfileonline.com** and use the code on your Access Card to log into the Online Practice.

Workbook

Practice *Grammar*, *Vocabulary*, and *Pronunciation* for every lesson.

Practice the *Practical English* for every episode.

Do the *Can you remember...?* exercises to check that you remember the Grammar, Vocabulary, and Pronunciation every two Files.

Online Practice

← Look again at the Grammar, Vocabulary, and Pronunciation from the Student Book before you do the Workbook exercises.

→ Listen to the audio for the Pronunciation exercises.

→ Use the Sound Bank video to practice English sounds.

← Watch the Practical English video before you do the exercises.

→ Use the interactive video for more Practical English practice.

→ Look again at the Grammar, Vocabulary, and Pronunciation if you have any problems.

Practice Reading, Listening, Speaking, and Writing.

Starting a new job is always scary. It's like the first day of school.
Sean Maher, American actor

G uses of the infinitive | **V** verbs + infinitive: *try to, forget to,* etc. | **P** weak form of *to*, linking

1 VOCABULARY verbs + infinitive

a Circle the correct verb.

A lesson for Charlie

Charlie didn't really like his job, so he ¹*started* / *pretended* to apply for new jobs. A few weeks later, a company called him and ²*needed* / *offered* to interview him. Charlie ³*didn't want* / *didn't remember* to tell his boss, so he ⁴*pretended* / *hoped* to be sick. He told his boss that he had a stomachache, and that he ⁵*tried* / *needed* to go to the doctor. He ⁶*promised* / *learned* to call his boss later and tell him how he was feeling. Charlie was really hoping to get the job, so he was a little nervous. He ⁷*promised* / *planned* to drive to the interview, but when he saw that there was a lot of traffic, he ⁸*decided* / *hoped* to take the subway. He was very late, and he ⁹*forgot* / *tried* to turn his phone off. Unfortunately, it rang while he was in the interview. The interview didn't go well, and on the way home, his boss saw him. It was a terrible day, and Charlie ¹⁰*tried* / *learned* not to lie to his boss again and to prepare well for job interviews.

b Complete the conversations with a verb from the list.

~~clean~~   close   go   improve   learn   stay   tell   rain

1 A Do I look OK for my interview?
   B Not really! You need to _clean_ your shoes.

2 A Can you drive?
   B No, but I'm planning to _____ this year.

3 A Why did you talk to Sophie about this?
   B Don't worry, she's promised not to _____ anybody.

4 A Are you going to go to night classes?
   B Yes, I want to _____ my French.

5 A Did you remember to _____ the window?
   B I'm not sure. I think so.

6 A What's the weather like where you are?
   B Not very nice. It's starting to _____.

7 A What's Jacinda going to do when she graduates from high school?
   B She's hoping to _____ to college.

8 A Have your parents moved yet?
   B No, they've decided to _____ where they are.

2 GRAMMAR uses of the infinitive

a Complete the sentences with the adjective and the correct form of the verb.

1 important / not say
   It's _important not to say_ the wrong thing at an interview.
2 difficult / talk
   Do you find it _____ to my mom?
3 easy / buy
   It's _____ presents for my nephew. He's only two.
4 great / hear
   Thanks for calling. It was _____ from you.
5 fun / be
   It's _____ with your family.

b Complete the sentences with the infinitive of a verb from the list.

~~do~~   find   not finish   not tell   rent   see   take out

1 John's very polite. He offered *to do* the dishes after the meal.
2 Thanks for coming. We hope _____ you again soon.
3 She wasn't enjoying the lasagna, so she decided _____ it.
4 My boyfriend is unemployed. He needs _____ a job.
5 I'll tell you what she said, but please promise _____ anybody.
6 They want to live together. They're planning _____ an apartment.
7 You forgot _____ the garbage last night. It's still in the kitchen.

c Complete the sentences with a question word from the list and the infinitive of the verb in parentheses.

~~how~~   how many   how much
what   when   where   who

1 Lucy gave me her address, but I don't know *how to get* there. (get)
2 My brother is always busy so I don't know _____ him. (call)
3 My mom asked me to get some eggs, but she didn't say _____. (buy)
4 We'd like to travel around the world, but we don't know _____ first. (go)
5 Yuna wants to go to college, but she doesn't know _____. (study)
6 Who's going to be here for lunch? We're having pasta, but I need to know _____. (make)
7 We have an extra ticket for the concert, but we don't know _____. (take)

d Read the conversations. Re-order the words to make answers.

1 What countries would you like to visit?
like / New / I'd / visit / to / Zealand
I'd like to visit New Zealand.
2 What are you planning to do this weekend?
tennis / to / I'm / friends / my / play / with / hoping
_____.
3 What are you doing tonight?
to / planning / stay / in / I'm
_____.
4 Are you learning anything that is very difficult right now?
learn / trying / Japanese / to / I'm
_____.
5 Why are you learning English?
get / to / a / job / better
_____.
6 What do you find difficult about English?
difficult / vocabulary / it's / to / remember
_____.

e Answer the questions in **d** about you.

1 I'd like to visit _____.
2 I'm hoping to _____.
3 I'm planning _____.
4 I'm _____.
5 To _____.
6 It's _____.

3 PRONUNCIATION weak form of *to*, linking

a 🔊 7.1 Listen and write six sentences.

1 *It started to rain as soon as we left.*
2 _____.
3 _____.
4 _____.
5 _____.
6 _____.

b 🔊 7.1 Listen again and repeat the sentences. Copy the rhythm.

🔴 **Go online** for more practice

7B Happiness is…

> Happiness is when what you think, what you say, and what you do are all in harmony.
> *Mahatma Gandhi, Indian political leader*

G uses of the gerund (verb + *-ing*) **V** verbs + gerund **P** *-ing*, the letter *o*

1 VOCABULARY verbs + gerund

a Match sentences 1–5 to a–e.

1 He hates doing housework.   _c_
2 He feels like going for a run.   ____
3 He doesn't mind cooking all the meals.   ____
4 He's stopped playing soccer.   ____
5 He loves being with his friends.   ____

a He doesn't do it anymore.
b It isn't a problem for him to do it.
c ~~He really doesn't like it.~~
d He wants to do it now.
e He really likes it.

b Circle the correct words.

1 Jenny never goes to parties because she *doesn't mind / doesn't enjoy* meeting new people.
2 Please don't *start / go on* eating until everyone has their food.
3 I can go with you, but I need to *stop / spend* an hour doing homework first.
4 My dad always gets to the airport very early because he *hates / loves* arriving late.
5 I really *start / love* taking photos. It's probably my favorite hobby.
6 My brother doesn't play many sports, but he *spends / likes* watching them on TV.
7 Let's rent a car when we get there. I *don't mind / don't like* driving.
8 I'm going to *go on / stop* studying English next year. I'm really enjoying the classes.
9 I don't *like / feel like* going out tonight. I'm too tired.
10 **A** Why did you *stop / start* going to the gym?
  B It was too boring!

2 GRAMMAR uses of the gerund (verb + *-ing*)

a Complete the sentences with the *-ing* form of the verb in parentheses.

1 I hate _being_ (be) late for meetings. I think it's really rude.
2 We stopped _____ (study) German because we didn't like the classes.
3 James is celebrating because he's finished _____ (write) his book.
4 I'm bored. I feel like _____ (go) for a walk.
5 I don't mind _____ (get) up early in the morning.
6 Kate really enjoys _____ (listen) to music while she's running.

b Match sentences 1–6 to a–f.

1 Do you ever think about   _c_
2 Read the instructions before   ____
3 He started his speech by   ____
4 I'm not very good at   ____
5 Ana left the party without   ____
6 I'm really looking forward to   ____

a using the machine for the first time.
b seeing you tonight.
c ~~stopping work and retiring?~~
d thanking everybody for coming.
e saying goodbye to me.
f parking my dad's car. It's very big.

c Complete the text with the *-ing* form of the verbs from the list.

drive   feel   go   have   imagine   leave   listen   not get up
not talk   read   ~~send~~   stay   take   turn off   walk   work   ~~write~~

feel good?
What makes you

We asked our readers, and here's what they said.

* [1] *Writing* and then [2] *sending* a funny email or text message to my friends. And of course, [3] _____ their faces when they read it.
* I really like [4] _____ my car at night when there's no traffic, [5] _____ to my favorite music. I feel completely free.
* [6] _____ in bed on Sunday morning and [7] _____ the newspaper. [8] _____ until about 12 and then [9] _____ my dog for a long walk.
* I enjoy [10] _____ to the gym and really [11] _____ hard, and then [12] _____ a nice cold drink followed by a long, hot shower. There's nothing better.
* I love [13] _____ alone in the mountains, [14] _____ the wind in my hair and [15] _____ to anyone.
* [16] _____ my computer at the end of the day and [17] _____ work! It's the best moment of the day. I love it!

d How do you feel about the following activities? (Circle) the best answer for you, a, b, or c.

1 Going to the gym
   a 😃   b 😐   c 😠

2 Talking to my friends on social media
   a 😃   b 😐   c 😠

3 Being alone
   a 😃   b 😐   c 😠

4 Walking on the beach
   a 😃   b 😐   c 😠

5 Going shopping for clothes
   a 😃   b 😐   c 😠

6 Getting up late
   a 😃   b 😐   c 😠

e Use your answers in **d** to write sentences. Say what you love, don't mind, or hate doing.

1 I _____ going to the gym.
2 I _____ talking with my friends on social media.
3 I _____.
4 _____.
5 _____.
6 _____.

3 PRONUNCIATION *-ing*, the letter *o*

a 🔊 7.2 Listen and complete the sentences.

1 There's *nothing* _____ to eat.
2 I hate _____.
3 We're _____ this afternoon.
4 What are you _____?

b 🔊 7.2 Listen again and repeat the sentences.

c 🔊 7.3 Listen to four sentences. Write the number of the sentence next to the correct picture.

d 🔊 7.3 Listen again and repeat the sentences.

Go online for more practice

The limits of my language are the limits of my world.
Ludwig Wittgenstein, Austrian philosopher

G *have to, don't have to, must, must not* | **V** adjectives + prepositions: *afraid of*, etc. | **P** stress on prepositions

1 GRAMMAR *have to, don't have to, must, must not*

a Look at the pictures. Complete the conversations with the correct form of *have to*.

Nanny Agency

1 A <u>*Do*</u> teachers in your country <u>*have to*</u> dress formally?
  B Not very formally. They _____ wear suits, but they _____ look neat.

2 A _____ American taxi drivers _____ work long hours?
  B Yes, we _____ work twelve hours a day, but we _____ work every day.

3 A _____ I _____ cook meals?
  B No. You _____ do the cooking, but you _____ help the children to eat.

4 A _____ your daughter _____ travel abroad in her job?
  B No, she _____ travel abroad, but she _____ speak foreign languages.

b What do these signs mean? Write sentences with *must* or *must not*.

1 <u>*You must*</u> _____ pay in cash.
2 _____ turn left here.
3 _____ make a noise.
4 _____ use your cell phone.
5 _____ stop here.
6 _____ play soccer here.

c Complete the sentences with *must not* or *don't have to*.

1 The museum is free. You <u>*don't have to*</u> pay.
2 You have to wear formal clothes. You _____ wear jeans.
3 The speed limit is 55 mph. You _____ drive faster.
4 Your hours will be 9–5 Monday to Friday. You _____ work on weekends.
5 That river is dangerous. You _____ swim in it.
6 It's a very small house. You _____ clean it every day.

d Complete the second sentence so it has a similar meaning to the first sentence. Use the **bold** verb in the affirmative or negative form.

1 Our school has no uniform.
  have
  We <u>*don't have to*</u> wear a uniform at our school.
2 The rules say we must be at school by 8.
  have
  We _____ be at school by 8.
3 It's very important that you start exercising.
  must
  You _____ start exercising.
4 For homework tonight, you can skip exercise 1, but do exercises 2 and 3.
  have
  For homework tonight, you _____ do exercise 1, but do exercises 2 and 3.
5 It's important that you don't eat any chocolate on this diet.
  must
  You _____ eat any chocolate on this diet.

2 VOCABULARY adjectives + prepositions

a Complete the sentences with a phrase from the list.

bad at (x2)   bad for   good at (x2)   good for

1 My sister's always been _bad at_ math. She hates numbers.
2 Wow! You're very _____ English. Where did you learn it?
3 I really like playing the guitar, but I'm not very _____ it.
4 Everybody knows that smoking is _____ you.
5 Our school soccer team is great, but we're very _____ basketball. We've lost every game this year.
6 Biking is lots of fun, and it's _____ you, too.

b Complete the sentences with a word from the list.

~~for~~   from   in   of (x2)   to   with

1 The town of Pisa in Italy is famous _for_ its leaning tower.
2 I'm very different _____ my younger brother. Sometimes people can't believe we're brothers.
3 We went to a nightclub that was full _____ tourists.
4 People always get angry _____ my uncle because he drives so slowly.
5 My husband is afraid _____ flying, so we always travel by car or train.
6 I love going to Boston because I'm very interested _____ American history.
7 Jack's parents were very nice _____ me when I stayed with them.

c Complete the tips with the words in parentheses and the correct prepositions.

1 If you're _interested in_ visiting museums, Berlin has some great ones, and the Alte Nationalgalerie is _____ amazing paintings. (full / ~~interested~~)
2 New York is _____ its top restaurants. If you're _____ spending too much money, there are lots of cheaper places to eat, too. (afraid / famous)
3 In most countries, people who live in the country are _____ people in cities. They're often friendlier and much _____ tourists. (nice / different)
4 Renting a car in a new city can be difficult. Even if you're very _____ driving, it's easy to make mistakes, and other drivers can get _____ you. (good / angry)

d Read the teacher's notes on students in an English class and then write the reports.

	Marc	Hugo	Ana
Good at	grammar	speaking	speaking
Bad at	listening	doing homework	grammar
Interested in	writing	reading English magazines	watching English / American movies
Must	check work	work harder	read more

1 _Marc's worked hard this year. He's good at_ _grammar, but he's still bad at listening. He's_ _interested in writing, but he must check his work._
2 I haven't been happy with Hugo this semester. He's good at speaking, but _____ _____ _____.
3 In some ways, Ana is doing well in class. _____ _____ _____ _____.

e Write your report and say how well (or badly) you think you are doing in your English class.

I'm good at _____.

I'm bad at _____.

I'm interested in _____.

I must _____.

3 PRONUNCIATION stress on prepositions

a Check (✓) the sentences where the preposition is stressed.

1 What's she famous **for**?   ✓
2 Why are you angry **with** him?
3 There's nothing to be afraid **of**.
4 I'm good **at** tennis.
5 Sugar is bad **for** your teeth.
6 You're always full **of** great ideas.
7 What are you interested **in**?
8 They weren't very nice **to** me.

b 🔊 7.4 Listen and check. Then listen again and repeat the sentences.

Go online for more practice   Go online to check your progress   51

Practical English At the pharmacy

1 VOCABULARY feeling sick

Re-order the letters to make words that complete the sentences.

1 Daniel feels terrible. He thinks he has the _flu_ (ulf).
2 I need to buy some tissues. I have a _____ (lcdo).
3 That fish wasn't very good. Now I have a _____ (achochmstae).
4 You feel very hot. I think you have a _____ (emretupetra).
5 Please turn that music down. I have a _____ (chaeheda).
6 Kate's had a bad _____ (oguhc) for three weeks now.

2 GOING TO A PHARMACY

Complete the conversation with words from the list.

allergic better every have ~~help~~ much often
symptoms take well

A Good afternoon. Can I ¹_help_ you?
B I'm not feeling very ²_____.
A What are your ³_____?
B I have a bad cough.
A Do you ⁴_____ a temperature?
B No, I don't.
A Are you ⁵_____ to any drugs?
B No, I don't think so.
A Take this cough medicine. It'll make you feel ⁶_____.
B How much do I have to ⁷_____?
A Four teaspoons ⁸_____ six hours.
B Sorry? How ⁹_____?
A Every six hours.
B OK, thanks. How ¹⁰_____ is that?
A That's $8.50, please.

3 HAVE GOT

Complete the conversations with the correct form of *have got*.

1 A _Have you got any aspirin?_
  B Sorry, we haven't got any aspirin, but we've got some ibuprofen.

2 A _____?
  B Yes, my brother's got two children, a girl and a boy.

3 A Have you got any pets at home?
  B No, we _____.

4 A What kind of car _____?
  B I've got a Ford.

5 A _____?
  B I've got one sister, but I haven't got any brothers.

6 A Have you got a printer?
  B Yes, I _____.

4 SOCIAL ENGLISH

Complete the conversations.

1 A That was a _lovely_ meal. And my cough has gone, too!
  B I'm gl_____ you're feeling better.

2 A Can I have some more coffee, please?
  B There isn't any more. Anyway, drinking too much coffee isn't good f_____ you.

3 A I think I sh_____ get back to the hotel now.
  B Would you like me to drive you back?
  A No, I'll walk. I'm s_____ I'll be fine. Thanks again for a gr_____ evening.

Go online to practice the Practical English phrases

Can you remember...? 1–7

1 GRAMMAR

Circle a, b, or c.

1 The weather isn't great, but it was ____ last year.
   a bad   **b** worse   **c** the worst

2 We want to go to Vietnam because ____ there before.
   a we've never been   **b** we weren't   **c** we went

3 I have problems sleeping because I drink ____ coffee.
   a enough   **b** too much   **c** too many

4 Do you think ____ tomorrow? It's cold enough.
   a it'll snow   **b** it's snowing   **c** it snows

5 Do you know ____ can come to the party?
   a that   **b** what   **c** who

6 In the US, you ____ carry your passport or ID with you, but you can if you want to.
   a haven't   **b** must not   **c** don't have to

2 VOCABULARY

Circle the word or phrase that is different.

1 enjoy   like   love   hate
2 interesting   depressing   relaxing   exciting
3 heart   muscle   harbor   teeth
4 dangerous   clean   crowded   polluted
5 bald   mustache   beard   long
6 rent a car   do the ironing   sunbathe   go sightseeing

3 PRONUNCIATION

Circle the sound that is different.

🦔 singer	1 thi**ng** si**ng** tha**nk** ri**ng**	
🦓 **z**ebra	2 like**s** read**s** feel**s** know**s**	
👧 **g**irl	3 **g**uarantee **g**ate **g**ift **g**eneral	
👢 b**oo**t	4 g**o**ing d**o**ing m**o**ving l**o**sing	
⬆ **u**p	5 en**ou**gh bl**oo**d p**u**t sh**u**t	
🌳 tr**ee**	6 **ea**sy br**ea**k m**ea**n b**ea**ch	

4 GRAMMAR & VOCABULARY

Read the article. Circle a, b, or c.

Bhutan Kingdom of happiness

The mountain kingdom of Bhutan is a very small country with a population of only 800,000 people.

Countries usually want [1]____ more cars and planes, build more houses and roads, and have more teachers and doctors, because this all improves the economy. However, in Bhutan, King Jigme Wangchuck decided [2]____ the 1970s that other things were more important, and the government had to think about what makes people happy.

The people of Bhutan are now healthier, and they live longer than they did before. The country has [3]____ roads, schools, and hospitals, but the people also believe [4]____ looking after the environment. In fact, it's one of the [5]____ polluted countries in the world.

Education is also very important. Almost 100% of children go to elementary school. The children take classes in math and science, and they also learn about farming and the environment. The teachers say that school must not just be about [6]____ exams; it should be about teaching students to be good people.

The people of Bhutan want to keep their special culture. Some [7]____ ideas and inventions have come to Bhutan, but they've come [8]____. Bhutan finally got TVs, but that [9]____ only in 1999. Only a small number of tourists can visit, and they [10]____ to pay $250 each a day just to be there.

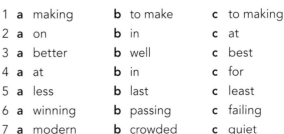

1	**a** making	**b** to make	**c** to making
2	**a** on	**b** in	**c** at
3	**a** better	**b** well	**c** best
4	**a** at	**b** in	**c** for
5	**a** less	**b** last	**c** least
6	**a** winning	**b** passing	**c** failing
7	**a** modern	**b** crowded	**c** quiet
8	**a** slow	**b** slowly	**c** more slow
9	**a** was	**b** is	**c** has been
10	**a** has	**b** must	**c** have

✓ **Go online** to check your progress

8A Should I stay or should I go?

G should   V get   P /ʊ/ and /u/

1 GRAMMAR *should*

a Read problems A–G. Complete the advice in 1–7 with *should / shouldn't* and a verb from the list. Then match the sentences to the problems.

~~~
call   drink   ~~get~~   give   go   see   tell
~~~

1 You *should get* _____ a cat.
2 You _____ coffee all day.
3 You _____ to bed earlier.
4 You _____ a doctor.
5 Don't worry. You _____ him how you feel.
6 You _____ them candy.
7 You _____ her and invite her to dinner.

PROBLEMS, PROBLEMS, PROBLEMS...

A I find it really difficult to get up in the morning, and I'm often late for work. My boss has noticed, and she's really angry with me. What should I do?
____

B Yesterday, I hurt my foot while I was playing soccer. It didn't seem very serious at the time, but now my foot is black and blue. What's your advice? ____

C I want to get a pet, but I work all day and there is nobody at home. What should I do? _1_

D I really like one of my colleagues at work, and I think she likes me, too. I'd really like to go out with her, but I don't know how to ask her. Any advice? ____

E I have three children, and they all have terrible problems with their teeth. We're always at the dentist, and each visit costs a lot of money. Any advice? ____

F I have problems sleeping at night. I take a lot of coffee breaks during the day. Maybe it's the caffeine? What should I do? ____

G I had an argument with my boyfriend, and I don't know what to do. I feel very stupid, and I really want to see him again. What do you think I should do? ____

b Rewrite the sentences with *should* or *shouldn't* and the verb in **bold**.

1 It isn't a good idea for you to **apologize**. You haven't done anything wrong.
I don't think you *should apologize* . You haven't done anything wrong.

2 It's always a good idea to **wear** a hat in the sun.
You _____ a hat in the sun.

3 It's a bad idea to **buy** that old house.
You _____ that old house.

4 If you're in Los Angeles, it's a good idea to **visit** the Los Angeles County Museum of Art.
If you're in Los Angeles, you _____ the Los Angeles County Museum of Art.

5 I know it isn't a good idea for me to **have** another chocolate.
I know I _____ another chocolate.

6 It's a good idea for us to **get** a new car.
We _____ a new car.

2 PRONUNCIATION /ʊ/ and /u/

a Circle the word with a different sound.

🐂 bull	1 p**u**ll (f**oo**d) w**ou**ld	
👢 boot	2 c**ou**ld y**ou** s**oo**n	
🐂 bull	3 w**o**man w**ou**ldn't s**ou**p	
👢 boot	4 b**oo**k sh**oe**s tw**o**	

b ▶ 8.1 Listen and check. Then listen again and repeat the words.

3 VOCABULARY *get*

a Match the **bold** phrases to the meaning of *get*.
Write a, b, c, or d.

a buy / obtain   b receive   c become   d arrive

1 When did you **get married**? _c_
2 Jack had an interview and he **got the job**. ____
3 It's going to **get colder** next week. ____
4 I **get very nervous** when I have to speak in front of a lot of people. ____
5 It's a really great book. I'm sure it'll **get a prize**. ____
6 Sorry to hear you're sick. I hope you **get better** soon. ____
7 Do you think we'll **get to the airport** on time? ____
8 When you go to the store, could you **get a newspaper**? ____
9 I **got an email** from an old school friend yesterday. ____
10 It was almost 3:00 in the morning when we **got home** from the party. ____

b Complete the sentences with the correct form of *get* and a word from the list.

along   ~~divorced~~   in shape   lost   ready   text message
tickets   to work   up   worse

1 Her parents aren't happy together, so they're going to _get divorced._
2 I don't feel like _____ today. I'm going to stay in bed.
3 Our GPS wasn't working and we _____ on the way to our friends' house.
4 I've started going to the gym because I want to _____.
5 The pain in my neck was _____, so I went to the doctor.
6 This morning I _____ for the concert online. They're very good ones in the front row!
7 How well do you _____ with your brothers and sisters?
8 I _____ a _____ from my boyfriend saying he's going to be late.
9 Do you always have a coffee as soon as you _____?
10 Lucy's in her bedroom. She's _____ for the party.

c Read Dana's problems. Then make sentences with *should* and the phrases in the list.

get in shape   get a new job   get up earlier
~~get better~~   get the bus   not get stressed

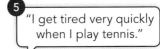

① "I spend too much on going out and new clothes."

② "I'm bored at work."

③ "I never have enough time for breakfast."

④ "It's difficult for me to relax."

⑤ "I get tired very quickly when I play tennis."

⑥ "It takes me an hour to walk to work."

1 She _should get better_ at saving money.
2 She _____.
3 _____.
4 _____.
5 _____.
6 _____.

d Write three things you think you should do to make your life better.

1 I think I should _____ _____.
2 I think _____ _____.
3 I _____ _____.

Go online for more practice

Murphy's Law

If everything seems to be going well,
you have obviously overlooked something.
Murphy's Law

G *if + present, will + base form (first conditional)* **V** confusing verbs **P** homophones

1 GRAMMAR *if + present, will + base form*

a Match 1–6 to a–f to make sentences.

Here are six more examples of MURPHY'S LAW

1 If you lose something, ___c___
2 If you arrive early at a party, _____
3 If you make an appointment to see a doctor, _____
4 If you don't do your homework, _____
5 If you buy a new rug, _____
6 If you get into a hot bath, _____

a you'll feel better before you see him or her.
b you'll drop something on it the first day.
c you'll find it in the last place you look.
d your phone will ring.
e all the other people will be late.
f your teacher will ask you for it.

b Circle the correct words.

1 If the plane arrives late tonight, I'll miss / I miss the last bus home.
2 If you see / you'll see an accident, call the police!
3 We won't get lost if we use / we'll use our GPS.
4 We don't get / won't get to the movie theater in time if we don't leave now.
5 If you don't take / won't take an umbrella, it'll definitely rain!
6 If there isn't / won't be much traffic when we leave, it won't take long to get there.

c Complete the sentences with the correct form of the verb in parentheses. Then match the sentences to the correct pictures, A–F.

Good luck, bad luck

1 Giving a knife D
If a friend _gives_ (give) you a knife as a present and you _give_ (give) your friend a coin, you_'ll always be_ (always be) friends.

2 Horseshoe ☐
If you _____ (find) a horseshoe and _____ (put) it above your door, it _____ (bring) good luck to you and your family.

3 Ladders ☐
If you _____ (walk) under a ladder, you_____ (have) bad luck.

4 Throwing a coin into a well ☐
If you _____ (throw) a coin into a well or fountain and _____ (ask) for something, your dreams _____ (come) true.

5 Falling leaves ☐
If you _____ (catch) a falling leaf, you_____ (not be) sick all winter.

6 Mirrors ☐
If you _____ (break) a mirror, you_____ (have) bad luck for seven years.

2 VOCABULARY confusing verbs

a Complete the sentences with a verb from the list.

~~carrying~~ earns found heard
listened to looking at looking for
watching ~~wearing~~ wins

1 **a** She's *carrying* a coat
  b She's *wearing* a coat.

2 **a** He's _____ a picture.
  b He's _____ TV.

3 **a** She's _____ her keys.
  b She's _____ her keys.

4 **a** He _____ a lot of boxing matches.
  b He _____ a lot of money.

5 **a** We _____ the ambulance.
  b We _____ the radio.

b Complete the sentences with the **bold** verbs in the correct tense.

1 **look, look like**
You *look* very nice in that suit. In fact, you *look like* a businessman!

2 **miss, lose**
I _____ my ticket and had to buy another one, so I _____ the train.

3 **say, tell**
My son doesn't often _____ lies, but if he does, he always _____ that he's sorry.

4 **hope, wait**
I'm _____ for the bus. I _____ it'll come soon because it's raining.

5 **know, meet**
Laura _____ Sam on a safari last summer, so she's _____ him for a year now.

6 **borrow, lend**
If you need to _____ some money, I can _____ you $50.

7 **bring, take**
I can _____ you to the shopping mall, but I can't _____ you home.

c Complete the questions with a verb from **a** or **b** in the correct tense.

1 What will you do if there's nothing to *watch* on TV tonight?
2 Have you ever _____ something important and then found it? What was it?
3 How often do you _____ old photos?
4 What kind of music do you _____ to?
5 Have you ever _____ a prize? What for?

d Answer the questions in **c** about you.

1 _____ .
2 _____ .
3 _____ .
4 _____ .
5 _____ .

3 PRONUNCIATION homophones

a 🔊 8.2 Listen and check (✓) the words you hear.

1	know	✓	no		5	right		write	
2	where		wear		6	meat		meet	
3	sea		see		7	wait		weight	
4	war		wore		8	one		won	

b 🔊 8.3 Listen and check your answers. Then listen again and repeat the words.

🔵 **Go online** for more practice

8C Who is Vivienne?

Life is ours to be spent, not to be saved.
D.H. Lawrence, British writer

| **G** possessive pronouns | **V** adverbs of manner | **P** reading aloud |

1 PRONUNCIATION reading aloud

a 🔊 **8.4** Listen to the sentences. You will hear each one twice. (Circle) the better version, a or b.

1 "Mr. Watson," she said slowly, "I am beginning to understand."
Version a / (Version b)

2 "Sit down," he said calmly, "and tell me what you know."
Version a / Version b

3 "Catherine," he said nervously, "there's something I have to tell you."
Version a / Version b

4 "Here you are," the old woman said kindly, "a nice cup of tea for you."
Version a / Version b

5 The detective looked at her suspiciously. "Tell me, what were you doing at 12:00 on May 11ᵗʰ?"
Version a / Version b

b 🔊 **8.5** Listen and repeat the sentences. Copy the rhythm and intonation.

2 GRAMMAR possessive pronouns

a Complete the questions and answers in the chart.

Whose...?	Possessive adjective	Possessive pronoun
1 *Whose bag is that?*	It's my bag.	It's *mine* .
2 *Whose books are those?*	They're your books.	They're _____ .
3 _____?	It's his laptop.	It's _____ .
4 _____?	They're her keys.	They're _____ .
5 _____?	It's our car.	It's _____ .
6 _____?	They're your coats.	They're _____ .
7 _____?	It's their house.	It's _____ .

b Complete the sentences with a possessive adjective (*my, your,* etc.) or pronoun (*mine, yours,* etc.).

1 **A** Are those *my* _____ glasses?
  B No, they're *mine.* _____
    Yours _____ are in your pocket!

2 **A** Whose coats are these? Are they _____?
  B Yes, they're _____. Thanks a lot.

3 **A** Is that your boyfriend's car? It looks like _____.
  B No, it isn't. _____ car is bigger than that.

4 **A** Whose cat is that? Is it _____?
  B No, it isn't. I've seen it in the neighbor's yard. I think it's _____.

c Complete the sentences with a possessive adjective (*my, your,* etc.) or pronoun (*mine, yours,* etc.).

1 You have to fill out this form in with a black pen. Do you want to use *mine?*

2 I left _____ wallet at home. Can I borrow some money?

3 You'll have to ask Sergio if you want to use this bike. It's _____, not mine.

4 Melissa can't come out tonight because she has to look after _____ sisters.

5 Min and I bought this house, so now it's _____.

6 I'll clean up my room if you do _____.

7 My sister bought a new phone, and now _____ is better than mine.

8 Toby and Sam had to get a taxi because _____ car's in the garage.

3 VOCABULARY adverbs of manner

a (Circle) the correct word.

1 I haven't done anything wrong. I don't know why you are (angry) / *angrily*.

2 "Come with me, my darling," he said *masterful / masterfully.* "You'll always be safe with me."

3 I had a very *lazy / lazily* morning. I didn't get up until 10:30.

4 Paulo had a *serious / seriously* accident, but he's fine now.

5 This movie is very *sad / sadly.* I can't watch any more!

6 There were no seats on the train. It was *complete / completely* full.

b Make adverbs from the adjectives in the list and complete the sentences.

_____
calm dream lazy quiet serious ~~slow~~
_____

1 Please walk *slowly.* You're going too fast!

2 Sorry? I can't hear you. You're speaking very _____.

3 Maria hardly ever laughs. She takes things very _____.

4 "I don't feel like doing anything today," he said _____.

5 "I'd like to retire early and live by the beach," Mark said _____.

6 Although the passengers were worried, the flight attendant spoke _____ and explained the problem.

c Complete the sentences with words from the list.

_____
ours / calmly   mine / completely   ~~ours / slowly~~
mine / well   ours / seriously   mine / quietly
_____

1 The other teacher talks too fast! It's difficult to understand her. We're lucky because *ours* speaks very *slowly*.

2 I'm surprised your plane was so empty yesterday. Today _____ was _____ full.

3 Your soccer coach seems very angry. _____ always talks to us _____.

4 I'm sorry to hear your exams went badly. _____ went really _____.

5 Your teacher doesn't think pronunciation is important, but _____ takes it very _____.

6 Your dog is very noisy. _____ just lies _____ in front of the fire and sleeps.

Go online for more practice   Go online to check your progress   59

All animals are equal – but some
animals are more equal than others.
*From Animal Farm, by George Orwell,
British writer*

| **G** if + past, would + base form (second conditional) | **V** animals and insects | **P** word stress |

1 VOCABULARY animals and insects

a Complete the crossword.

ACROSS →

DOWN ↓

b (Circle) one or two animals in each set to answer the questions.

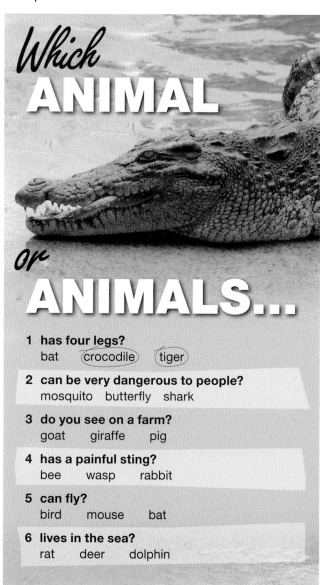

Which **ANIMAL** *or* **ANIMALS...**

1 has four legs?
bat (crocodile) (tiger)

2 can be very dangerous to people?
mosquito   butterfly   shark

3 do you see on a farm?
goat   giraffe   pig

4 has a painful sting?
bee   wasp   rabbit

5 can fly?
bird   mouse   bat

6 lives in the sea?
rat   deer   dolphin

c Complete the sentences with the missing animal.

1 A g*iraffe* has a very long neck so it can eat leaves from the top of trees.
2 Cows are usually calm, but b_____ can be dangerous.
3 African e_____ are the largest land animals.
4 When we were in Australia, we saw lots of k_____ jumping near the road.
5 Put that food in the refrigerator or there will be fl_____ all over it!
6 In the desert, c_____ are good working animals because they don't need water every day.

2 PRONUNCIATION word stress

a Underline the stressed syllable in each word. If they all have the same stressed syllable, check (✓) the group.

1 je|lly|fish   cro|co|dile   e|le|phant   ✓
2 mon|key   ti|ger   gi|raffe
3 bu|tter|fly   kan|ga|roo   mo|squi|to
4 ca|mel   dol|phin   li|on
5 spi|der   ra|bbit   chi|cken

b 🔊 9.1 Listen and check. Then listen again and repeat the words.

3 GRAMMAR if + past, would + base form

a Circle the correct words.

1 If a bee *flew* / *would fly* into my bedroom, *I'd open* / *I opened* the window.
2 If my sister *would see* / *saw* a mouse in the kitchen, *she screamed* / *she'd scream*.
3 *We'd have* / *We had* pets if *we wouldn't travel* / *we didn't travel* for work all the time.
4 If my brother *wouldn't be* / *wasn't* allergic to animals, *he got* / *he'd get* a cat.
5 If *I'd live* / *I lived* in the country, *I learned* / *I'd learn* to ride a horse.
6 What *did you do* / *would you do* if a bull *attacked* / *would attack* you?
7 If *I got* / *I'd get* a dog, *I chose* / *I'd choose* a small one.
8 If *I'd see* / *I saw* a crocodile, *I'd swim* / *I swam* away fast.

b Complete the second conditional sentences with the correct form of the verbs in parentheses.

1 If you _went_ (go) on safari, what animals _would you hope_ (you / hope) to see?
2 If you _____ (have) the chance to have any pet, what animal _____ (you / get)?
3 What _____ (you / do) if you _____ (see) a shark in the water when you were at the beach?
4 How _____ (you / feel) if someone _____ (ask) you to look after their dog for a week?
5 What _____ (you / do) if you _____ (find) a snake in your house or yard?
6 If there _____ (be) a mosquito in your room at night, what _____ (you / do)?

c Answer the questions in **b** about you. Use contractions where possible.

1 If I went on safari, I'd _____
_____.
2 If I had the chance to have any pet, I'd _____
_____.
3 I'd _____
_____.
4 _____
_____.
5 _____
_____.
6 _____
_____.

🔵 **Go online** for more practice

> I am not afraid of death. I just don't want to be there when it happens.
> *Woody Allen, American film director*

| **G** present perfect + *for* and *since* | **V** words related to fear, phrases with *for* and *since* | **P** sentence stress |

1 GRAMMAR present perfect + *for* and *since*

a Complete the conversations with the correct form of the verbs in parentheses. Use contractions where possible.

1 **A** Is Laura still frightened of flying?
  B Yes, she *hasn't been* (not be) on a plane for about ten years.

2 **A** Do you like snakes?
  B No, I _____ (have) a phobia of them since I was a child.

3 **A** How long _____ (you / live) in Miami?
  B We've been here since 2005.

4 **A** Does your sister work at the local school?
  B Yes, she _____ (work) there since she graduated from college.

5 **A** How's John these days?
  B I don't know. I _____ (not hear) from him since he moved to Washington, D.C.

6 **A** Is that a new coat?
  B No, I _____ (have) it for years.

b Rewrite the sentences and correct the mistakes in the **bold** phrases.

1 How long **do you have** your dog?
  How long have you had your dog?

2 **Valeria hates spiders** since she was a child.
  _____ .

3 **How much time** has your brother been an actor?
  _____ ?

4 **We're married** for ten years, and we're very happy.
  _____ .

5 My cousin's been in the US **for February**.
  _____ .

6 He's had the same job **since eight years**.
  _____ .

7 I've had this bike **since a long time**.
  _____ .

c Complete the sentences with the correct form of the words in parentheses and *for* or *since*. Use contractions where possible.

1 Juliet and I were in the same class at school. We *'ve known each other for* (know each other) 20 years.

2 This is our new dog. We _____ (only have him) October.

3 The yard is very dry. It _____ (not rain) weeks.

4 I think Dan and Jin will get married soon. They _____ (be together) three years now.

5 Christina is very excited about going to Morocco. She _____ (not be on vacation) a long time.

6 I don't ever want to leave Seattle. I _____ (live here) I was five.

7 I'm really hungry. I _____ (not eat anything) breakfast.

8 He _____ (play in the band) two years.

2 VOCABULARY phrases with *for* and *since*

a Circle the correct words.

1 I've been afraid of snakes since I *am* / *was* a child.
2 I haven't seen Amy for *age* / *ages*.
3 We've known Suki for *a long time* / *long time*.
4 I'm worried about our cat. It hasn't been home since *the weekend* / *a week*.
5 I saw Jacob on Friday, but I haven't spoken to him since *then* / *after*.

b Use today's time and date to rewrite the **bold** phrases with *for* or *since*.

1 José hasn't been to school **since Christmas**.
José hasn't been to school for _____.
2 Peter hasn't visited his sister **for ten years**.
Peter hasn't visited his sister since _____.
3 I haven't watched TV **for three days**.
I haven't watched TV since _____.
4 Omar's been abroad **since last Monday**.
Omar's been abroad for _____.
5 They've been at the airport **since eight o'clock**.
They've been at the airport for _____.
6 I went to Paris **three years ago**.
I haven't been to Paris since _____.

c Write questions with *How long* and the present perfect.

1 you / have / your phone
How long have you had your phone?
2 you / know your best friend?
_____?
3 you / have your computer or tablet?
_____?
4 you / live where you live now?
_____?
5 you / be in your English class?
_____?
6 you / be on Facebook or Twitter?
_____?

d Answer the questions in **c** about you. Use *for* or *since*.

1 I've had my phone _____.
2 I've known my _____.
3 I've _____.
4 _____.
5 _____.
6 _____.

3 PRONUNCIATION sentence stress

a 🔊 9.2 Listen and complete the sentences with the missing words.

1 *He's had* _____ a serious phobia *since he was* _____ a child.
2 I've _____ for _____ years.
3 _____ here for _____.
4 _____ married?
5 _____ Andrew?
6 _____ here?

b 🔊 9.2 Listen again and repeat the sentences. Copy the rhythm.

In films the director is God;
in documentaries God is the director.
Alfred Hitchcock, British movie director

G present perfect or simple past? (2)   **V** biographies   **P** word stress, /ɔr/

1 VOCABULARY biographies

a Match 1–8 to a–h to make sentences.

1 My grandfather was ___c___
2 He went ____
3 He fell ____
4 He graduated from ____
5 He got ____
6 He and my grandmother got ____
7 They had ____
8 He retired ____

a on his 65th birthday.
b in love with my grandmother at school.
c born in 1945.
d to elementary school when he was five.
e three children.
f high school in 1962.
g a job when he was 17.
h married in 1968.

b Complete the sentences with the missing words. Use the past tense where necessary.

1 I think my grandmother is about 70, but I can't remember exactly when she was *born.*
2 Victor and Carla's marriage wasn't happy; they s_____ in 2017 and g_____ d_____ a year later.
3 I would like to h_____ ch_____ one day. I'd like a boy and a girl.
4 After she graduates from high school, Kate wants to g_____ to c_____.
5 I'll never forget my first girlfriend. I f_____ i_____ l_____ with her at first sight.
6 My dad worked for the same company for years, but he r_____ last year when he was 65.
7 When Jackie was 13, she went to a big h_____ sc_____ with around 800 students.
8 My grandfather had a long and happy life, but sadly he d_____ last year at the age of 96.

2 PRONUNCIATION word stress, /ɔr/

a <u>Underline</u> the stressed syllable in the words.

1 di|vorced
2 marr|ied
3 gra|du|ate
4 e|le|men|ta|ry
5 chil|dren
6 re|tire
7 co|llege
8 se|pa|rate

b ◀)9.3 Listen and check. Then listen again and repeat the words.

c Check (✓) the sentences where the last two words have the /ɔr/ sound.

1 Look in the newspaper for the **sports scores**.   ✓
2 My new car has **four doors**.
3 Your hair looks **worse short**.
4 I have to do **more work**.
5 When was this **horse born**?
6 I can't tell if the wi-fi is better **or worse**.

d ◀)9.4 Listen and check. Then listen again and repeat the sentences.

3 **GRAMMAR** present perfect or simple past? (2)

a Read the sentences. Write **F** if the sentence is about finished actions and **U** if it's about unfinished actions.

1 Margarita was married to Juan for 11 years. _F_
2 I've been friends with Luke for a long time. ____
3 We've lived here since 2010. ____
4 Our family lived in Pakistan from 2008 to 2010. ____
5 I've had this phone for almost two years. ____
6 I only had two days off from school last year. ____
7 Maria's worked here since 2017. ____
8 My first wife and I separated for a year and then got divorced. ____

b Complete the sentences with the simple past or present perfect form of the verb in parentheses. Use contractions where possible.

1 A How long _have_ you _studied_ English? (study)
  B Since I was little. I _started_ learning it at school. (start)

2 A Are Tom and Gail married?
  B Yes, they are.
  A When _____ they _____ married? (get)
  B Last year. But they _____ together for about ten years now. (be)

3 A Is that man the new assistant?
  B Yes, he is.
  A How long _____ he _____ here? (work)
  B Only for two months. He _____ from college in June. (graduate)

4 A How long _____ you _____ your car? (have)
  B A long time! I _____ it about ten years ago, I think. (buy)

5 A When _____ Sandra _____ her boyfriend? (meet)
  B When she was in college. She _____ him for three years now. (know)

6 A How long _____ you _____ in New York? (live)
  B Not long. I _____ six months ago. (arrive)

c Write questions from the notes. Change the form of the verb if necessary.

1 Where / you born?
  Where were you born?
2 Where / you live when you were a child?
  _____?
3 When / you go to elementary school?
  _____?
4 / you enjoy school?
  _____?
5 Where / you go to high school?
  _____?
6 Where / you live now?
  _____?
7 How long / you live there?
  _____?
8 Where / you work or study?
  _____?
9 How long / you be there?
  _____?

d Write a paragraph about your life. Answer the questions in **c**.

I was born in _____
_____
_____
_____
_____
_____
_____

Go online for more practice | Go online to check your progress

Practical English Getting around

asking how to get there | **V** directions

1 VOCABULARY directions

a Match the pictures and phrases.

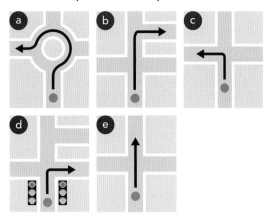

1 Turn left. __c__
2 Go straight ahead. ____
3 Take the second turn on the right. ____
4 Turn right at the traffic lights. ____
5 Go around the traffic circle and take the third exit. ____

b Complete the directions.

To get to the hotel, you need to ¹t**urn**_____
right and go ²str_____ ahead until you
get to the traffic circle. Go ³a_____ the
traffic circle and take the fourth ⁴e_____.
Then turn right at the traffic ⁵l_____ and
⁶t_____ the second turn on the
⁷l_____. The hotel is called The Garden
Inn and it's on the ⁸r_____.

2 ASKING HOW TO GET THERE

a Match 1–4 to a–d to make sentences.

1 How do I get to __d__
2 Sorry, could you ____
3 So first, I get to Columbus Circle. ____
4 How many stops ____

a OK. And then?
b is that?
c say that again?
d ~~the Museum of Natural History on the subway?~~

b Complete the conversation with the sentences from the list.

~~How do I get to SoHo on the subway?~~
OK, thanks. See you later.   OK. And then?
How many stops is that?   Could you say that again?   Where is it?

A ¹_How do I get to SoHo on the subway?_
B Go to the subway station at Grand Central – 42nd Street. Take the 6 towards Brooklyn Bridge – City Hall. Get off at Spring Street.
A ²_____
B OK. Take the 6 from Grand Central – 42nd Street to Spring Street.
A ³_____
B Seven.
A ⁴_____
B Then you can walk to the restaurant.
A ⁵_____
B Come out of the subway on Spring Street. Go straight ahead for about 80 yards and the restaurant is on the right. It's called Balthazar.
A ⁶_____
B And don't get lost.

3 SOCIAL ENGLISH

Complete the conversation with the words from the list.

feel   long   mean   said   ~~so~~

A I'm ¹_so_____ sorry I'm late. I missed the bus.
B But you're always late! I've already eaten.
A I ²_____ I'm sorry. Look, why don't we go for a walk? I can get a burger or something.
B I don't ³_____ like a walk. It's been a ⁴_____ day and I'm tired.
A Listen. I'll take you home now. And tomorrow I'll make dinner for you at my house.
B OK. I suppose that way you can't be late! Sorry, I didn't ⁵_____ to say that! I'm sure that'll be nice.

🔊 **Go online** to practice the Practical English phrases

1 GRAMMAR

Circle a, b, or c.

1 I think you ____ take the job. It's a great opportunity.
   a would   **b** should   **c** need

2 I love my new phone. It's the ____ phone I've ever had.
   a good   **b** better   **c** best

3 Louisa ____ at our school for three months now.
   a was   **b** 's   **c** 's been

4 We couldn't find ____ to park near the movie theater.
   a anywhere   **b** somewhere   **c** nowhere

5 We ____ get up early tomorrow because there's no school.
   a must not   **b** don't have to   **c** must

6 If I had more time, ____ all the housework myself.
   a I'll do   **b** do   **c** I'd do

2 VOCABULARY

Circle the word that is different.

1 married   divorced   separated   retired
2 get in shape   get to work   get to school   get home
3 butterfly   wasp   goat   mosquito
4 extroverted   friendly   talkative   cheap
5 castle   terminal   temple   palace
6 windy   dirty   foggy   cloudy

3 PRONUNCIATION

a Circle the word with a different vowel sound.

ɜː bird	1 w**or**d b**ear**d sk**ir**t l**ear**n	
ʊ bull	2 g**oo**d w**oul**d bl**oo**d p**u**sh	
eə chair	3 wh**ere** w**ere** w**ear** b**ear**	

b Circle the word that is stressed on a different syllable.

1 slow|ly   af|ter   a|long
2 ex|ci|ting   ex|pen|sive   beau|ti|ful
3 de|cide   prac|tice   re|pair

4 GRAMMAR & VOCABULARY

Read the text. Circle a, b, or c.

Words of wisdom

There's one thing that everybody is happy to give you – their advice. But [1]____ people love giving advice, not many people [2]____ for it, and even fewer people actually take it.

If we were lucky, our parents probably gave us some good advice when we were children. I remember [3]____ a good luck card from my mother before my school exams. It said "You can only do your best, but DO it!" It was just a mother's way of saying "Be the best you can be!"

Here are some words of wisdom [4]____ celebrities have found useful over the years.

My mother, Eve, always taught me you should never look back and worry about the mistakes you have [5]____. When something goes wrong, it's just another one of life's lessons. Move on to the next thing.
Sir Richard Branson, businessman

A long time ago, my grandmother told me, "When you [6]____ somebody for the first time, try to [7]____ something nice to say about them. It always makes them happy." She really made people happy, and I've always tried to be like her.
Jilly Cooper, writer

The [8]____ way to give advice to your children is to find out what they want and advise them to do it.
Harry S. Truman, US President

"Everything matters, but nothing matters very much." I read this [9]____ and love it because it seems just right.
Deborah Moggach, writer

[10]____ give up, because if you keep believing and trying, anything can happen.
Goran Ivanisevic, tennis player

1	**a** because	**b** although	**c** so
2	**a** ask	**b** tell	**c** answer
3	**a** got	**b** to get	**c** getting
4	**a** who	**b** where	**c** that
5	**a** made	**b** done	**c** been
6	**a** meet	**b** know	**c** look
7	**a** found	**b** finding	**c** find
8	**a** easy	**b** easily	**c** easiest
9	**a** someone	**b** somewhere	**c** something
10	**a** Never	**b** Ever	**c** Always

A lifetime of training for just 10 seconds.
*Jesse Owens, American athlete and
winner of the Olympic 100 meters in 1936*

G expressing movement   **V** sports, expressing movement   **P** word stress

1 VOCABULARY sports, expressing movement

a Match the sports to the photos.

baseball   basketball   cycling   gymnastics
karate   rugby   ~~tennis~~   windsurfing

1 *tennis*   2 _____

3 _____   4 _____

5 _____   6 _____

7 _____   8 _____

b Complete the phrases with *play*, *go*, or *do*.

1 *play*   soccer
2 _____   cycling
3 _____   handball
4 _____   yoga
5 _____   gymnastics
6 _____   skiing
7 _____   volleyball
8 _____   track and field

c Complete the crossword.

ACROSS →

DOWN ↓

2 PRONUNCIATION word stress

a Underline the stressed syllable in each word. Then check (✓) the groups where all three stress patterns are the same.

1 <u>ski</u>|ing <u>yo</u>|ga <u>tenn</u>|is   ✓

2 gym|na|stics ka|ra|te bas|ket|ball

3 cy|cling hand|ball rug|by

4 so|ccer base|ball te|nnis

b 🔊 10.1 Listen and check. Then listen again and repeat the words. <u>Co</u>py the <u>rhy</u>thm.

3 GRAMMAR expressing movement

a Circle the correct words.

1 The goalkeeper stopped the ball from going *into* / *out of* the net.

2 In the 800 meters, athletes go *along* / *around* the track twice.

3 My ex-girlfriend ran *over* / *past* me, but she didn't say hello.

4 The soccer player kicked the ball *across* / *through* the field to a player on the other side.

5 I was running *down* / *under* the bridge when I saw a big, black dog coming *toward* / *across* me.

6 Go *up* / *over* the stairs to the next floor.

7 My sister said, "Go *back* / *away*! I don't want to talk to anybody."

8 The tunnel goes *through* / *under* the mountain and out the other side.

b Look at the pictures. Complete the sentences with the simple past of the verb and the correct preposition from the list.

~~cycle~~ go hit kick run throw
across into over through under ~~up~~

---

1 They *cycled*   *up*   the hill.

2 She _____ the ball _____ the net.

3 He _____ the ball _____ the goal.

4 The boy _____ the ball _____ the car.

5 The train _____ _____ the tunnel.

6 The children _____ _____ the road.

c Complete the sentences with a preposition from the list and the words in parentheses.

~~down~~ into over around through up and down

---

1 In skiing, you have to *go down hills fast*   .
(go / hills fast)

2 In volleyball, you have to _____.
(hit / the ball / the net)

3 In cycling, you have to _____.
(ride / hills)

4 In track and field, you have to _____.
(run / the track)

5 In soccer, you have to _____.
(kick / the ball / the goal)

6 In basketball, you have to _____.
(throw / the ball / the hoop)

🔵 **Go online** for more practice

Woke up, got out of bed,
dragged a comb across my head.
*John Lennon and Paul McCartney,
British songwriters*

G word order of phrasal verbs **V** phrasal verbs **P** linking

1 VOCABULARY phrasal verbs

a Complete what the people are saying in each picture.

1 Can you turn *down* the radio? It's very loud!
2 Don't worry! The game will be _____ soon.
3 We need someone who can look _____ our dog while we're on vacation.
4 Take _____ your shoes before you come in!
5 Can you fill _____ this form, please?
6 Why don't you put _____ a different jacket? That one looks awful!

b Complete the sentences with a verb from the list.

~~find~~ get go look set take throw turn

1 Chris listens to the radio to *find* out about the traffic in the morning.
2 I never _____ away old books, I sell them on eBay.
3 It's very cold in here. Can you _____ up the heat?
4 Use your dictionaries to _____ up the words you don't understand.
5 I don't _____ along with my boss. He thinks he's always right.
6 They always _____ off really early when they go to the airport because they don't want to miss their flight.
7 Can you wake me up if my alarm doesn't _____ off?
8 We're going to _____ back our new coffee machine because it doesn't work well.

c Complete the conversations with a phrasal verb from the list.

~~don't get along~~ drop you off give it up
goes off looking forward to it
pick you up run out try it on turn it off

1 A To tell you the truth, John and I don't like each other.
  B I know. I think it's sad that you two *don't get along.*

2 A I don't drink soda anymore.
  B That's fantastic. Good job! When did you _____?

3 A Jamilla is excited about our vacation!
  B Yes, she's really _____.

4 A Can you help me? I want to see if this dress fits.
  B Sure. You can _____ in the fitting room over there.

5 A When you go to bed, please don't leave the TV on all night.
  B Don't worry. I promise I'll _____.

6 A Our neighbor's car alarm started in the middle of the night.
  B That's really annoying. Our neighbor's house alarm _____ all the time.

7 A Jack's dad can't take me to school today. He's sick.
  B Don't worry. I can _____ on my way to work and _____ this afternoon.

8 A I'm a little worried that we don't have enough gas.
  B It's only 10 miles to the next gas station. I don't think we'll _____.

2 GRAMMAR phrasal verbs

a Match 1–7 to a–g to complete the sentences.

1 I'm really sorry I'm late. My alarm clock didn't go ___b___.
2 I wasn't sure how to spell "practice," so I looked ____.
3 The sound in this movie theater is too loud! I don't understand why they don't turn ____.
4 It was a really boring movie. I couldn't wait until it was ____.
5 Jemma can't take her cat on vacation, so I'm going to look ____.
6 I have the application form, so now I just have to fill ____.
7 I've lost my debit card. Can you help me look ____?

a it out
b off
c it up
d over
e for it
f after it
g it down

b Read the sentences. If both options are correct, check (✓) the sentence. If only one option is correct, circle the correct words.

1 Our flight's at 9:00 tomorrow, so we need to *get up early* / *get early up*.
2 My diet's going OK, but *giving up bread* / *giving bread up* has been really difficult.
3 My daughter isn't very well, so I'm staying at home today to *look her after* / *look after her*.
4 Sorry! I didn't know you were on the phone. I'll *turn down the TV* / *turn the TV down* a little.
5 It's freezing. *Put your coat on.* / *Put on your coat.*
6 You're wearing shoes. If you want to go into the mosque, you'll have to *take them off* / *take off them*.

c Rewrite the sentences with a pronoun. Change the word order if necessary.

1 Can you write down **your email address**?
   Can you write it down?
2 The teacher will give back **the exams** on Friday.
   _____.
3 Are you looking forward to **your weekend in Mexico**?
   _____?
4 I called **my mother** back when I arrived at the train station.
   _____.
5 We don't get along with **our new neighbors**.
   _____.
6 Can you turn on **the TV**?
   _____?

d Complete the questions with a phrasal verb from the list.

get up   go away   ~~go off~~   go out   set off

A What time does your alarm clock
   ¹*go off*_____?
B At 6:30, but I usually stay in bed for a little longer.
A What time do you ²_____?
B Usually at about 6:45.
A What time do you ³_____ for work?
B At 8:00. I take the 8:15 train.
A Do you usually ⁴_____ on Saturday night?
B Yes, I often meet up with friends and we go to a dance club or have dinner.
A Do you ever ⁵_____ for the weekend?
B Not often – I don't have enough money!

e Answer the questions in **d** about you.

1 My alarm goes off _____.
2 I _____.
3 _____.
4 _____.
5 _____.

3 PRONUNCIATION linking

a 🔊 10.2 Listen and write the missing words.

1 I eat too much chocolate. I'm going to try and *give it up.*_____
2 My laptop's broken. I can't _____.
3 That's my jacket! _____!
4 This camera cost a lot of money. Please _____!
5 This sweater looks nice. Is there anywhere I can _____?
6 Your pen doesn't work. You should _____.

b 🔊 10.2 Listen again and repeat the sentences.

Go online for more practice

71

10C International inventions

Necessity is the mother of invention. *Anonymous*

G the passive **V** people from different countries **P** /ʃ/, /tʃ/, and /dʒ/

1 VOCABULARY people from different countries

a Complete the chart with the missing words.

Country	Adjective	People
Turkey	Turkish	the Turks
America		the Americans
	Chinese	the
		the Brazilians
Morocco		the
	Japanese	the
		the Spanish
	Thai	the
	Argentinian	the
Italy		the
	English	the

b Complete the sentences with the correct nationality adjective.

1 We love going to places like Paris because the _French_ have the most amazing markets.

2 I really enjoyed living in Thailand, and I think the _____ are the best cooks.

3 If you visit Durham, East London, and Cornwall, you'll realize that the _____ have lots of different accents.

4 I loved New York, and all the _____ I met were really friendly.

5 When we visited Istanbul, we learned a lot about the _____ and their culture and history.

6 You can understand why the _____ are proud of cities like Buenos Aires and Córdoba.

7 The _____ have super-fast trains that run between cities like Tokyo and Osaka.

2 PRONUNCIATION /ʃ/, /tʃ/, and /dʒ/

a (Circle) the word with a different sound.

ʃ shower	1 (Belgian)	Spanish	musician
dʒ jazz	2 Japanese	German	British
tʃ chess	3 shop	watch	cheese
tʃ chess	4 chocolate	chair	shut
ʃ shower	5 ship	cheap	Russia

b 🔊 10.3 Listen and check. Then listen again and repeat the words.

c 🔊 10.4 Listen and write the sentences.

1 *Fish and chips is an English dish.*
2 _____.
3 _____.
4 _____.
5 _____.

d 🔊 10.4 Listen again and repeat the sentences.

3 GRAMMAR the passive

a Circle the correct words.

1 In 1848, gold *discovered* / *was discovered* in California.
2 Today most of the food we eat *is bought* / *bought* in supermarkets.
3 Spanish *speaks* / *is spoken* widely in North and South America.
4 The Indian movie industry *calls* / *is called* Bollywood, and they *make* / *are made* lots of movies every year.
5 When *were the pyramids built* / *built the pyramids* and who *built* / *was built* them?
6 My grandfather *gave* / *was given* me this beautiful, old watch.

b Write sentences and questions in the present or past passive.

1 what / your new baby / name?
   What's your new baby named?
2 contact lenses / invent / a Czech chemist
   _____.
3 where / olives / grow?
   _____?
4 the VW Beetle / design / in the 1930s
   _____.
5 diamonds / find / in many different colors
   _____.
6 when / vitamins / discover?
   _____?

c Complete the conversations with a verb from the list in the correct present or past passive form.

~~be born~~   build   grow   invent   make

1 A *Were you born* in Mexico?
   B Yes, in Monterrey, but I moved to the US when I was 11.

2 A Are these airplanes 100% American?
   B No, the engines _____ in Japan.

3 A Does tea come from China?
   B Some of it does, but it _____ in India and some other countries, too.

4 A Is the Tower of London very old?
   B Yes, the oldest part _____ in 1078.

5 A Who invented the ballpoint pen?
   B It _____ by a Hungarian named László Bíró.

d Write sentences about the inventions.

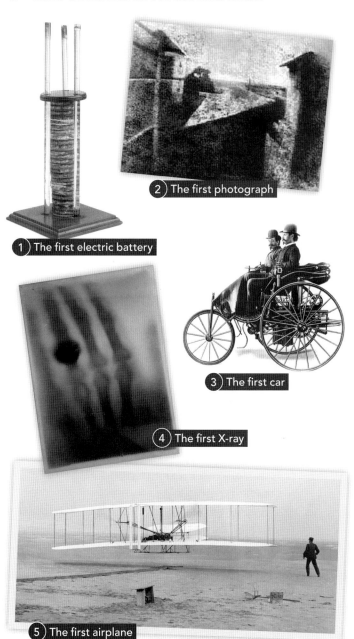

1 The first electric battery
2 The first photograph
3 The first car
4 The first X-ray
5 The first airplane

1 make / Alessandro Volta / 1800
   The first electric battery was made by Alessandro Volta in 1800.
2 take / Joseph Niépce / 1826
   _____
   _____.
3 drive / Karl Benz / 1886
   _____
   _____.
4 take / Wilhelm Röntgen / 1895
   _____
   _____.
5 fly / Wright brothers / 1903
   _____
   _____.

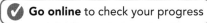 Go online for more practice   Go online to check your progress

11A Ask the teacher

> The beautiful thing about learning is that no one can take it away from you.
> *BB King, American musician*

G *used to* **V** school subjects **P** *used to / didn't use to*

1 VOCABULARY school subjects

a Match the school subjects to the questions.

1 foreign languages __c__
2 geography ____
3 history ____
4 literature ____
5 math ____
6 PE ____
7 chemistry ____
8 IT ____
9 art ____
10 biology ____

a What's 15 times 99?
b Who wrote *Macbeth*?
c How do you say "Thank you" in Portuguese?
d How do you create an XML document?
e When did Abraham Lincoln die?
f How many miles is eight laps around a standard track?
g Where was Pablo Picasso from?
h Are snakes warm-blooded or cold-blooded?
i What's the chemical symbol for water?
j What's the capital of Argentina?

b Match the questions in **a** to the answers.

1 Buenos Aires __j__
2 Spain ____
3 *Obrigado* ____
4 1,485 ____
5 William Shakespeare ____
6 H_2O ____
7 2 miles ____
8 Click on the link and find out. ____
9 1865 ____
10 Cold-blooded ____

c Look at sentences 1–8 and complete the puzzle with school subjects. What's the mystery word?

```
            ¹L A N G U A G E S
  2 □ □ □ □ □ □ □
       3 □ □ □ □
       4 □ □ □ □
  5 □ □ □
         6 □ □ □ □ □
  7 □ □ □ □
    8 □ □ □ □ □
```

1 I enjoy Spanish and Japanese, so I'm going to study foreign ____ at college.
2 Jason loves studying American ____ – especially writers like F. Scott Fitzgerald.
3 ____ is my worst subject. I'm terrible with numbers.
4 Kitty loves ____. She's really good at painting and drawing.
5 You have to be good at ____ if you want to be a doctor.
6 In our ____ class we're learning about the Russian Revolution.
7 I think Mai likes programming because her Information ____ teacher is really good.
8 For the ____ test tomorrow, we have to remember the names of all the big rivers in the US.

74

2 GRAMMAR used to

a Complete the sentences with the correct form of *used to* and the words in parentheses.

1 [?] *Did you use to be* _____ (you / be) a good student at school?
2 [−] I _____ (work) hard at school.
3 [+] We _____ (wear) a uniform at school.
4 [?] _____ (you / have) a favorite teacher at school?
5 [−] Children _____ (not study) IT when I was at school.
6 [+] My school _____ (be) smaller than it is now.
7 [−] We _____ (not play) soccer in PE.
8 [?] _____ (your teachers / give) you a lot of homework?

b Correct the mistakes in the **bold** phrases.

1 **I use to** sit at the back of the class.
   I used to _____
2 **Jon used go** to school on Saturday mornings.
   _____
3 **We didn't used to understand** our Spanish teacher.
   _____
4 **Did you used to** go to school by bus?
   _____
5 **School use to** start at 7:45 but now it starts at 7:15.
   _____
6 **Did your friends use help** you with your homework?
   _____

c Make questions about *your* old school with the words below and the correct form of *used to*.

1 what school / you / go?
   What school did you use to go to? _____
2 What subject / you / like most?
   _____?
3 What subjects / you / hate?
   _____?
4 Which teacher / you / like most?
   _____?
5 Did / you / work hard?
   _____?
6 What sports / you / play?
   _____?
7 What / you / do after school?
   _____?

d Answer the questions in **c** about your own experience at a school. If you're in high school, write about your elementary school.

1 _____
_____ .
2 _____
_____ .
3 _____
_____ .
4 _____
_____ .
5 _____
_____ .
6 _____
_____ .
7 _____
_____ .

3 PRONUNCIATION used to / didn't use to

a ◉ 11.1 Listen and write the sentences.

1 *I used to be good at math.* _____
2 _____ .
3 _____ .
4 _____ .
5 _____ .
6 _____ .

b ◉ 11.1 Listen again and repeat the sentences. Copy the rhythm.

Go online for more practice

Help! I can't decide!

The first step to getting what you want out of life is this: Decide what you want to do
Ben Stein, American actor

G *might* **V** word building: noun formation **P** diphthongs

1 GRAMMAR *might*

a Complete the sentences with *might* or *might not* and a verb from the list.

be come fail get give
go ~~go out~~ have miss rain

1 I'm really tired so I *might not go out*
   tonight.
2 Miguel speaks English very well, so he
   _____ the job with the
   American company.
3 If you have a temperature, you
   _____ the flu.
4 If the taxi doesn't come soon, we
   _____ the train.
5 I haven't seen Ryan with Nora for a
   long time. They _____
   together anymore.
6 Mike and Karen _____ to
   our party. They're thinking of going on
   vacation then.
7 We love skiing, so we _____
   to Colorado for our next vacation.
8 Hana hasn't had much time to practice, so
   she _____ her driver's test
   tomorrow.
9 Let's have something to eat before we
   board our flight. They _____
   us a meal on the plane.
10 Take an umbrella. I think it
   _____ later.

b Complete the article with words from the lists.

THE FUTURE IS ROBOTS

~~might be~~ might see might succeed

In the future, robots [1]*might be*_____ good for us or bad
for us, but we can be sure about one thing – we're going
to see a lot more of them. The Henn-na Hotel in Japan is
known as the world's first robot hotel. They hope robots will
do 90% of the work. The robots, which look like humans,
already greet people, answer questions, and help guests with
their bags. If the hotel does well, and there are signs that it
[2]_____, then this is the kind of thing that we
[3]_____ in other kinds of business soon, too.

might learn might not be might start

We used to think that robots could only do simple jobs
like cooking or cleaning, but there are signs that this
[4]_____ true. Now some scientists are saying
that robots [5]_____ how to do more difficult jobs
and [6]_____ doing the kind of work that doctors,
teachers, and other professionals do now.

might begin might have might lose

If businesses start using robots, a lot of people
[7]_____ their jobs, but it's also true that people
[8]_____ to do new and more interesting jobs
– making robots, for example. If robots do a lot of the boring
work, people [9]_____ more free time to enjoy
themselves and get away from the computer screen.

2 PRONUNCIATION diphthongs

a Look at the words in the square. Circle any three sounds in a row that are the same. The lines can go across, down, or diagonally.

m**igh**t	de**ci**de	b**uy**	ann**oy**	s**ou**th
w**o**n't	alth**ough**	kn**ow**	**ow**l	h**ere**
br**ea**k	sc**are**d	n**ow**	sl**ow**	d**eer**
m**ay**	w**ear**	h**air**	th**ere**	souven**ir**
f**ai**l	n**oi**sy	enj**oy**	b**oy**	s**ure**

b ◑11.2 Listen and check. Then listen again and repeat the words.

3 VOCABULARY word building: noun formation

a Complete the chart with the correct nouns.

Verb	Noun
choose	¹ choice
confuse	2
decide	3
die	4
compete	5
educate	6
invite	7
live	8
invent	9
fly	10
succeed	11
elect	12
advise	13
pronounce	14

b Complete the sentences with a verb or noun from **a**.

1 I made the right *choice* to continue studying when I graduated from high school. I loved college.
2 After the _____ of our dog, we were all really sad for weeks.
3 They're going to _____ all their friends to their party.
4 The _____ was very long, but I watched three movies on the plane.
5 The documentary was about the _____ of the track star, Jesse Owens.
6 I can't _____ between the steak or the fish. They're both delicious at this restaurant.
7 The computer was a very important _____.
8 The new Chinese restaurant has been a big _____. It's full every night.

c Complete the sentences with *might* or *might not* and a noun from **a**.

1 I'd love to go to Louisa's party, but I *might not* get an *invitation*. We had an argument last week.
2 We _____ win the _____ tomorrow. The team we're playing isn't very good.
3 The children _____ get a better _____ if we teach them at home. The local school is terrible.
4 I _____ book the _____ to Miami. It's very expensive and I don't have much money.
5 I _____ take Marta's _____. She's usually wrong.
6 Carlos _____ watch some English movies to improve his _____.

🔍 **Go online** for more practice

There are two things in life for which
we are never truly prepared: twins.
Josh Billings, American writer

G *so, neither* + auxiliaries   **V** similarities and differences   **P** /ð/ and /θ/

1 VOCABULARY similarities and differences

a Circle the correct word.

1 My sister and I are *similar / identical* twins. Even our mom sometimes doesn't know who's who!
2 I have the same color eyes *as / that* my dad.
3 My brother and I are *both / same* in a band. I'm a guitarist and he's a drummer.
4 My cousin and I are very *similar / identical*, but she's taller than me.
5 Do you look *like / as* your mother?
6 When we went back to the house where we used to live. It seemed very different *from / as* how I remembered it.

b Complete the text with words from the list.

as   both   different   identical   like   ~~similar~~

The same *but different*

People think my best friend Sam and I are
sisters because we're very ¹ *similar* . Sam's
from the same town ² _____ me, and we
look ³ _____ each other, but we aren't
⁴ _____ because her eyes are ⁵ _____
from mine. We ⁶ _____ like shopping,
and we have the same taste in clothes, too.
We even have the same last name – Johnson.
This confuses a lot of people!

2 GRAMMAR *so, neither* + auxiliaries

a Match the sentences with the replies.

1 I'm from New York.   *g*
2 I really hated the movie.   ____
3 I'm going to be 21 this month.   ____
4 I was really bad at history at school.   ____
5 Dave doesn't have time to take me to the airport.   ____
6 I had a great time at the party.   ____
7 Gina has never been to Mexico.   ____

a So did I. It was very boring.
b So am I. What day is your birthday?
c So did I. I stayed until one in the morning.
d So was I. I could never remember all those dates.
e Neither have I. That's why we want to go there.
f Neither do I. Why don't you take the bus?
g ~~So am I. Where do you live?~~

b Complete the conversation with phrases from the list.

~~Neither did I~~   Neither have I   Neither was I
So am I (x2)   So would I

A Hi, Tom. Do you ever watch *Who Do You Think You Are?* You know, that TV series about celebrities who find out about the history of their families?
B Yes, I do. But I didn't see it last night.
A ¹ *Neither did I.* I wasn't at home.
B ² _____. But I'm going to watch it on demand later.
A ³ _____. I think it's really interesting. I'd love to find out about my family.
B ⁴ _____. I'm thinking about doing some research online.
A ⁵ _____. But I haven't done anything about it yet.
B ⁶ _____.

c Respond to the statements with *So* or *Neither* to say that you are the same.

1 I'm going out tonight.

So am I.

2 I went away last weekend.

_____.

3 I haven't done my English homework.

_____.

4 I got up late today.

_____.

5 I'm not very hungry.

_____.

6 I can't drive.

_____.

7 I'd love to travel around the world.

_____.

8 I don't have any pets.

_____.

9 I didn't sleep very well last night.

_____.

10 I hate standing in line.

_____.

3 PRONUNCIATION /ð/ and /θ/

a Circle the word with a different sound.

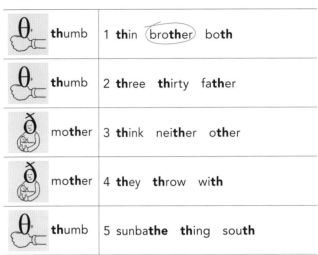

thumb	1 thin (brother) both
thumb	2 three thirty father
mother	3 think neither other
mother	4 they throw with
thumb	5 sunbathe thing south

b 🔊 11.3 **Listen and check. Then listen again and repeat the words.**

c 🔊 11.4 **Listen and respond. Say you're the same.**

I'm going away for the weekend.

So am I.

I don't like spicy food.

Neither do I.

 **Go online** for more practice  **Go online** to check your progress

Practical English Time to go home

on the phone

1 ON THE PHONE

a Circle a, b, or c.

1 Hello, marketing. _____ can I help you?
   a Which **b** Who **c** How

2 Can I speak _____ Laura Jones, please?
   a on **b** at **c** to

3 I'll put you _____ now.
   a across **b** over **c** through

4 Hello, _____ is Laura Jones.
   a here **b** these **c** this

5 Oh sorry. I have the _____ number.
   a wrong **b** bad **c** false

6 Can I _____ a message for Anna, please?
   a make **b** say **c** leave

7 Don't worry. I'll call _____ later.
   a over **b** back **c** into

8 I'm sorry, the line's _____ right now.
   a occupied **b** busy **c** full

9 I'm afraid Teresa isn't _____ her desk right now.
   a by **b** with **c** at

10 Sure. I'll _____ him a message for you.
   a say **b** tell **c** give

b Complete the conversations.

1 **A** I'm sorry, I can't t_ake_____ your call right
      now. Please l_____ a message after the
      beep.
   B Hi, Tomo, this is Mark r_____ your call.

2 **A** Hi, Amy.
   B I'm s_____, you have the wr_____
      number.

3 **A** Hello, this is reception. How can I help you?
   B Good morning. Mr. Clarke, please.
   A I'm sorry, the l_____ is b_____.
   B OK, can I l_____ a m_____?
   A Yes, of course.
   B Can you tell him Fiona called? I'll c_____
      b_____ later.

4 **A** Good morning, New York 24seven.
   B Hello, can I speak to Alison, please?
   A Just a second. I'll p_____ you through.

c Write the correct question or response for the situations.

1 In a hotel, you want the receptionist to let you talk to the manager on the phone.
   Can I _speak to the manager, please?_

2 Someone calls you, but they haven't called the right number.
   I'm sorry, you _____.

3 Someone calls you at work. You offer to help them.
   How can _____?

4 You call an office, but Mrs. Jones is not at her desk. You want to tell her something.
   Can I _____?

5 Someone asks you if it's OK for you to wait. You want to say that's fine.
   OK, I'll _____.

6 The person you want to talk to is not there. You want to say that you will call again in a few hours.
   I'll call _____.

7 Someone says your colleague is not answering her office phone. Suggest calling her cell phone.
   You could _____.

2 SOCIAL ENGLISH

Circle the correct word or phrase.

1 **A** Does your girlfriend know you're here?
   B No, I'll *call her* / *call to her* now.

2 **A** I have a new job!
   B That's *great news* / *a great news*.

3 **A** I have something to tell you.
   B Me, too. But you *do first* / *go first*.

4 **A** What are you doing here?
   B I'll explain *after* / *later*.

5 **A** Is everything all right?
   B *Never better* / *Ever better*.

⊙ **Go online** to practice the Practical English phrases

Can you remember...? 1–11

1 GRAMMAR

Circle a, b, or c.

1 If we ____ Chicago, I'd have to find another job.
a would leave   b will leave   c left

2 We can't find the TV remote control, so we can't ____.
a turn on it   b turn up it   c turn it on

3 Leonardo da Vinci ____ in France from 1516 to 1519.
a was living   b has lived   c lived

4 These glasses are very expensive because ____ by hand.
a they are made   b they make   c they have made

5 I'm lucky because I don't ____ work on weekends.
a have to   b should   c must

6 Farrah is a woman I ____ know a long time ago.
a used   b use to   c used to

2 VOCABULARY

Circle the word that is different.

1 geography   history   classroom   art
2 cycling   sightseeing   tennis   skiing
3 noisy   exciting   dangerous   polluted
4 fairly   quickly   very   really
5 checkout   fitting room   garbage   receipt
6 cap   sandals   sneakers   boots

3 PRONUNCIATION

Circle the word with a different sound.

ð mother	1 nei**th**er wea**th**er ba**th** **th**ose	
ɛr chair	2 h**air** w**ear** th**ere** n**ear**	
ɔr horse	3 d**oor** p**ar**t sc**ore** f**our**	
dʒ jazz	4 ima**g**ine **j**eans **G**erman **G**reek	
/ɪd/	5 invit**ed** need**ed** arriv**ed** want**ed**	
ɜr bird	6 p**er**son sneak**ers** sweat**er** arr**i**ve	

4 GRAMMAR & VOCABULARY

Read the article. Circle a, b, or c.

Cycling superstar

Danny MacAskill, who comes from Dunvegan in Scotland, is one of the ¹____ trials bike riders in the world.

If you don't know what a trials bike is, it's a little smaller than a mountain bike, and you can do some amazing things on it. Or at least, Danny MacAskill can. When he ²____ on his bike, he can go up or down steps, fly over walls, or climb mountains. Sometimes it's difficult ³____ that this is just a bike and not a ⁴____ of magic machine.

Danny's professional career began when he was 23 and his roommate David Sowerby made a short video of him on his bike. Danny put it up on YouTube, where it ⁵____ by millions of people. From that moment on, Danny discovered that he was ⁶____ becoming an internet superstar. In the United States, the *New York Times* and *National Geographic* wrote stories about him. He ⁷____ up his job as a bicycle mechanic and moved to Edinburgh to ride his bike full time. He ⁸____ lots of awards, and he was chosen to carry the Olympic torch through the city of Glasgow.

Since then, Danny ⁹____ other great videos such as "Way Back Home" and "The Ridge." He is now ¹⁰____ to travel across Europe, and this new video will show people some of his most famous tricks.

1 a well   b good   c best
2 a got   b gets   c will get
3 a to believe   b believe   c believing
4 a kind   b way   c piece
5 a has seen   b saw   c was seen
6 a quick   b quickly   c quicker
7 a gave   b set   c got
8 a earned   b won   c beat
9 a has made   b made   c makes
10 a planning   b deciding   c pretending

✓ Go online to check your progress

12A Unbelievable!

G past perfect **V** time expressions **P** the letter *i*

> For truth is always strange;
> stranger than fiction.
> *Lord Byron, British poet*

1 VOCABULARY time expressions

a Match sentences 1–5 with a–e.

1 I made plans to meet Jack at the movie theater at 8:00, but he was late. ___d___

2 He was in the living room, relaxing and reading a book. ____

3 On the way to the train station, he realized he didn't have his wallet. ____

4 Sonia fell off her bike, and Peter was worried when he heard. ____

5 Frank's date with Wendy was a disaster. He was at the café on 14th Street, and was waiting there. ____

a He called her right away to find out how she was.

b He turned around immediately and went back to pick it up.

c Meanwhile, she was waiting for him at the café on 40th Street.

d ~~He eventually arrived, but the movie was almost finished.~~

e Suddenly there was a loud noise outside and someone was shouting.

b Complete the sentences with a word from the list.

---
eventually   ~~immediately~~   meanwhile   right away
suddenly
---

1 "You're going to miss the bus!" Max's mother shouted. "Get up *immediately.* "

2 We were watching TV last night. _____. the electricity went off, so we missed the end of the movie.

3 Dave was in his room hoping that Bella might call. _____, Bella was in her room waiting for her phone to ring.

4 Eri waited and waited for Sam to arrive at the restaurant. _____, after two hours, she gave up and went home.

5 I'm sorry, I forgot to go to the supermarket. I'll do it _____.

2 GRAMMAR past perfect

a Complete the sentences with the past perfect form of the verb in parentheses.

1 The streets were white because it *had snowed* during the night. (snow)

2 I suddenly remembered that I _____ the windows before I left the house. (not close)

3 We got to the movie theater ten minutes after the movie _____. (start)

4 Tina felt nervous when she got on the plane because she _____ before. (not fly)

5 Omar lent me the book after he _____ it. (read)

6 When Jack got back to the parking lot, he saw that someone _____ his car. (take)

b Circle the correct words.

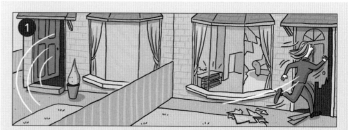

Last week my neighbor was on vacation. One night [1] *I heard* / I'd heard a strange noise in her house.
[2] *I opened* / I'd opened her front door to take a look, and I immediately saw that someone [3] *broke* / had broken into the house.

Luckily, he (or she!) [4] *already left* / had already left when I got there, and they [5] *didn't steal* / hadn't stolen very much – just the TV.

I was looking for my phone yesterday morning, but I couldn't find it. I was sure [6] *I didn't lose* / I hadn't lost it because [7] *I saw* / I'd seen it twenty minutes before. Then I realized that [8] *I left* / I'd left it in my jeans pocket, and [9] *I put* / I'd put my jeans in the washing machine!

c Read the stories. Then write mini-paragraphs of two or three sentences.
Use the past perfect and time expressions where necessary.

1

MISSING A BUS, TRAIN, OR PLANE

CHECK-IN CLOSED

This happened when we were going on vacation to Brazil. We were driving to the airport, but the traffic was terrible. Eventually, we got to the airport, but our flight had already left.

Write about a time when you missed or almost missed a bus, train, or plane.

- say where and when this happened to you
- say why you were delayed
- say what eventually happened

_____
_____
_____
_____

2

TRYING TO MEET A FRIEND

GAME TODAY

A few weeks ago, I made plans to meet my friend Jack at the soccer stadium. I arrived at 6:30, but he wasn't there. He was at home watching TV because he'd forgotten. Eventually, I went in and watched the game, but I was really angry with him.

Write about a time when you tried to meet a friend but things went wrong.

- say who you were meeting and where
- say what went wrong with your plans
- say what your friend was doing or had done in the meantime
- say what eventually happened

_____
_____
_____
_____

3 PRONUNCIATION the letter _i_

a Circle the word with a different sound.

🚲 bike	1 arrive drive (signal)	
🐟 fish	2 driven surprise miracle	
🚲 bike	3 kill spider outside	
🐟 fish	4 notice while miss	

b ▶12.1 Listen and check. Then listen again and repeat the words.

Think before you speak

Gossip is what no one claims to like, but everyone enjoys.
Joseph Conrad, Polish writer

G reported speech   **V** say or tell?   **P** vowel + double consonant

1 GRAMMAR reported speech

a Match the direct speech to the reported speech.

1 "I work hard."   e
2 "I worked hard."   ____
3 "I'm working hard."   ____
4 "I can work hard."   ____
5 "I'll work hard."   ____

a Emma said that she had worked hard.
b Emma said that she could work hard.
c Emma said that she would work hard.
d Emma said that she was working hard.
~~e Emma said that she worked hard.~~

b Complete the reported speech.

Direct speech

1 "I want to leave my husband."
2 "I don't like my wife's parents."
3 "I'm getting divorced."
4 "I've been to the hospital."
5 "I haven't met my brother's girlfriend yet."
6 "I saw James with another woman."
7 "I can't cook."
8 "I won't tell anyone."
9 "I'll speak to my boss."
10 "I have a lot of work to do."

Reported speech

Suriya said that she *wanted to leave her husband.*
Gi-joon told me that he _____.
Katie told me that she _____.
Matt told me that he _____.
Anita said that she _____.
Robert said that he _____.
Lucy told me that she _____.
Enrique said that he _____.
Katherine said that she _____.
My boyfriend told me that he _____.

c Write the sentences in direct speech.

1 Mei-Ting said she was busy.
   She said: *"I'm busy."* _____

2 Amelia said that she wanted a cup of coffee.
   She said: "_____"

3 They told me that they hadn't seen their new neighbors yet.
   They said: "_____"

4 Steve told me that he didn't want to go to the movies.
   He said: "_____"

5 Natalia and Paul said they would come to the party.
   They said: "_____"

6 Fabio said that he had broken his arm.
   He said: "_____"

7 The guide told me that the building was very old.
   She said: "_____"

8 My friends said that they couldn't help me.
   They said: "_____"

2 VOCABULARY *say* or *tell*?

a Circle the correct word.

1 They *said* / *told* us that they were getting married next month.
2 Did Angela *say* / *tell* you that she wasn't happy?
3 Mia's husband *said* / *told* that he was working late.
4 You *said* / *told* that you didn't like men with beards.
5 I *said* / *told* you that I had a new girlfriend.
6 We *said* / *told* that we were going away this weekend.
7 Did Yuto *say* / *tell* that he couldn't come tonight?
8 I *said* / *told* Mary that you were in a meeting.
9 The teacher *said* / *told* that we had to do exercise 5.
10 You didn't *say* / *tell* me that Mike had called this morning.

b Complete the sentences with *said* or *told*.

1 Saki *said* ________ that she'd been to a friend's house.
2 We ________ our parents that we wouldn't be home for lunch.
3 I ________ you that the man she was with wasn't her brother.
4 They ________ that they were going to Turkey this summer.
5 Jack ________ me that he didn't have a girlfriend.
6 You ________ that you weren't going out tonight.
7 Marco ________ that he was busy tonight.
8 I ________ that the movie started at eight o'clock not seven o'clock.
9 We ________ our friends that we were going to get married.
10 Olivia ________ me that she'd seen Sam with another woman.

c Match 1–5 with a–e to make sentences.

1 My neighbor told ___c___
2 The teacher said that ___
3 My parents told ___
4 When I saw my friend, I told ___
5 My friend Sophie said that ___

a her that she looked nice in her new dress.
b I needed to speak more in class.
c ~~me that he was going away for the weekend.~~
d she hadn't enjoyed her vacation.
e me that they'd always be there for me.

d Complete the sentences about things people have said to you recently, or that you have said to them. Use reported speech and *say* or *tell*.

1 My neighbor told me ________________.
2 My teacher ________________.
3 My parents ________________.
4 When I saw my friend, I ________________.
5 My friend ________________.

3 PRONUNCIATION vowel + double consonant

a Look at the words in the square. Circle any three vowel sounds in a row that are the same. The lines can go across, down, or diagonally.

m**i**ss	b**i**tten	m**i**ddle	**o**pposite	r**o**bber
l**u**ggage	l**e**tter	wr**i**tten	l**i**ttle	g**o**ssip
h**a**ppy	d**i**fferent	t**e**nnis	b**o**ttle	r**u**nner
egg	m**a**rried	c**o**llege	l**e**ggings	f**u**nny
b**a**ggage	**a**ccident	r**a**bbit	b**i**gger	s**u**mmer

b 12.2 Listen and check. Then listen again and repeat the words.

Go online for more practice

12C The American English File quiz

Who am I to judge?
Douglas Adams,
English author

G questions without auxiliaries **V** review of question words **P** question words

1 PRONUNCIATION question words

a Check (✓) the words that start with the same sound.

1 who how ✓   3 what whose   5 how whose   7 which whose
2 where when   4 when who   6 why what

b ◁ 12.3 Listen and check. Then listen again and repeat the words.

2 VOCABULARY review of question words

Complete the questions in the *American English File* quiz with a word from the list.

how what when ~~where~~ which who whose why

The **American** *English* File Quiz

1 Q <u>Where</u> did Jim Springer meet his twin brother?
A In a café in Dayton.

2 Q _____ does Maggie Alderson do?
A She's a journalist.

3 Q _____ was in the movie *Frozen*?
A Kristen Bell.

4 Q _____ is orange juice bad for your teeth?
A Because there's a lot of acid in it.

5 Q _____ was the saxophone invented?
A In 1846.

6 Q _____ of these sports uses a net: volleyball, rugby, or karate?
A Volleyball.

7 Q _____ long has Chloe been afraid of buttons?
A Since she was a baby.

8 Q _____ illustrations of happiness have appeared on Facebook?
A Ralph Lazar and Lisa Swerling's.

3 **GRAMMAR** questions without auxiliaries

a Circle the correct form of the question.

1 **a** Who did paint *The Kiss*?
   b Who painted *The Kiss*?

2 **a** How many lives do cats have?
   b How many lives have cats?

3 **a** Who did become president of France in 2017?
   b Who became president of France in 2017?

4 **a** Which American singer did die on April 21, 2016?
   b Which American singer died on April 21, 2016?

5 **a** Who did Amal Alamuddin marry in 2014?
   b Who Amal Alamuddin married in 2014?

6 **a** What animal went into space in 1957?
   b What animal did go into space in 1957?

7 **a** What invented Elisha Otis in 1854?
   b What did Elisha Otis invent in 1854?

b Match the questions in **a** to these answers.

a Nine. *2*
b Prince. ____
c Emmanuel Macron. ____
d Gustav Klimt. ____
e George Clooney. ____
f A safety device for elevators. ____
g A dog named Laika. ____

c Complete the questions for the answers.

1 What *made Mark Zuckerberg* _____ famous?
   Facebook made Mark Zuckerberg famous.

2 How many Oscars _____?
   The movie *La La Land* won six Oscars.

3 Where _____?
   Polar bears live in the Arctic.

4 Who _____ *Sunflowers*?
   Vincent van Gogh painted *Sunflowers*.

5 How many Olympic medals _____
   for swimming?
   Michael Phelps won 28 Olympic medals for
   swimming.

6 Which country _____ in the world?
   India produces the most bananas in the world.

7 Who _____ the World Wide Web?
   Tim Berners-Lee invented the World Wide Web.

8 When _____?
   World War II ended in 1945.

d Write questions.

1 What / you / usually do on the weekend?
   What do you usually do on the weekend?

2 Who / sit next to you in class?
   _____?

3 How often / you / usually go to the movies?
   _____?

4 Which city in your country / have the most beautiful
   buildings?
   _____?

5 What / you / like watch on TV?
   _____?

6 How many times a week / you / play sports or
   exercise?
   _____?

e Answer the questions in **d** about you.

1 I usually _____.
2 My friend _____.
3 I usually _____.
4 _____.
5 _____.
6 _____.

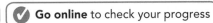

OXFORD
UNIVERSITY PRESS

198 Madison Avenue
New York, NY 10016 USA

Great Clarendon Street, Oxford, OX2 6DP, United Kingdom

Oxford University Press is a department of the University of Oxford. It furthers the University's objective of excellence in research, scholarship, and education by publishing worldwide. Oxford is a registered trade mark of Oxford University Press in the UK and in certain other countries

ISBN: 978 0 19 490653 1 MULTI-PACK 2B (PACK COMPONENT)

ISBN: 978 0 19 490652 4 MULTI-PACK 2B (PACK)

ISBN: 978 0 19 490631 9 ONLINE PRACTICE ACCESS CARD (PACK COMPONENT)

ISBN: 978 0 19 490638 8 ONLINE PRACTICE (PACK COMPONENT)

Printed in China

This book is printed on paper from certified and well-managed sources

STUDENT BOOK ACKNOWLEDGMENTS

Back cover photograph: Oxford University Press building/David Fisher

The authors would like to thank all the teachers and students around the world whose feedback has helped us to shape this series. The authors would also like to thank: all those at Oxford University Press (both in Oxford and around the world) and the design team who have contributed their skills and ideas to producing this course. Finally very special thanks from Clive to Maria Angeles, Lucia, and Eric, and from Christina to Cristina, for all their support and encouragement. Christina would also like to thank her children Joaquin, Marco, and Krysia for their constant inspiration.

The publisher and authors would also like to thank the following for their invaluable feedback on the materials: Jane Hudson, Brian Brennan, Isabel Orgillés Trol, Philip Drury, Rachael Smith, Robert Anderson, Maria Vanessa Ferroni, Jeremy Meehan, Lesley Poulad, Cristina Cogollos, Magdalena Muszyńska, Dagmara Łata, Sandy Millin, Pavlína Zoss, Ruth Valentová, Elif Barbaros, Zahra Bilides, Polina Kuharenko, Ellen Van Raemdonck, Gyula Kiss, Wagner Roberto Silva dos Santos, Sarah Giles, Roberto Sanchez, Pham Thi Bao Hoa

The authors and publisher are grateful to those who have given permission to reproduce the following extracts and adaptations of copyright material: p.8 'Why I want to find a date for Mum this year' by Rhiannon Cosslett Williams, Rhiannon Lucy Cosslett, theguardian.com, 14 February 2015. Copyright Guardian News & Media Ltd 2017. p.9 'I let Ma pick my dates on Tinder and guess what? It worked' by Elspbeth Gordon copyright Elspbeth Gordon, the Sunday Independent and Independent News and Media. p.16 'Jane Rangeley is snapped by Henri Cartier-Bresson, Paris, 1973' by Hannah Booth, theguardian.com. Copyright Guardian News & Media Ltd 2017. p.21 Adapted from 'Tips on Travel Photography: how to take better Holiday photos' by Geoffrey Lawrence from 'www.geofflawrence. com. Reproduced by permission. p.22 Extract from 'The guided tours for people waiting for a connecting flight' by Sarah Treleavan from http://www.bbc.co.uk/news. Reproduced by permission. p.34 '#Wild weekend? Why we lie on social media' from http://www.express.co.uk. Reproduced by permission of the Press Association. p.38 'I want it and I want it now! Why are we so impatient?' by Patrick McLenean, Metro. Reproduced by permission of Solo Syndication. p.41 'Most Honest Cities' by Damon Beres, originally published on RD.com. Copyright © 2013 by Trusted Media Brands, Inc. Used by permission. All rights reserved. p.43 'The A–Z of (conflicting) health advice: We try to get to the bottom of all those contradictory medical theories' by Jeremy Laurance, The Independent. Reproduced by permission. p.53 'The woman who inspired Martin Luther King's 'I have a dream' speech' by Emily Crockett. Vox Media & Vox Media, Inc, www.vox.com. Reproduced by permission. p.54 'The Ultimate Guide to Surviving Your First Day at a New Job' by Siobhan Harmer from http://www.lifehack.org. Reproduced by permission. p.56 Extract from 'Happiness Is … How it all began' from http://lastlemon.com/happiness/backstory/. Reproduced by permission. p.62 Extract from 'Dear Graham Norton: 'I feel like my older boyfriend has done it all before' by Graham Norton from http://www.telegraph.co.uk/© Telegraph Media Group Limited 2016. Reproduced by permission. p.69 Extract from 'Get in line for clues to being a queue winner' by Ian Dey and James Gillespie, Sunday Times, 8 November 2015. Reproduced by permission of News Syndication. p.79 'Why Aren't Women's Sports as Big as Men's? Your Thoughts' (excerpt) by Chris Bodenner © 2015 The Atlantic Media Co., as first published in The Atlantic Magazine. All rights reserved. Distributed by Tribune Content Agency. p.86 Extract from 'Fame Academy: They grew up to become stars of stage and screen, of literature and politics, of art and sport. But what were today's celebrities like as children? Did they already have that spark that sets them apart? We track down their former teachers to find out' by Liese Spencer, Becky Barnicoat, Heidi Blake and Dave Simpson. The Guardian, 13 September 2008. Copyright Guardian News & Media Ltd 2017. Reproduced by permission. p.90 'Twin Strangers: The website can find your doppelganger – but you may not be pleased with your matches' by Maggie Alderson from http://www.independent.co.uk. Reproduced by permission. p.94 'Cat delivered alive and well after spending eight days in the post' by James Tapper, theguardian.com, 27 March 2016. Copyright Guardian News & Media Ltd 2017. p.94 'Police rush in after man heard screaming 'I'm going to kill you'; discover noise caused by him attacking spider' by Michael Safi, theguardian.com, 26 November 2015. Copyright Guardian News & Media Ltd 2017. p.104 Adapted extract from 'How to survive meeting your partner's parents for the first time'. http://www.wikihow.com. This material is available under the Creative Commons license, http://creativecommons.org/licenses/ by-nc-sa/3.0/.

Sources: www.hsph.harvard.edu, www.planetdeadly.com, www.fearof.net www.bbc.com, http://ed.ted.com, www.richardwiseman.com/quirkology

The publisher would like to thank the following for their kind permission to reproduce photographs: Cover: Hobbit/Shutterstock. 123RF pp.34 (young man/vlue), 34 (friends/William Perugini), 34 (girl with camera/kho), 34 (woman with red hair/William Perugini), 35 (woman in hat/Fabio Formaggio), 113 (man/Daniel Ernst); 20th Century Fox p.74 ('SCREAM QUEENS' 2015 Twentieth Century Fox Television. All rights reserved.); Adrian Peacock p.90 (Maggie Alderson/Adrian Peacock); Airi Kivi p.57 (Airi Kivi); Alamy Stock Photo pp. 26 (woman/Westend61 GmbH), 32 (Uniqlo/zhang jiahan), 32 (Zara/Alex Segre), 32 (Apple logo/B Christopher), 32 (Topshop/Trevor Benbrook), 32 (The Body Shop/Newscast Online Limited), 32 (H&M/incamerastock), 32 (Nike/Keenretail), 32 (Ikea/Kristoffer Tripplaar), 37 (burger/Cultura Creative (RF)), 40 (cleaners/Paul Quayle), 40 (taxis/imageBROKER), 40 (Times Square/Urbanmyth), 40 (Skansen/ZUMA Press, Inc.), 41 (dropped wallet/Sean Locke), 53 (Mahalia Jackson & Martin Luther King/Everett Collection Inc), 60 (woman coughing/BSIP SA), 63 (silhouette/Benoit Daoust), 75 (Duncan Jones and David Bowie/WENN UK), 78 (Yelena Chernyavskaya/Jerry Lamper/Reuters), 78 (skiing/MARKA), 78 (velodrome/velosport), 82 (Konrad von Soest, (circa 1370), Wildungen altar, central panel, The Last Supper, detail/INTERFOTO), 82 (early Lego/INTERFOTO), 82 (CD/NearTheCoast.com), 83 (Penny Black/YAY Media AS), 83 (Penny Black stamp/Chronicle), 83 (wipers/E.D. Torial), 83 (intercom/Evgeniy Kleymenov), 83 (sea rescue/), 83 (washing machine/Roman Milert), 83 (lipstick/Lourens Smak), 86 (JK Rowling/WENN Ltd), 102 (woman/blickwinkel), 119 (runners/Sam Stephenson), 150 (toddler/Cultura Creative), 150 (young man/PhotoAlto sas), 151 (dress/Kevin Wheal), 151 (coat/Oleksiy Maksymenko Photography), 151 (leggings/Ruslan Kudrin), 151 (stripy t-shirt/Anatoliy Sadovskiy), 151 (vest/Judith Collins), 151 (pants/Phanuwat Nandee), 151 (pyjamas/Creative Control), 152 (plane ticket/B.A.E. Inc.), 152 (transport/Tristar Photos), 154 (shopper/Nicosan), 154 (tidying/Jacky Chapman), 154 (cleaner/Phovoir), 155 (sale banners/AKP Photos), 155 (cotton bag/Pat Tuson), 155 (shop assistant/Kzenon), 155 (shop display/ronstik), 155 (self service checkout/British Retail Photography), 156 (VF Outlet Village in Reading, Pennsylvania/Philip Scalia), 157 (man with money/Image Source), 157 (new home/D. Hurst), 157 (athletes/Image Source), 157 (broken iPhone/Lucian Milasan), 157 (results success/EnVogue_Photo), 157 (remote/Torontonian), 157 (teacher/Cultura Creative (RF)), 157 (Australian netball team/Alan Oliver), 157 (airport arrivals/RosaIreneBetancourt 12), 160 (handbag/Blaize Pascall), 160 (watching tv/Image Source), 160 (friends/Anna Berkut), 160 (girl with bag/ableimages), 160 (Andy Murray/Malcolm Park editorial),160 (business people/OJO Images Ltd), 160 (toddler/B&Y Photography), 160 (smiling woman/Commercial Megapress Collection), 160 (listening/Vadym Drobot), 61 (mosquito/Stefan Sollfors), 161 (Great Tit/Herbert Kehrer); Anya Chomacki p.17 (Instagram photos); Bridgeman Images p.10 (The Milkmaid, c.1658–60 (oil on canvas), Vermeer,Jan (Johannes) (1632–75)/ Rijksmuseum, Amsterdam,The Netherlands), 82 (Alto Saxophone, c.1848 (brass),Sax,Adolphe (1814–94)/Museum of Fine Arts,Boston, Massachusetts,USA/Leslie Lindsey Mason Collection), 102 (Girl at a Window Reading a Letter (oil on canvas),Vermeer,Jan (Johannes) (1632–75)/Gemaeldegalerie Alte Meister,Dresden, Germany/© Staatliche Kunstsammlungen Dresden); Catherine Blackie p.154 (pick up clothes), 160 (two men), 160 (men); Christina Latham-Koenig p.114 (storks); Chronicle Books LLC p.56 (Happiness is…by Ralph Lazar & Lisa Swerling); Eagle Radio p.80 (Peter Eagle); Fearof.net p.72 (Fear of net logo/Jacob Olesen); Geoff Lawrence pp.21 (Bruges), 21 (Forbidden City, Beijing), 21 (Paris); Getty Images p.6 (students/Tom Merton), 14 (smiling woman/Rafael Elias), 39 (cyclist/ Hinterhaus Productions), 49 (handyman/Sue Barr), 49 (barbecue/Hill Street Studios), 49 (refusing chocolates/Fuse), 49 (doctor/Peter Dazeley), 63 (Chinese Shadows By Jean-Pierre Chevenement/Alexis DUCLOS/Gamma-Rapho), 63 (map reading/Adrian Weinbrecht), 64 (queue/Rubberball/Mike Kemp), 65 (tiger/Safique Hazarika Photography), 72 (feet on ledge/Leslie-Ann Smith/EyeEm), 72 (butterfly/Adrian Dennis), 72 (learner driver/Jupiterimages), 78 (Anastasija Sevastova/Tim Clayton/Corbis), 78 (basketball/sodapix sodapix), 78 (handball/Marwan Naamani/AFP), 78 (Cecil Afrika/Stephen McCarthy), 79 (Matthias Ostrzolek/Stuart Franklin), 79 (Garbine Muguruza/Matthew Lewis), 82 (Illustration of man's first free ascent from Earth on November 21, 1783/Bettmann), 83 (Martin Cooper/Simon Flamigni/Contour), 83 (babies/Zephyr Picture), 85 (Angel Valodia Matos/JUNG YEON-JE/AFP), 86 (Alex Turner/Simone Cecchetti/Corbis), 90 (twin brothers/m-imagephotography), 108 (happy woman/andresr), 115 (Family/David P. Hall), 115 (family/Thomas Grass), 118 (Matt Damon/Gregg DeGuire/WireImage), 154 (bin bags/Fuse), 154 (friends/Leander Baerenz), 154 (runners/Zia Soleil), 154 (whiteboard/Duncan Smith), 155 (woman paying/Yellow Dog Productions), 155 (changing room/Siri Stafford), 157 (looking at clock/Commercial Eye), 157 (send button/alubalish), 157 (missed train/Simon Marcus Taplin), 160 (mother & daughter/Laura Doss), 160 (listening/Tom Merton), 160 (Kim Kardashian/Stephen Lovekin), 161 (Short-tailed Bat/Frank Greenaway), 161 (giraffe/Hans Neleman), 161 (Humpback whale/Paul Souders), 161 (bull/Picavet), 161 (lion/John Giustina), 161 (dolphin/Mike Hill), 161 (Holstein-Friesian cow/Peter Cade), 161 (Africa Rock Python/Visuals Unlimited, Inc./John Abbott), 161 (Tobiano paint horse/Kelly Funk), 161 (mouse/Tim Flach), 161 (Grey reef shark/Jeff Hunter), 161 (kangaroo/Tier Und Naturfotografie J und C Sohns); Guardian News & Media pp.8 (Charlotte with her father Clint Bouchez/Thomas Butler), 8 (Charlotte with her father Clint Bouchez/Thomas Butler); Independent Newspapers Marketing Ltd. p.9 (Elspbeth Gordon/David Conachy); iStockphoto p.63 (female silhouette/zenaphoto); Johann Watzke p.103 (Vermeer remake); Justine Rioufrait p.11 (Le Laitier/Justine Rioufrait); Kate Mount p.80 (Ella White); Magnum Photos p.16 (The Jardin des Plantes gardens/Henri Cartier-Bresson); Oxford University Press pp. 17 (punting), 49 (teen bedroom/Gareth Boden), 151 (socks/Gareth Boden), 151 (blue shirt/Gareth Boden), 151 (jeans/Gareth Boden), 151 (suit/Gareth Boden), 151 (denim jacket/MM Studios), 151 (tracksuit/Gareth Boden), 151 (chinos/Gareth Boden), 151 (stripy jumper/MM Studios), 151 (sandals/Gareth Boden), 151 (shoes/Gareth Boden), 151 (boots/Gareth Boden), 151 (flip-flops/Gareth Boden), 151 (tie/Gareth Boden), 151 (red gloves/MM Studios), 151 (scarf/MM Studios), 151 (baseball cap/Gareth Boden), 151 (hat/Gareth Boden), 151 (belt/Gareth Boden), 152 (family/Juice Images), 154 (greeting friends/Digital Vision), 154 (laying table/Image Source), 154 (putting away/Monalyn Gracia/Corbis), 154 (cooking/Relaximages), 154 (washing/Digital Vision), 154 (spelling/MM Studios), 154 (man on phone/Pixland), 155 (receipt/Tetra Images), 157 (visitor/MM Studios), 157 (women/Gareth Boden), 160 (businessman/Digital Vision), 160 (couple/Image Source), 160 (found glasses/Gareth Boden), 160 (student/MM Studios), 161 (tiger/Corbis/Digital Stock), 161 (chicken/Photodisc), 161 (spider/Eureka), 161 (butterfly/Digital Vision), 161 (elephant/Digital Vision); Patek Philippe p.82 (first Patek wristwatch); Regina Speer p.102 (The Poor Poet by Regina Speer, Annika Mittelmeier & Mattea Stahl); Reuters News Agency, Thomson Reuters p.85 (Robert Bauer/Marcos Brindicci); Rex Shutterstock pp.74 (Janet Leigh Psycho 1960/Paramount/Kobal), 154 (washing up/Burger/Phanie), 160 (Óscar Cardozo dejected/Sipa Press); Shutterstock pp. 6 (Living room/Gaf_Lila), 6 (San Francisco/Tupungato),6 (hospital/Spotmatik Ltd), 6 (studying/Stokkete), 6 (tablet/Kaspars Grinvalds), 14 (Peruvian Andes/Joerg Steber), 15 (backpack/design56), 17 (Wooden baseball bat/Slavko Sereda), 23 (airport/Tupungato), 25 (woman on phone/Andrey Arkusha), 25 (iPhone 7/guteksk7), 25 (Oxford/Offcaania), 25 (hotel bedroom/Eviled), 27 (kite/Roblan), 27 (bin/Selin Aydogan), 27 (stone/donikz), 27 (grapes/Phicai), 27 (mug/terekhov igor), 30 (mop/fotohunter), 34 (social media icons/solomon7), 35 (man with glasses/creativemarc), 35 (painter/David Pereiras), 37 (texting/Andrey_Popov), 37 (latte/Dmitry Galaganov) , 40 (Dubai Mall shopping mall/Elnur), 40 (street signs/Kizel Cotiw-an), 40 (wallet/IB Photography), 40 (Trevi Fountain/r.nagy), 57 (Tallinn/kavalenkava), 58 (Man in Café/AboutLife), 58 (American Flag/Milan M) , 60 (ill man/Elnur), 60 (man with headache/Borysevych.com), 60 (man with cold/Estrada Anton), 60 (sick kid/Ermolaev Alexander), 60 (ill woman/Tepikina Nastya), 62 (Female silhouette/Butsaya), 63 (Young woman silhouette/Alexey_M), 65 (Bus in the tunnel/Sondem), 66 (blank book/bonchan), 72 (syringe/funnyangel), 72 (web/melis), 72 (crowd/Frederic Legrand – COMEO), 73 (buttons/ZoranKrstic), 75 (Janet Leigh & Janet Leigh Curtis/Featureflash Photo Agency), 81 (alarm clock/Ko Backpacko), 82 (Fireworks/yotin Pakthongchai), 83 (dishwashing/Garsya), 83 (House roof with solar panels/manfredxy), 83 (stockings/Vladimir Gjorgiev), 86 (exam/Chinnapong), 87 (Kristen Bell/JStone), 89 (ripped jeans/elenovsky), 89 (straight jeans/elenovsky), 89 (female jeans/elenovsky), 116 (Kayseri, Turkey/Anujak Jaimook), 117 (Quincy Market/Stefan Uglijevarevic), 117 (students/Rawpixel.com), 150 (ginger haired woman/Lucky Business), 150 (young woman/Olena Z), 150 (smiling man/Uber Images), 150 (hipster guy/giorgiomtb), 150 (blonde woman/nobelio), 150 (overweight man/Monkey Business Images), 150 (young man/Tracy Whiteside), 151 (shorts/Stockforlife), 151 (blouse/Maffi), 151 (skirt/Karkas), 151 (cardigan/Tarzhanova), 151 (trainers/Jiang Hongyan), 151 (tights/Olga Popova), 151 (earrings/Ben_Neumann), 151 (bracelet/Fotosoroka), 151 (ring/Smirnof), 151 (necklace/Elnur), 152 (camping/gorillaimages), 152 (Black Forest/Juergen Wackenhut), 152 (friends/AYA images), 152 (queue/MarKord), 152 (skiing/gorillaimages), 152 (girls swimming/Monkey Business Images), 154 (making bed/Monkey Business Images), 154 (ironing/Africa Studio), 154 (Preparing Lunch/ Photographee.eu), 154 (Crossword Puzzle/Jne Valokuvaus), 154 (mop/Morrowind), 154 (vacuum/sezer66), 154 (dishwasher/Lolostock), 155 (Cash Register/Ozgur Coskun), 155 (shopping basket/Syda Productions), 155 (trolley/Big Jamnong), 156 (Reading, Pennsylvania Map/Globe Turner), 156 (Venice/Olga Kashubin), 157 (Lending Money/ Serg Zastavkin), 157 (found keys/cunaplus), 157 (download icon/Kumer Oksana), 157 (Student Passing Test/Antonio Guillem), 160 (woman/Yuricazac), 160 (handshake/Asia Images Group), 160 (Running for the bus/VGstockstudio), 160 (Exchanging Money/Thakkura P), 160 (Pay Stub/viewcapture), 161 (wasp/ Timin), 161 (piglet/yevgeniy11), 161 (rabbit/RimDream), 161 (goat/Anna Tkach), 161 (camel/Konstantnin), 161 (crocodile/Naypong), 161 (Squirrel Monkey/l i g h t p o e t), 161 (grizzly bear/Adam Van Spronsen), 161 (bumblebee/Juraj Kovac), 161 (jellyfish/H.Tanaka), 161 (green fly/irin-k), 161 (deer/InnaVar), 161 (sheep/Studio Grand Quest), 161 (rat/anatolypareev); South West News Service pp.48 (Steve Smith & Carmen Ruiz-Perez 1993/SWNS), 48 (Steve Smith & Carmen Ruiz-Perez wedding day/David Smith), 48 (long-lost love letter/SWNS); Telegraph Media Group Limited p.62 (Graham Norton/Andrew Crowley); Thomas S. England Photography p.91 (Springer Twins/Tom England); Twinstrangers.com pp.90 (Cordelia Roberts & Ciara Murphy), 90 (Niamh Geaney & Luisa Guizzardi); Universal Studios Licensing LLC p.74 (Psycho Still License); Wikimedia Commons; 108 (The Poor Poet by Carl Spitzweg).

Pronunciation chart artwork by: Ellis Nadler

Illustrations by: Bill Brown/Illustration Division pp.127, 130, 131, 135, 139, 140, 141, 144, 146, 147, 148, 149, 153, 159, 162, 163; Peter Bull pp.76, 78, 156; Stephen Collins pp.30, 31, 54, 55, 104; Gemma Correll/Anna Goodson Illustration pp.46, 47; Sveta Dorosheva/Illustration p.97; Jon Fletcher pp.24, 38, 69; Ivan Gillett/NB Illustration p.96; Joanna Kerr/New Division pp.42, 43; Mark Ruffle pp.22, 33; Vari Telleria/New Division p.50; Kipper Williams pp.94, 95, 101; Jonathan Woodward pp.70, 71.

Commissioned photography by: Gareth Boden pp.18 (restaurant, nightclub), 49 (teen in untidy room), 88 (packing), MM Studios: 23, 25 (Jake), 26/7 (games letters), 86, 89 (bootcut,boyfriend), 96, 151 (blouse, ; Practical English stills photography by: Rob Judges, Jacob Hutchings, and Richard Hutchings: pp.12, 13, 28, 44, 45, 60, 61, 77, 92, 93; Other video stills: Oxford University Press: pp.18, 19, 37 (vox pops), 51, 53, 66, 67, 69, 5, 101.

WORKBOOK ACKNOWLEDGMENTS

Back cover photograph: Oxford University Press building/David Fisher

The authors would like to thank all the teachers and students around the world whose feedback has helped us to shape this series.

The authors would also like to thank: all those at Oxford University Press (both in Oxford and around the world) and the design team who have contributed their skills and ideas to producing this course.

Finally very special thanks from Clive to Maria Angeles, Lucia, and Eric, and from Christina to Cristina, for all their support and encouragement. Christina would also like to thank her children Joaquin, Marco, and Krysia for their constant inspiration.

The authors and publisher are grateful to those who have given permission to reproduce the following extracts and adaptations of copyright material: p.11 Extract from 'Liu Bolin: The Real Life Invisible Man', www.boredpanda. com. Reproduced by permission. p.67 Adapted from 'The 101 best pieces of advice ever received' by Olivia Parker, Anna Tyzack and Celia Walden, 29 December 2012 © Telegraph Media Group Limited 2012. http://www.telegraph.co.uk. Reproduced by permission.

Sources: www.guardian.com, www.dannymacaskill.co.uk

The publisher would like to thank the following for their permission to reproduce photographs: Cover: Hobbit/Shutterstock. Alamy: pp. 8 (ex 1a 10/Kevin Wheal), 26 (ex 1a 3/Nicosan), 34 (1/Fotomaton), 39 (Georgetown Canal/B. Christopher), 46 (Radius Images), 53 (Jordan Siemens), 64 (boy/Mark Sykes, man/UpperCut Images), 68 (ex 1a 7/Aflo Co., Ltd.), 73 (battery/Dorling Kindersley Ltd, photograph/Paul Fearn, car/World History Archive, X ray/Arterra Picture Library, plane/Archive Pics), 77 (M.Sobreira), 79 (Andrew Fox); Getty: pp 25, 59 (Greg Elms), 60 (cow/Peter Cade, whale/Paul Souders, horse/Kelly Funk, snake/Visuals Unlimited, Inc./John Abbott), 76 (Akio Kon/Bloomberg), 81, 87 (Michael Phelps/Christophe Simon/AFP); Oxford University Press pp 8 (ex 1a 1-9, 11, 12), 13 (ex 3a 1, 2, 4, 6, 8), 17/Mark Mason Studios), 26 (ex 1a 1, 2, 4-7), 45, 60 (monkey, spider, bee, sheep, jellyfish, bear, crocodile); Rex Features: pp 11 (Liu Bolin/Quirky China News), 13 (ex 3a 5/Monkey Business Images); Shutterstock: pp 8 (Friends taking a Selfie/ Mavo), 5 (both), 7, 12, 13 (ex 3a 2, 7, 9), 16 (both), 21, 23, 28, 33, 34 (2-6), 35 (all), 37, 39, 7 (Friends walking in City/Stock Studio), 48, 49, 55, 61, 62, 63, 65 (all), 68 (ex 1a 1-6, 8), 69, 72, 74, 78, 85, 86 (buttons, juice, saxophone), 87 (polar bears, bananas).

With thanks to: Jim Springer p86; Joshua Louis Simon p 8 (remake of The Bedroom/Re-creation by Joshua Louis Simon).

Pronunciation chart artwork by: Ellis Nadler

Illustrations by: Bill Brown pp. 9, 15, 19, 27, 43, 49, 58, 68, 83; Peter Bull p 50 (ex 1b), 66; Joanna Kerr/New Division pp 33, 34, 36, 41, 50 (ex 1a), 57; Jerome Mirault p 31; Roger Penwill p 70; Gavin Reece p 42; Kath Walker p 56, 69, 82; Anders Wenngren p 49 (emojis).

Although every effort has been made to trace and contact copyright holders before publication, this has not been possible in some cases. We apologise for any apparent infringement of copyright and, if notified, the publisher will be pleased to rectify any errors or omissions at the earliest possible opportunity.